D0915412

COMMUNITY TREATMENT AND SOCIAL CONTROL

COMMUNITY TREATMENT AND SOCIAL CONTROL
A Critical Analysis of Juvenile Correctional Policy

Paul Lerman

THE UNIVERSITY OF CHICAGO PRESS
Chicago and London

Paul Lerman is professor of social work and sociology, and chairman
of the doctoral program in social work, Rutgers University.

The University of Chicago Press, Chicago 60637
The University of Chicago Press, Ltd., London
© 1975 by The University of Chicago
Printed in the United States of America
80 79 78 77 76   98765432

Library of Congress Cataloging in Publication Data

Lerman Paul.
  Community treatment and social control.

  (Studies in crime and justice)
  Bibliography: p.
  Includes index.
  1. Rehabilitation of juvenile delinquents—California
2. Corrections—California.   3. Social control.
I. Title.   II. Series.
HV9105.C2L47   364.36'09794   74-11629
ISBN 0-226-47307-4

Contents

List of Tables vii
Foreword by Lloyd Ohlin
             ix
Preface   xiii

1   Introduction 1

PART ONE   THE COMMUNITY TREATMENT PROJECT
2   The Community Treatment Project: The Ideal Program
             19
3   The CTP in Operation: Changing the Ideal Design
             30
4   Assessing the Impact of CTP
             55
5   CTP and Issues for Correctional Policy
             78

PART TWO   PROBATION SUBSIDY
6   Probation Subsidy: Assumptions and Operating Criteria
             107
7   The Social Impact of Probation Subsidy
             126

8   The Fiscal Impact of Probation Subsidy
                    157
9   Probation Subsidy: Issues for Correctional Policy
                    188

10   Summary and Conclusions
                    204

     Appendix A. A Methodological Note on the CTP Analysis
                    229
     Appendix B. Tables B-1 and B-2
                    238

     Bibliography   241
     Index   249

Tables

1. Overview of I-Level Typology and Selected Treatment Strategies 26
2. Use of Program Elements in CTP, as of 1 January 1963 35
3. Exposure to Detention and Treatment Program Elements 39
4. CTP Experimentals and Controls Released to Sacramento and Stockton 60
5. Costs of Original CTP Deisgn, Actual CTP Program, and Control Group, Assuming a Successful Career 68
6. CYA Institutional Wards, 1965 and 1970 133
7. Percentage of Parole Violators, by Population Characteristics of 1969 Release Cohort 134
8. Sustained Offense of Juvenile Cases in Regular and Subsidy Active Judicial Probation Caseloads on 31 December 1970 137
9. Number and Admission Rates of County Camps, Ranches, and Schools, 1943-70 141
10. California Police, Probation, and Court Responses to Youth Behavior for 1960-65 and 1965-70 143
11. Juvenile Arrest: Specific Rates for 1960, 1965, and 1970 146
12. California Detention: Specific Rates for 1960, 1965, and 1970 148
13. State and County Rates of Admissions and Institutional Youth Days for All Sources, 1960, 1965, and 1970 153

14. Commitment Reductions under the California Probation Subsidy Program, including State Costs and Potential Savings to State, for Fiscal Years, 1966–70   160
15. Assessing 1969–70 Fiscal Impact of Subsidy on the State by Two Types of Career Cost Policies   164
16. Assessing the Fiscal Impact of Subsidy on State by Using Two Assumptions Concerning Rise in CYA Career Costs   168
17. Career Costs of CYA and CDC, by Components and Fiscal Years 1963–64 and 1967–68   173
18. Historical Data on Average Operating Institutional Costs According to Average Cost per Bed and Average Cost per Ward Paroled   175
19. Per Capita Career Costs for Successful CYA Careers for Three Correctional Policies   177
20. Institutional Beds Closed and Opened in CYA Institution, 1966–72   179
B-1. Time on Parole Prior to Violation for Two Cohorts of CYA Boys Released to Parole by Sentencing Court   238
B-2. Violence Risks of CYA Male Parolees, 1961, 1962, 1963, and 1970   239

Foreword

This is a timely book and already a controversial one, for it addresses basic issues in the current development of correctional policies. The author does this somewhat indirectly by carefully reanalyzing the correspondence between the intentions and the actual accomplishments of two of the most highly regarded and innovative correctional experiments of the 1960s.

The first half of the book reexamines data relevant to the achievements claimed for the Community Treatment Project launched in the Sacramento-Stockton area of California in 1961, while the second half is devoted to a similar analysis of the Probation Subsidy program enacted by the California legislature in 1965. The Community Treatment Project has been repeatedly cited by national crime commissions as a model program for substituting community-based treatment services for institutional confinement. Similarly, the Probation Subsidy program provided a model for diverting offenders from state correctional institutions to an expanded set of local facilities and services.

The author evaluates claims that these projects have been successful in reducing confinement of offenders in institutions and in lowering recidivism rates, all at less social and economic cost to the state. It is a tribute to the criminal justice research and

information system in California that Lerman was able to
complete his analysis and interpretation of the impact of these
programs relying wholly on published and unpublished public
documents, records, and reports of research studies. The result is
a thoughtful, provocative, and highly persuasive treatise. It is
tough-minded and critical in its detailed exploration of the way
implementation measures or unintended consequences can subvert the accomplishment of project goals. In this brief foreword it
is not possible to review the conclusions reached by Lerman's
analysis. The author has stated them carefully and clearly enough
in the pages that follow. I am confident they will be the subject of
spirited debate over the next few years and will greatly aid the
clarification of choices and priorities in correctional policies and
programs.

This type of probing reevaluation of the policy implications of
research and action projects is altogether too rare an enterprise in
the field of criminal justice. We need many more studies that
weigh and assess costs and benefits of new programs and policies
in a thoughtful, searching fashion. As in this instance, such
studies should be concerned not only with public policy implications but also with the dilemmas, choices, and consequences of
the operational decisions made in implementing new projects.

This analysis also clearly demonstrates the necessity of a
systems approach to the evaluation of the results of new policies
or programs. A narrow preoccupation with data relevant only for
assessing achievement of the manifest goals of a project may lead
to erroneous policy judgments. Lerman shows the importance of
evaluating the effects on the total system in which the project is
embedded. In fact, he urges a deliberate search for evidence of
unintended consequences and accommodations within the project
and in other parts of the system that may serve to enhance or to
subvert project objectives.

Finally, whatever may be the ultimate resolution of the con-
flicting assessments of the two projects analyzed in this book,
Lerman has clearly shown the necessity for careful distinctions
between policies and programs of social control versus rehabilitative treatment. For the correctional field he demonstrates the
confusion and erroneous judgments that may result unless we
take greater care in clarifying not only our intentions in this
regard but the manifest and latent consequences of our decisions

and acts. Indeed, it would not be inappropriate to regard this book as offering us two major case studies documenting this thesis in a variety of different ways.

LLOYD E. OHLIN

Preface

In writing and editing this manuscript I have tried to focus on ideas and policy issues rather than on persons or organizations associated with these ideas. A critical policy analysis such as this may seem harsher toward such persons and organizations than intended. Actually, this study was possible only because California corrections is open and competent in reporting research and statistical information. The administrators of the California correctional organizations deserve a good deal of credit for collecting and openly disseminating information and documents. Obviously they bear no responsibility for the way I used documents produced by public agencies.

The analytic framework, data analyses, and inferences are, of course, my responsibility and are not attributable to any of the persons or organizations that directly assisted me. This assistance warrants acknowledgment, which I can best express by providing a brief chronology of the evolution of this book.

In 1971, at the suggestion of Dr. George Weber, Deputy Chief, Center for the Studies of Crime and Delinquency, National Institute of Mental Health (NIMH), I agreed to conduct an assessment of the Community Treatment Project (CTP) and to study Probation Subsidy, with the aid of NIH Contract 71-908. I spent the summer of 1971 in California gathering data and documents and conducting interviews on these two programs, in Sacramento, Alameda, San Francisco, San Mateo, San Jose, Los Angeles, Orange, and San Diego counties.

Officials and staff of the California Youth Authority were extremely helpful in providing information and facilitating contacts. I also spent time in the library of the Office of the Legislative Analyst. Robin Lamson, an analyst, gained access for me to public documents not otherwise readily available and facilitated my meeting with staff members of the Bureau of Criminal Statistics (BCS). W. H. Hutchins, Walter K. Giesecke, and Charles Bridges of BCS helped me to understand the BCS codes and procedures used in the collection of statewide statistical data.

My research assistant in California was Jay Nyhuis, a doctoral student at Rutgers University School of Social Work and a Los Angeles County probation officer (on leave). In addition to writing up descriptions of county programs, he helped me gain an understanding of the intricacies of the operation of probation subsidy at the county level.

In 1972 I presented a final report to NIMH. Saleem Shah, Chief of the Center for Studies of Crime and Delinquency, and staff member Loren Roth reacted to the document with critical sensitivity. After reflecting on the merit of their questions and comments, I rewrote the report and submitted it as a manuscript for publication. The present work is an outgrowth of this report, but it is clear that the NIMH Center for Studies of Crime and Delinquency bears no responsibility for the book's contents.

After formally accepting the manuscript, the University of Chicago Press rendered editorial assistance through the services of Norval Morris and his select group of critical readers. In response to their questions and reactions, I again rewrote and reorganized substantial parts of the manuscript. During the revision stage I had the benefit of the astute editorial skills of Barbara Christenberry, a member of my extended family.

In the fall of 1973, while I was working in the final stages of my manuscript, the University of Chicago Press and I received a critique of my assessment of CTP from the principal investigator, Ted Palmer. After analyzing *his* critique of *my* critique, I concluded that my assessment remained sound—but required some further editorial changes to avoid being misconstrued. I also prepared an appendix to deal with unpublished, "updated," empirical data contained in Palmer's critique. I chose this form to keep the text free from personal squabbling but still to provide interested readers with an opportunity to examine the bases for my skepticism regarding the updated data proffered by Palmer.

Laudably, the University of Chicago Press was not deterred by the attempt of interested parties to hinder the manuscript's publication. In the finest tradition of freedom of expression, the publisher provided me with the opportunity to write as my interpretation of the data warranted.

Closer to home, colleagues, friends, and family were also helpful. Donald Dickson, a triple-threat thinker in the fields of sociology, law, and social work, was unusually deft in raising questions and pointing out ambiguities in the data-analysis sections. His wife, Mary, typed the manuscript with error-free fidelity.

I lived with the various stages of this manuscript for over four years. During that time my wife, Carla, and my children, Nina and Joshua, were extremely patient with my preoccupation with the project. While all the people I have noted were helpful, as always my best and most faithful critic remains Carla.

London, England
October 1974

1   Introduction

This study is about societal responses to youthful deviants. Of particular interest are the assumptions, choices, and consequences related to implementing program strategies designed as alternatives to traditional institutional programs. With the aid of empirical evidence, derived from an analysis of two nationally respected programs, the relative advantages and disadvantages associated with executing a community treatment strategy will be assessed. By subjecting conventional and unexamined beliefs about this new correctional strategy to a critical analysis, we may considerably broaden the customary level of discourse about correctional policy toward juveniles. An empirically oriented policy analysis may also offer insights that can improve policy making while simultaneously extending our knowledge about alternative forms of social control.

The data used in this study stem primarily from a reanalysis of official government documents that are in the public domain. Many of the documents have a limited distribution and exist in file drawers rather than on library shelves—but that does not necessarily mean they are either secret or confidential. The analyses conducted for this study may yield surprising conclusions for many readers, but it is important to emphasize that all of the data presented were found in documents that were made freely available by either state or county agencies of government. However, the conceptual framework used in collecting, sorting, analyzing, and reporting the data will not be found in the documents. Since this analytic perspective is just as crucial to the study as are the multiple sources of official data, an overview of guiding ideas and examples of major findings will be used to introduce the two parts of this study.

During the past decade an increasing number of correctional leaders in the United States have expressed disillusionment in the rehabilitative potential of state and local prisons and juvenile reformatories and training schools. This loss of faith in American correctional institutions was provided a national forum by two federal fact-finding commissions: the President's Commission on Law Enforcement and the Administration of Justice (1967a) and the National Commission on the Causes and Prevention of Violence (1969). Both commissions, relying on leading scholars and correctional spokesmen to assess an array of evidence and correctional knowledge, concluded that incarceration was associated with high rates of recidivism and failed to function as a deterrent to crime. Besides citing these institutional failings, the writers of these national documents also argued that lengthy incarceration may be compounding the problem of crime and delinquency—since inmates may emerge from correctional institutions even more committed to deviant practices than when they entered.

The national reports recommended that the old correctional strategy of continued reliance on institutionalization be discarded in favor of an alternate policy, particularly for offenders requiring more than routine probation supervision. The new policy was termed "community treatment." In its initial formulation, community treatment referred to alternatives in lieu of traditional institutionalization. As the concept became more popular, the term "community treatment" has been expanded to refer to change or innovation in local correctional programming (National Institute of Mental Health, 1971a). As laudable as innovative probation, parole, and half-way house programs may turn out to be, in practice they are not deemed to qualify as examples of a new policy direction—unless offenders are placed in these programs in lieu of traditional institutionalization. The challenge to

American corrections, set forth by the national commissions, was to construct *in lieu* programs rather than programs with a catchy label.

By recommending the policy of inaugurating in lieu programs (i.e., community treatment), the writers of the commission reports were not unmindful of other reforms that might improve society's response to the crime and delinquency problem. Besides advocating broad-scale social and economic reforms to address the problems of high crime neighborhoods and communities, the reports also detailed reforms that would improve all parts of the criminal justice system. As important as improvements in social condition, law enforcement, statutes, the bail system, prosecution, and the courts were deemed to be, it appears reasonable to infer that the writers of the commission reports were convinced that American corrections could be reformed and could be made to correct—even if other reforms were not readily realized.

The community treatment strategy was apparently based on the central assumption that *individual* offenders—particularly youth—could be corrected, even if the crime and delinquency problem per se remained untouched by the failure to mount more fundamental reforms in the criminal justice system and in American society. The writers of the commission reports appeared to be optimistic about the possibility of individual reformation if it took place outside traditional institutional walls. The policy of community treatment appears to be uniquely American, expressing optimism about the future, the corrigibility of dealing with problems, pragmatism in finding solutions, and a belief in the individual reformation of youthful deviants.

While the policy of community treatment was probably influenced by beliefs and value assumptions, it was also guided by an informed intelligence regarding reports of potential community treatment prototypes. In urging the inauguration of a new correctional policy, particularly for juveniles, proponents gave a great deal of emphasis to the empirical findings emerging from a nationally known experimental/demonstration program—California's Community Treatment Project. Operated as a special parole unit within the California Youth Authority (CYA), the project was explicitly designed to provide individually programmed, intensive treatment services in lieu of commitment to a CYA facility. The Community Treatment Project (CTP) had been launched in 1961, with an experimental research design that randomly allocated eligible youth to an experimental or traditional correctional program, after youths had spent an average of four weeks in a reception center. Control youth spent an average of eight months in an institution, while experimentals were released to community placements.

By the time of the writing of the two national reports, CTP had been evaluated as highly effective in reducing recidivism rates. In addition, CTP had been assessed as practical and acceptable to local community agencies. These favorable evaluations were backed up by the claim that these results had been achieved at a fiscal cost per capita that was much lower than the traditional CYA program of institutionalization and regular parole. This favorable assessment of an ongoing, organizationally practical project was based primarily on the empirical evidence and research reports presented by CTP research personnel.

Besides being impressed by the favorable evaluations emerging from 1961-67 CTP research reports, it appears plausible that the President's Commission and the National Violence Commission were also encouraged by the authenticity of the research sponsorship. While the CYA funded the major demonstration aspects of CTP, the research proposal was approved by the National Institute of Mental Health's Center for the Study of Crime and Delinquency, and the entire research effort was supported by NIMH funds. It appeared that the CTP efforts were being symbolically supported, as well as funded, by two of the most prestigious organizations involved in correctional research in the United States—the CYA and the NIMH. In 1967 and again in 1969, federal commissions lent added prestige and significance to CTP by explicitly recommending it as a community treatment prototype (President's Commission, 1967a, p. 179; and National Commission, 1969, pp. 578-80).

The first indication that the claims of CTP effectiveness were premature appeared in 1968 in an article of my own, published in the professional journal *Social Work* (Lerman, 1968). Using CTP data, I reassessed the evidence by making a sharp distinction between renewed offenses known to law enforcement officials and the responses by CTP parole agents and CYA Board representatives to the known offenses. This analysis indicated quite clearly that the two groups of youth—CTP experimentals and institutionalized controls—had comparable rates of being noticed by the police for legal infractions. However, the adult organizational decision makers reacted differentially to the two groups of youth, thereby producing apparent differences in rates of recidivism (i.e., revocation of parole, dishonorable discharge, and incarceration). The article concluded that CTP had demonstrated that it could change the discretionary decision-making behavior of adults—but had been unable to demonstrate that it had any appreciable impact on youth behavior. The evidence presented in part 1 of this study extends this line of analysis even further by specifying how parole organizations, within limits, can inadvertently create their own rates of success and failure.

While only a limited number of scholars and correctional practitioners are aware of the findings that question CTP claims of effectiveness, it is significant that none of these knowledgeable experts (including myself) had been willing to examine other claims about CTP as a community treatment prototype (Robison and Smith, 1970; National Institute of Mental Health, 1971a; Beker and Heyman, 1972; and Schur, 1973). Scholars and practitioners may have been reluctant to examine this primary example of community treatment because they were convinced that CTP was still a less financially expensive alternative to traditional institutionalization. In addition, they may have been convinced, not unreasonably, that it was also less costly in a social sense—since unnecessary deprivation of liberty had been avoided by substituting individual treatment in the community for an eight-month incarceration.

However, a reexamination of the evidence as set forth in part 1 indicates that the assumption concerning lower fiscal costs cannot be automatically made. By means of a critical perspective, evidence is examined to find out whether the in lieu strategy proved to be less fiscally expensive, per treated youth, than a traditional program would have been. The evidence indicates that if the CTP operation had adhered to the original, ideal policy (or program design), fiscal savings could have been realized that would have been significant. However, the program did not follow the design and proved to be much more costly.

The cost overrun was probably neither intended nor anticipated. However, discrepancies between the conception of ideal policies and their execution is not an unusual occurrence in human affairs; nor is the emergence of unanticipated outcomes uncommon. Both occurrences may be concomitants of efforts at realizing ideal policies. A reasonable policy analysis must strive to identify nonideal practices and outcomes—even if the evidence involved upsets conventional assumptions.

A critical search for nonideal practices and outcomes requires the tracing of systemic, organizational consequences of discretionary decision making. Discretionary decision making in varying degrees occurs in virtually all policy execution, since operational choices must be made to transform an ideal policy conception into an actual, ongoing program (Davis, 1967). Discretionary choices, however, if unmonitored or left unregulated by policy designers, can modify or create new program policies. The results can be costly or beneficial, or even mixed in outcome. In the case of CTP, the operational decision to extend the period of intensive treatment for experimental youth had a significant impact on the organization. Extending treatment time from eight months to close to three years (while maintaining caseloads at a ratio of one CTP agent to ten youth) entailed the following systemic consequences: rates of turnover of cases were kept low; additional personnel were required to handle the desired number of offenders; and the amount of personnel time expended on a case over time increased. The initial operational decision was deemed to be compatible with the ideal policy design of providing intensive treatment, but the systemic consequences were not without added costs. These consequences led to a significant cost overrun, but the undesired increase in fiscal costs appears to be associated with a desired exercise of discretionary decision making in the operation of the program. A critical perspective can assist in the location of discretionary sources of undesired cost overruns, as well as specify the actual total costs incurred in operationalizing the ideal program design.

An examination of social costs and benefits indicates that community treatment can also include an appreciable amount of deprivation of liberty. A detailed presentation of the evidence presented in part 1 discloses that offenders placed in the CTP experimental group experienced more detention stays than those youth placed in the regular CYA parole program. CTP parole agents were much more likely to bring their wards physically to a lock-up facility for reasons that did not pertain to renewed

Introduction 7

delinquency. The reasons given included violations of treatment expectations, accommodation to community complaints, administrative convenience, diagnostic purposes, and the prediction and prevention of "acting out" behavior. The broad scope of the reasons, the loose procedures for initiating a lock-up, the failure to distinguish between serious and nonserious deviance, and other practices produced an array of discretionary decisions that appeared to be arbitrary and unfair.

The evidence of part 1 indicates that CTP youth spent more time in detention facilities than they did with their community treatment agents. In practice, this nationally admired correctional prototype included a degree and duration of social control that outweighed the amount of treatment offered. While the CTP delivered to its youth much more social control than treatment, however, CTP youth spent fewer total days in an institutional setting than if they had experienced the traditional CYA program in its totality (i.e., institutionalization plus parole).

It appears that a critical perspective, utilizing available empirical evidence, is capable of broadening the discussion of alternative correctional policies. Besides reassessing the issue of program effectiveness and fiscal efficiency, it is necessary to examine whether a new policy relies on the employment of new methods of social control that are fair, just, and reasonable. The evidence indicates that the new correctional policy implemented in California modified—but did not entirely exclude—the type, degree, duration, and even the scheduling of negative sanctions administered by official agents of the state. The evidence appears to be at odds with the ideal conception of community treatment, whereby reliance on traditional forms of incarceration were to be avoided. Community treatment, in practice, has involved intermittent doses of short-term detention that bears a marked resemblance to aspects of the traditional correctional policy.

Increased reliance on alternative modes of social control can also influence the practices of the regular parole organization. Evidence is presented in part 1 below that CTP, as a special project, helped the regular CYA parole organization learn how to legalize, use, and incorporate into its daily operations the discretionary use of "therapeutic detention." This type of spillover effect was, of course, also unintended by the designers of community treatment.

Significant portions of part 1 attempt to describe and assess the problems of social control associated with CTP (and, potentially, with other community treatment programs). This inquiry and discussion assumes, at an analytic level, that it is possible to make a clear distinction between social control and treatment as correctional program elements. Unless this distinction is made, it is possible to label conveniently all intended treatment efforts as examples of "treatment"—regardless of the coercive impact on wards of the state. The community treatment literature has failed to make this important distinction. As a result, in programs like CTP it is possible to label as "treatment" the detention of youth for therapeutic purposes. An informed and critical policy analysis ought to be able to distinguish between overt dimensions of social control and therapy. To do otherwise may risk describing outcomes only on the bases of stated benign intentions—leaving out an assessment of a new source of individual and social cost.

Distinguishing between Social Control and Treatment

From a sociological perspective, social control refers to either informal social processes or the formal organizational efforts utilized to induce compliance with social standards. The social standards that are capable of being enforced by threat or the use of positive or negative sanctions can refer to group norms, organizational rules and regulations, or community norms and laws. Many social standards are enforced by self-regulation or by informal mechanisms of sanction—praise, blame, shame, ridicule, and social isolation. These more informal forms of social control rely on the processes of extended socialization and primary group interaction to induce compliance with the demands of others. This form of social control also tends to rely on the acceptance of the customs, folkways, and mores of the society. Lemert refers to this mode of social control as "passive," in contradistinction to "active social control" where organized efforts by formal regulatory agencies are created to enforce compliance (Lemert, 1967). Police and judges, as well as housing inspectors and public health officers, are ready examples of agents of active social control.

As an integral part of the active social control system set up for juveniles, corrections may be conceived of as potentially participating in the enforcement of standards and the administration of negative sanctions at three levels of social organization: (1) the dispositional level, (2) the correctional organizational level, and (3) the subunit level of the correctional organization. At the first level, correctional workers are responsible for assisting in the informal or formal administration of the dispositions of cases judged by police, court intake workers, or judges. These dispositions may involve informal or formal detention, informal probation, formal probation without placement, formal probation with placement, institutionalization, fines, or weekend work assignments. To the extent that the dispositions involve threats or actual restrictions on normal living arrangements, freedom of movement, or other deprivations of rights, privileges, and resources, they are definable as indications of social control. At the dispositional level of social control, the correctional worker is helping to enforce the standards interpreted by other decision makers of the juvenile justice system. It is evident that even at this level the sanctions can vary by *type* (e.g., probation at home or "probation" in a correctional camp or group home), *degree* (e.g., probation at home with one supervisory visit a month versus "probation" at a correctional camp with twenty-four-hour surveillance), and *duration* (e.g., probation at home for one year versus "probation" at a camp for six months).

The second potential level of negative sanctions is related to the specific rules and regulations of the correctional organization. Agencywide rules and regulations that are *not* set forth by law or the court confront offenders with additional social standards to comply with and correctional officers with new standards to enforce. Probation organizations vary by what they define as "conditions of probation," and correctional camps, ranches, schools, and reformatories can vary by their definitions of "institutional adjustment." Noncompliance with these organizational rules can lead to another level of sanctions that may vary by type, degree, and duration. Isolation or solitary confinement in an "adjustment cottage," for example, is normally a correctional administrative decision—not a judicial disposition (Fox, 1972).

The third potential level of sanctions is related to the subunit of the correctional organization. Besides agencywide rules and regulations, there exist subunit variations in interpretations of rules. Robison and Takagi, for example, found that parole units within a state organization can vary in their rates of using revocation of parole (Robison and Smith, 1971).

From a sociological perspective, it is important to recognize that *any* actual application of negative sanctions may provide useful indicators of the existence of social control. While the general goal of active social control is to induce compliance, the use of sanctions to deal with offenders can also be guided by the following kinds of specific aims: (1) to deter renewed noncompliance by offenders; (2) to deter others from noncompliance; (3) to highlight the social boundaries of right and wrong; (4) to reinforce the habits of compliance in offenders; (5) to build respect for the legitimacy of rules and laws (Zimring, 1971).

Whether social control efforts achieve these aims and are therefore effective is, of course, an important empirical issue. However, even without this knowledge it is possible to categorize negative sanctions as examples of organized control efforts—irrespective of the intent underlying the sanctions or the systemic level where coercion occurs. From this point of view, living in a foster home by virtue of a court order or a correctional decision is more controlling than living at home—regardless of intention. Or living in a detention facility (at the order of a parole officer or policeman) is more controlling than living in a group home that permits freedom of movement to attend a neighborhood school, a playground, or a friend's house—again irrespective of intention. By using this perspective, it is possible to categorize correctional efforts, at any level of operation, by the type, degree, and duration of negative sanctions that are actually employed.

According to Schwitzgebel,

> treatment ... is directed toward producing an enduring change in the behavior of an individual as he lives under natural conditions in the community. Included within the concept of treatment is an idea of restoration or improvement rather than restriction or disablement. Also intrinsic to treatment, especially behavior modification, is the requirement of measurable results. "Treatment" techniques that do not produce measurable results may be either an aspect of research or merely ineffective, and therefore probably inappropriate procedures. [Schwitzgebel, 1971]

If one were to utilize this approach outside of a correctional framework, there would be minimal difficulty in identifying procedures and programs associated with special efforts to resocialize or reeducate youth. Tutoring, remedial classes, counseling, token economy systems, and guided group interaction would all constitute examples of special efforts geared to affecting "enduring change." Implicit in these efforts is a deemphasis of "restriction" while emphasizing the skills or attitudes associated with improved functioning. However, as soon as these treatment procedures and efforts are removed from their nonrestrictive context in homes, schools, community centers, and clinics—and placed in a correctional context—difficulties emerge. These difficulties emerge from three sources: (1) compelling treatment, (2) delivering sanctions for noncompliance with treatment programs, and (3) using aversive techniques that resemble negative sanctions. In a broad sense, procedures or programs that are geared to teaching aspects of passive control (particularly self-regulation and self-compliance) can also become an intrinsic part of the organized effort of active social control.

The first difficulty in meshing treatment with a correctional effort is that the treatment can be forced on offenders. To the extent that offenders experience compulsion, force, or coercion, then the treatment effort has been transformed into a type of negative sanction. For example, placement in a relatively benign, semiopen, but "structured environment" is often recommended by probation officers as a treatment-oriented disposition. The experience of many "open settings" is that youngsters may perceive the "treatment" as if it were a potent type of punishment. One indicator of this difficulty is the relatively high rate of runaways. To what extent treatment can be imposed without becoming transformed into a potent type of sanction is an issue worth exploring.

A difficulty in keeping treatment free of social control relates to correctional responses to noncompliance in meeting treatment standards. For example, some probation organizations require attendance at a group meeting periodically, in order to discuss mutual problems (Weeks, 1958; Empey, Newland, and Lubeck, 1965). Nonattendance at group meetings is not usually considered a violation of juvenile delinquency statutes; however, it can be considered grounds for violating probation. How many absences from a group meeting will be countenanced before applying sanctions to gain compliance can vary by organizations. To the degree that offenders receive sanctions for this noncompliance, the treatment will again have been transformed into a type of social control. Differential involvement or participation in treatment programs can be a recurrent source of difficulty for agencies of active social control that also offer treatment services. The powers of the social control officer can be used to force compliance with the treatment norms of the treatment officer, as will become evident in part 1.

The third difficulty can relate to the procedures per se. For example, in current work with youthful offenders a variety of procedures within the repertoire of behavior modification are explicitly geared to a minisystem of rewards and punishments (Phillips, Wolf, Bailey, and Fixsen, 1972). To the extent that the present discussion of social control has focused on negative sanctions, the reward aspects of the procedures need not be perceived as an indication of problematic social control. Major difficulty arises when aversive procedures can serve a dual function—as sanctions for misbehaving and as a "contingency" for eliciting more appropriate behavior. If the balance of "negative contingencies" outweighs the granting of "positive contingencies," then the treatment program may be classified, as well as experienced, as a means of administering a regulatory agency. Competent action researchers, currently attached to universities, appear sensitive to this problem. They purposefully design token economy systems whereby youth receive more rewards than punishments for their behavioral performances. Whether alternative programs, using aversive procedures, can maintain this positive balance is a matter worthy of investigation (but which will not be addressed in this study).

Probation Subsidy

In 1967 there was no published evidence that contradicted the impression that CTP-type programs were effective, less costly than traditional correctional programs, and free of coercion. It is therefore understandable that the writers of the President's Commission report on corrections were not hesitant or cautious in urging states to finance county and local programs that were in consonance with the new community treatment policy. One financial strategy that appeared promising and capable of yielding a rapid implementation of the proposed strategy was singled out for attention. This was California's novel plan of "State Aid for Probation Service" (commonly referred to as "Probation Subsidy").

According to the California legislation of 1965, funds could be authorized for distribution to a county, from general state revenues, on the condition that a county reduce its actual first commitments to state correctional facilities below its expected rate of commitments. Besides reducing commitments below the expected "base rate," a county also had to be able to demonstrate that it had organized special probation units that offered intensive supervision. The legislation did not, however, mandate that only those offenders that could have been committed to state institutions were eligible to be included in the restricted caseloads of the special supervision units. While only certain categories of offenders could be counted for purposes of computing commitment reductions, the counties were free to include any type of offender as potential probation subsidy "cases" in their actual client workload.

This approach to financing community treatment alternatives was recommended by the President's Commission in the belief not only that it was fiscally sound, but that states could afford to pay subsidies out of the savings generated by receiving fewer offenders. In addition, of course, a state would also be expected to have reduced the institutionalization of offenders. The positive recommendation by a prestigious federal commission has recently been reinforced by the official endorsement of the Youth Development and Delinquency Prevention Administration of the U.S. Department of Health, Education, and Welfare (President's Commission, 1967b; Smith, 1972).

The designers of probation subsidy were quite aware that state subventions to counties would require an alteration in correctional decision making at the county level. In order for the subsidy program to be put into operation, counties would have to reduce commitments by altering a portion of the dispositional decisions pertaining to offenders. The incentive for obtaining new patterns of decision making was, of course, the sizable amount of money that could be obtained from noncounty funds. The data reported in part 2 indicate that the subsidy strategy appeared to be quite successful in reducing the commitment of offenders to the state; it also provided counties with "earnings" of over 20 million dollars in fiscal 1971-72.

While the designers of the subsidy policy were successful in influencing changed decision making at the county level, they apparently paid minimal attention to the discretionary decisions of the administration of state facilities. With a reduction in state commitments, the following organizational changes occurred in state correctional facilities during the subsidy years, 1966–71:

1. The length of institutional stay for youth that were still being committed to CYA facilities increased from an average stay of 8 months to 11.2 months in the CYA, and from 30 to 36 months in the adult institutions.

2. New bed capacity was permitted to be phased in while old beds were being phased out, with a net gain of at least 320 beds for CYA facilities.

3. The ratio of staff to wards was permitted to decrease in CYA facilities.

4. The time on parole, after a lengthier institutional stay, was also increased for CYA wards from an average of 24.9 months to 28.4 months.

5. The rates in the use of "temporary detention," for parole treatment purposes, increased markedly during this period.

These changes were not part of the ideal design. Instead, they reflected systemic responses to the altered rates of new commitments, as well as discretionary adaptations to job and organizational survival. The new fiscal costs of these cumulative, systemic effects were profound. By the end of the first year of operation of the subsidy program, the expected economic savings by the state had vanished, as the analysis in part 2 below makes clear. State officials claimed the opposite in reports to the legislature, even while admitting that per capita costs for operating state institutions had increased dramatically. In part 2 a detailed examination is made of the deficiencies in conceptualization and computational method that prevented the state Department of Finance from realizing that the state's operating correctional costs had increased significantly in the postsubsidy years. Evidently CTP was not the only community-oriented program capable of creating a cost overrun linked to unintended systemic consequences and unregulated discretionary decision making.

Probation subsidy had social consequences as well as those of a fiscal nature. The evidence presented in part 2 indicates quite clearly that postsubsidy youth commitments were probably experiencing more CYA institutional time as an offset to the lower rates of county commitments. In a sense, the postsubsidy commitments were incurring added individual costs as a result of the change in correctional policy. To the extent that unnecessary individual deprivation of liberty is also deemed to be a social liability, then social costs were also involved in the lengthening of institutional stay.

Besides these social costs, there is also evidence that at a county level many more youth were experiencing detention in county facilities than during the presubsidy years (controlling for population changes and the rise in drug arrests). This finding complicated the assessment of social costs even further: for while fewer youth were being deprived of their liberty at the state level, many more were being detained at the county level; and while fewer youth were experiencing lengthier lock-up periods at a state level, more were experiencing shorter lock-up periods at a county level. According to computations depicted in part 2, there is a lack of evidence that California has, in fact, reduced the net amount of statewide institutionalization when state and county figures are combined. It appears, contrary to conventional beliefs, that probation subsidy need not be associated with economic savings or a reduction in total institutionalization.

Conclusions and Summary

This study is prepared to examine the possibility that community treatment can include alternative modes of social control (as well as treatment). Paying attention to discrepancies between ideals and actual practices, unintended consequences, discretionary decision making, and systemic effects can aid in specifying the occurrence and range of uses of social control. In addition, a critical analytic perspective is capable of revealing a variety of other findings that challenge conventional assumptions about the social and fiscal costs and benefits of community treatment.

While this study can reveal surprising findings and raise policy issues that are usually left unexamined, there are limitations regarding the generality of the findings. These limitations pertain primarily to the limited sample of community treatment efforts chosen for this study. It is evident that two programs, conducted in one state, cannot adequately represent all of the many variations of a community treatment strategy that are currently occurring in other parts of the country. While the study has definite limitations, it seems reasonable to argue that the findings outweigh these limitations. For the findings pertain to two of the most highly prized examples of the new correctional policy. By examining these prototypes, we can begin to discern the range of choices and consequences that might occur in other states—when ideals are transformed into operational practices.

The following chapters will report and discuss the findings in greater detail, document their authenticity, and attempt to assess the emergent policy issues. A chapter summarizing the distinctive issues posed by CTP can be found at the end of part 1. A similar summary chapter, synthesizing the policy issues raised by Probation Subsidy, can be found at the end of part 2. The final chapter attempts to assess community treatment from a broad policy perspective, using the insights gained in parts 1 and 2. In addition, an attempt will be made to hypothesize about the theoretical implications associated with findings concerning alternative modes of social control.

PART ONE
The Community Treatment Project

2   The Community Treatment Project: The Ideal Program

The Community Treatment Project (CTP) began operation in September 1961 in the urban areas of Sacramento and Stockton, California. It was designed as a combined experimental and demonstration project to determine the impact of substituting an intensive program in the community in lieu of the traditional institutional programs conducted by the California Youth Authority (CYA). Initially conceived as a three-year endeavor, jointly financed by the National Institute of Mental Health and the State of California, CTP received renewed five-year funding in 1964 to continue its earlier efforts and to expand its research and demonstration work to an area in San Francisco. In 1966 a spin-off project focusing on the use of group homes in treatment supervision was approved for additional funding by NIMH and the State of California. In 1969 a modified project was jointly funded to replace the original program; this new program was designed to test the relative efficacy of starting treatment of selected juvenile offenders in a special institutional setting. The present study will deal only with the CTP as it functioned from 1961 to 1969. As noted in the Introduction, it is this phase of the CYA's community treatment efforts that received national attention and recognition (National Institute of

Mental Health, 1971a; President's Commission, 1967a, p. 170; National Commission, 1969, pp. 578–80).

Specific Aims and Working Assumptions

In the initial proposal three specific aims were set forth as major goals:

1. *To determine the feasibility* of releasing selected California Youth Authority wards directly from a reception center to a treatment program in the community; to see whether communities are willing to accept the return under treatment conditions of members who have just been "banished" as no longer tolerable in the community;

2. *To compare the effectiveness* of a period of community treatment with a period of incarceration as measured by parole performance and attitudinal and behavioral changes in the ward; and

3. *To develop hypotheses* regarding treatment plans for definite types of delinquents in specified kinds of settings. [Adams and Grant, 1961, p. 2]

These major goals were supported by five explicit assumptions regarding the kind of program design contemplated: (1) the belief that youth "acting out" because of "family tensions and community pressures" should keep "facing these tensions" and "make use of offered help," rather than be incarcerated and removed from confronting their problems; (2) the belief that specific treatment strategies and programs must be individually designed "to meet the needs and problems of a particular type of delinquent"; (3) the belief that each youngster could be classified into a specific "type" that would not only designate his Interpersonal Maturity Level (I-Level), but would suggest the goals, techniques, and programs to be applied to the individual CYA ward; (4) the belief that past efforts at attaining treatment success had been hindered by the failure properly to classify youth or to provide appropriate and adequate differential treatment resources to deal with the diagnosed problems; (5) the belief that existing parole agents could be selectively hired to become community agents, and that these primary treaters—chosen mainly for their flexibility in applying individual or group techniques and their ability to communicate with researchers—could be trained to engage in I-Level diagnosis and treatment strategies (Adams and Grant, 1961, pp. 1–2).

Proposed Program Design

In order to be successful in carrying out such a differentiated treatment strategy, proposed caseloads were extremely small (about eight wards to each agent). In addition, to handle the complexities of working with local community representatives, as well as to supervise agents in their complex assignments, two types of project supervisors were required: a program supervisor and a treatment supervisor. To ease the management and supervision task, only fifty wards would be assigned to a unit, with a staff of six agents, clerical assistance, and resources to purchase foster care, tutors, treatment consultants, transportation, etc.

To test the effectiveness of the program, a pool of eligible cases would be randomly assigned to experimental and control groups. All first-commitment wards sent to the Youth Authority's Northern Reception Center Clinic, from the juvenile courts covering the greater urban area of Sacramento and Stockton, were deemed eligible for inclusion in the experimental design. Within this general eligible group, the following categories were excluded from the CTP experiment: (1) wards whose most appropriate placement is outside metropolitan Sacramento and Stockton; (2) wards requiring transfer to the Department of Mental Hygiene; (3) wards who will likely move from the area within six months after release to the project; (4) cases of murder second degree, robbery first degree, forcible rape, manslaughter, vicious assault, and other serious offenses; and (5) cases involving intense community reaction (Adams and Grant, 1961, pp. 4–5).

Upon random assignment to CTP rather than to a CYA institution, wards would proceed through three stages of treatment. Stage A was to be an *intensive* period of treatment lasting about eight months after release from the Reception Center. Intensive contact was defined as including *from two to five agent-ward contacts per week*, as well as full or partial day-programming for youth. This stage was meant to approximate the average length of institutional stay of "control" wards—those youngsters who were eligible for CTP but who had been randomly allocated to receive the traditional CYA program. Stage B was planned as a transitional period "to help the ward work through any difficulties arising from the decrease in amount of support and supervision from the agent." Agent-ward contacts were expected to average *one per week*. Stage C was to be a *minimum supervision* period, "when treatment of experimental cases will compare with treatment accorded to regular parolees in the Youth Authority." Therefore, case contacts would average only *one per month*. It was expected that "success criteria comparisons" would be based on the "parole" experiences of experimentals and controls during stage C and the discharge period (Adams and Grant, 1961, p. 7).

In October 1961, after extensive planning and preparation, the first eligible experimental boys and girls entered the Community Treatment Project. By the time of the first progress report to NIMH, in August 1962, the program was able to provide evidence that the CYA board representatives had deemed 73 percent of the boys and all of the girls to be "eligible" CTP participants—even though they might be randomly assigned to an institutional facility. The ideal design would be tested in practice, since subsequent years provided comparable rates of eligible youth.

Proposed Indicators of Effectiveness

Besides proposing a treatment strategy and a research design to implement the aims and the assumptions of the project, the primary initiators of the proposal, Adams and Grant, also proposed to measure the impact of CTP. They described the impact measures as follows:

1. *Differential success rates of experimental and control cases in the second year of the program.* The parole criteria will be the major test of difference. Criteria include: suspension of parole, revocation of parole, good and bad discharge, parole officer ratings, number of months of reincarceration, and seriousness of recommitment offense.
2. *Differential personal and social adjustment of experimental and control subjects in the community.* Ratings will be made by the agent, research staff, and significant others in the ward's life.
3. *Differential changes in the psychological characteristics of wards under experimental and control conditions.* In this area, tests and ratings related both to classification material and to other variables which may be expected to show change with treatment, will make up the data. [Adams and Grant, 1961, p. 9]

Major Reasons Advanced for Funding

Besides arguing for the rationality of the proposed program and research design, the initiators of CTP appealed to funding sources as follows:

Overcrowding in the institutions plus the high cost of new construction is the combination of conditions most frequently cited as creating a demand for finding alternative programs to institutionalization of delinquents. Even if this very practical problem did not exist, there can be found real and urgent reasons for research to be conducted in this area. Little is known about the relative good or harm which may attach to the institutional experience for various kinds of youths, although it is known that the recidivism rate following release from state training schools remains constantly high. There exists no tested way of classifying juvenile offenders systematically into types who would benefit from training programs while incarcerated as opposed to types which could be more successfully treated in an intensive program in the community. There is widespread belief that maintaining a young person as an integral part of the community, while strengthening his ability to relate to family, school, and other normal social functions is a desirable goal whenever this is possible. This line of reasoning, then, led to the development of the proposal for the Community Treatment Project. [State of California Youth Authority, 1962-68, *CTP Research Report No. 1*, 1962, pp. 1-2]

This list of reasons indicates that practical, as well as clinical, empirical, and humanitarian interests, were linked to the initiation of this large-scale community treatment project. Building and maintaining traditional state training school programs was a correctional policy involving increasing economic costs. This practical concern over correctional costs suggests that CTP *could* be assessed by an additional indicator of effectiveness—the extent to which community treatment could reduce costs for handling CYA wards.

Administration and Sources of Funding
The program of CTP was organized as a special parole unit within the CYA's regional parole system; the research activities were undertaken by a special unit within the Division of Research. This meant that the CTP workers and supervisors were theoretically responsible for following established CYA procedures for writing reports, granting suspensions, recommending revocations, or requesting honorable or dishonorable discharges from supervision.

The major cost for financing the program was borne by the CYA. However, the funds for program operation did not come out of the existing institutional, parole, or administrative budgets. Rather, the monies represented additional appropriations added to the CYA parole budget by the State of California. In fiscal 1966–67, according to the Legislative Analyst to the Joint Budget Committee of the California State Legislature, the additional state funds required for CTP program operations amounted to more than $698,000 (State of California Legislative Committee, 1966, p. 170).

The entire cost of the research staff was borne by the NIMH from 1961 to 1969. In addition, NIMH also funded, from 1961 to 1964, special program costs that the state legislature refused to authorize: the salary of the treatment supervision personnel, part-time tutor positions and school costs, and treatment consultation costs. Proposal requests indicate that NIMH expended over a million dollars during the eight years of the project. The State of California probably expended at least four times that amount during the same time period, since the 1966–67 budget request indicates that each year cost at least half a million dollars.

I-Level Theory and the Treatment-Control Strategy

The typology used in the Community Treatment Project is called the "Interpersonal Maturity Level Classification: Juvenile." The classification of a delinquent youth is made in two steps. The individual is first diagnosed according to level of perceptual differentiation or degree of complexity in his view of himself and others. This step identifies the individual's Interpersonal Maturity Level (also called Integration Level or I-Level). In the second classification step, individuals within each I-Level are further diagnosed according to *response set* or way of responding to their perceptions of the world. There are two major ways in which the I-Level 2 (I_2) individual responds to his perceptual frame of reference. Similarly, there are three typical response sets among delinquent I_3s, and four typical response sets among delinquent I_4s. In this manner, nine delinquent subtypes have been identified. These subtypes have been described by lists of item definitions which characterize the manner in which the members of each group perceive the world, respond to the world, and are perceived by others. The descriptions of the subtypes, with predicted-most-effective intervention or treatment plans, combine to make up the *Differential Treatment Model* used in the Experimental program of the Community Treatment Project.

Brief descriptions of the three I-Levels and the nine subtypes are given below, as described by Warren (1969, pp. 47–59):

Maturity Level 2 (I_2): The individual whose interpersonal understanding and behavior are integrated at this level is primarily involved with demands that the world take care of him. He sees others primarily as "givers" or "withholders" and has no conception of interpersonal refinement beyond this. He has poor capacity to explain, understand, or predict the behavior or reactions of others. He is not interested in things outside himself except as a source of supply. He behaves impulsively, unaware of anything except the grossest effects of his behavior on others.

Subtypes: (1) *Asocial, Aggressive* (Aa) responds with active demands and open hostility when frustrated.
(2) *Asocial, Passive* (Ap) responds with whining, complaining and withdrawal when frustrated.

Maturity Level 3 (I_3): The individual who is functioning at this level, although somewhat more differentiated than the I_2, still has social perceptual deficiencies which lead to an underestimation of the differences among others and between himself and others. More than the I_2, he does understand that his own behavior has something to do with whether or not he gets what he wants. He makes an effort to manipulate his environment to bring about "giving" rather than "denying" response. He does not operate from an internalized value system but rather seeks external structure in terms of rules and formulas for operation. His understanding of formula is indiscriminate and oversimplified. He perceives the world and his part in it on a power dimension. Although he can learn to play a few stereotyped roles, he cannot understand many of the needs, feelings and motives of another person who is different from himself. He is unmotivated to achieve in a long-range sense, or to plan for the future. Many of these features contribute to his inability to accurately predict the response of others to him.

Subtypes: (3) *Immature Conformist* (Cfm) responds with immediate compliance to whoever seems to have the power at the moment. (4) *Cultural Conformist* (Cfc) responds with conformity to specific reference group, delinquent peers. (5) *Manipulator* (Mp) operates by attempting to undermine the power of authority figures and/or usurp the power role for himself.

Maturity Level 4 (I_4): An individual whose understanding and behavior are integrated at this level has internalized a set of standards by which he judges his and others' behavior. He can perceive a level of interpersonal interaction in which individuals have expectations of each other and can influence each other. He

TABLE 1
Overview of I-Level Typology and Selected Treatment Strategies

Level and Subtype	Critical Characteristics	Preferred Placement Plan	Desired Kinds of Agent Focus	Suggested Kind of Control Focus
I_2 *Level*	Unsocialized, disorganized personality; low level of frustration tolerance	Group home or foster home (both types)	Externally oriented, since ward needs structure and support rather than insight counseling. Extreme patience (both types)	Simple and concrete demands; gradual insistence on conformity with no great penalties for non-conformity (both types)
1. Asocial, aggressive (Aa)	Responds with active demands or open hostility when frustrated			
2. Asocial, passive (Ap)	Responds with complaining, whining or withdrawal when frustrated			
I_3 *Level*	Beginning to recognize that behavior has impact on others, but satisfied with his way of life and himself		Strict, but fair, with an impersonal approach toward youth	Well defined demands with possible use of weekend use of center or profects at center or use of local detention on a weekend basis (all three types)
3. Immature conformist (Cfm)	Responds with strong compliance to persons whom he thinks have the power at the moment	Own family if possible, but where behavior limits strict	Guided group counseling with emphasis on external world	
4. Cultural conformist (Cfe)	Responds with conformity to delinquent peers or specific reference group	(Same as subtype 3)	(Same as subtype 3)	

5. Manipulator (Mp)	Frequently attempts to undermine or circumvent authority and usurp power for himself	Strict home behavior limits and set up "communications network to include agent"		(Same as subtype 3)
I₄ Level				
6. Neurotic, acting-out (Na)	Responds to underlying fears or guilt with attempts to "outrun" or deny conscious feelings	Own home, if possible	Warm, supportive, trusting, with clear demands	Make firm demands and use approval/disapproval techniques
	Greater internalized standards and can focus on reasons for behavior; ability to relate		Internal, specialist in individual and group therapy with focus on gaining "insight"	Initially fairly strict, gradually loosening
7. Neurotic, anxious (Nx)	Responds with symptoms of emotional disturbance resulting from conflicts over feelings of inadequacy, fear, or guilt	(Same as 6)	(Same as 6)	(Same as 6)
8. Situation emotional reaction (Se)	Responds to immediate crisis by acting out	(Same as 6)	(Same as 6)	Loose, psychological
9. Cultural identifier (Ci)	Expresses identification with an anti or non-middle class values system by acting out delinquent beliefs	Foster home or group home away from delinquent peers	(Same as 6)	Loose, psychological; control by trusting him

Source: Adaptation of material detailed in Appendix of CTP Proposal submitted to NIMH 27 February 1961 (files of Center for Study of Crime and Delinquency, NIMH)

shows some ability to understand reasons for behavior, some ability to relate to people emotionally and on a long-term basis. He is concerned about status and respect, and is strongly influenced by people he admires.

  Subtypes: (6) *Neurotic, Acting-out* (Na) responds to under-
           lying guilt with attempts to "outrun" conscious
           anxiety and condemnation of self. (7) *Neurotic,
           Anxious* (Nx) responds with symptoms of emotional
           disturbance to conflict produced by feelings of
           inadequacy and guilt. (8) *Situational Emotional
           Reaction* (Se) responds to immediate family or
           personal crisis by acting-out. (9) *Cultural Identifier*
           (Ci) responds to identification with a deviant value
           system by living out his delinquent beliefs.

The delinquent subtypes, along with their code names, may be summarized as follows:

Code Name	Delinquent Subtype
I₂ Aa	Asocial, Aggressive
Ap	Asocial, Passive
I₃ Cfm	Conformist, Immature
Cfc	Conformist, Cultural
Mp	Manipulator
I₄ Na	Neurotic, Acting-out
Nx	Neurotic, Anxious
Se	Situational Emotional Reaction
Ci	Cultural Identifier

Accompanying each diagnostic type is a recommended treatment-control strategy that deals with the following kinds of considerations: (1) treatment goals, (2) placement plan, (3) family variables, (4) location of community supports, (5) job and school recommendation, (6) peer group and recreation variables, (7) kind of controls, (8) kind of agent, and (9) ward-agent interaction (Warren and staff, 1966).

Table 1 attempts to provide a brief overview of I-Level classification, by level and subtype, with three significant aspects of treatment strategy. The table may tend to underplay the complexity of the judgments involved in arriving at a level and subtype diagnosis. However, it highlights critical elements of the proposed program with the associated I-Level rationale.

The first two columns of table 1 provide the typology's nomenclature (or diagnostic labels) and summary descriptions of key modes of youthful functioning. The last three columns refer to three critical elements of treatment "prescriptions"—where the youth should live, type of agent and therapeutic style, and the kinds of approaches to take regarding the control of "acting out" behavior. For example, the rather impulsive, immature I_2 subtypes should not live at their own homes, nor should they receive insight therapy; instead, they should be treated rather patiently (according to their specific, concrete needs), and agent standards for nonconformity should be kept low. In contrast, the middle maturity subtypes (I_3) could live with their own families (if they were strict), could be treated impersonally in a group discussion context, and could, on occasion, even be locked up for a weekend of detention. Much more self-control is expected of I_4 wards; therefore, they can live at home, be treated to insight therapy on an individual or a group level, and controlled by psychological means of approval and disapproval. These general approaches were to be adapted, according to the specific needs and response modes of the subtypes at each level.

3   The CTP in Operation: Changing the Ideal Design

In the previous chapter the project's proposed program and research design was presented. From a policy perspective, this ideal design represents the initial, stated policy of CTP. As the policy is implemented, the original design can either be adhered to or altered. If the program is modified in practice, then it is possible to view the changes as indications of further policy development—and not just as policy implementation. These new policies may or may not be acknowledged by agency administrators or workers as signifying a shift in the original design, but the operating criteria of an administered program are as real as the ideals stated in the original design. From the perspective of the recipients of the operating program, the intentions of the program designers may be neither apparent nor real. The effects of discretionary decision making by CTP personnel on the program and on the original research design will be discussed in this chapter.

Shift from a Stage Strategy to a Lengthy Intensive Strategy

Under the original proposal it was expected that after youth had been declared eligible for the project, there would be a random assignment to either the experimental program or the control program (i.e., release to CTP or to a state training school). On a chance basis this would mean that eligible youth would have a 50-50 chance of being assigned as an experimental or control ward. However, this expectation was not realized.

As of 1 August 1963, about twenty-two months after the operation started, 73 percent of the boys and 97 percent of the girls had been declared eligible—using the criteria set up in the design. Of the 244 Sacramento and Stockton youth declared eligible, only 77 were assigned as experimentals and 167 were assigned as controls. According to *CTP Research Report No. 3*, the reasons for this were as follows:

The 50-50 ratio of experimental and control subjects anticipated has not been maintained for two reasons. The commitment rate increased considerably in Sacramento County from the time of the original proposal to the present. Also, the movement of cases through the experimental program has not been as fast as expected, and, as a result, intake of new cases into the community program has been low during the second year of operation. [State of California Youth Authority—hereafter SCYA—1962-68, *CTP No. 3*, p. 3]

As of 21 January 1964, the total experimental cases increased from 77 to 87. Reasons given for the slow build-up of CTP cases were as follows:

Several factors appear to contribute to keeping the number of cases in the experimental group low: (1) Although an attempt was made to minimize staff turnover within the operations staff, 11 individuals have filled the six community agent positions during the study period, and intake of new cases has been minimized during periods of agent replacement; (2) duration of treatment in the community program was originally underestimated for many types of cases; and (3) experimental cases whose parole had been revoked and who had been institutionalized, were returned to the project following incarceration and thus lowered total case turnover. [*CTP No. 5*, p. 1]

CTP Research Report No. 6 (October 1965) described efforts to build up the experimental caseload. These included changing eligibility criteria to exclude experimental youth whose parole had been revoked (as of a March 1964 cutoff date) and more than doubling the size of the CTP work staff. As of that report the originally planned 50-50 ratio of experimental to control cases had finally begun to materialize. On 1 July 1965, there were 204

experimentals and 272 controls, indicating that the imbalance
was being reduced. By 31 March 1966, the eligible youth that
were randomly assigned were closer to being equal in numbers,
243 experimentals and 283 controls. The two samples of eligible
youth were comparable regarding I-Level and subtype classification with one exception: the control group had seven youth that
were classified as unsocialized aggressive (Aa), but the experimental had none. Excluding these seven youth from statistical
analysis, the CTP researchers were able to demonstrate that the
eligible 243 experimentals and 276 controls were comparable
regarding the following population characteristics: sex, socioeconomic status, type of commitment offense, age, and I.Q.
(*CTP No. 6*, 1966, pp. 33–35). Regarding race, there was a
tendency for the two samples to differ, but this difference was not
statistically significant. While the population comparisons of the
two total eligible samples appeared satisfactory, a similar
inference, as of 31 March 1966, could not be reached when
comparisons were made between specific experimental and
control subtypes.

Analysis of subsequent reports indicate that population differences between specific experimental and control subtypes continued to occur. In addition, for unknown reasons, the population
comparability between the total experimental and control eligible
youth could *not* be demonstrated in subsequent reports. Because
of these operational difficulties, Appendix A documents further
why the present study relied primarily on data that were
associated with *total* experimental and control groups that were
comparable in 1966.

Another aspect of the original overall design that departed
from the ideal design was the staging of program service. Of the
active cases on 1 July 1965, 116 were classified in stage A, 13 in
stage B, and only 7 in stage C (*CTP No. 6*, table 1, p. 4). As of 31
March 1966, 139 youth were in stage A, 11 were in stage B, and
only 6 in stage C (*CTP No. 7*, table 2, p. 31). By 31 March 1967,
the skewed distribution of cases (most cases being classified in
stage A) had not changed appreciably (*CTP No. 8*, part 1, table 1,
p. 3). (Actually these statistical reports appear to have been
presented primarily for record-keeping purposes, since in the text
of the *Research Reports* discussion of levels of treatment by stages
was dropped after February 1964 (*CTP No. 5*, p. 5). In effect, a

new policy had replaced the original one: Provide intensive services for most CTP youth until they are discharged as CYA wards (i.e., for 2½ to 3 years).

This shift in policy influenced the research design. The period "in lieu of institutionalization" and the "parole" periods were to have been assessed separately. But these distinctions were not made in the *Research Reports*; the experimental and control groups were compared only by "total months of community exposure." Because of this shift it is impossible to make the type of analyses that were contemplated at the time the proposal was approved by NIMH.

The shift in policy also had an impact on costs. The longer the wards were kept on caseloads at an intensive level, the lower the turnover rate. The project was forced to hire more agents, thus increasing the total costs. The extent to which the per capita cost of treating experimentals was affected, as compared to controls, will be analyzed in chapter 4.

Operationalizing the Concept of Intensive Services
In the original proposal, intensive treatment services were defined in terms of frequency of contact by the parole agent: from two to five direct contacts per week. However, the proposal did not state how long each contact might last, nor how an agent would allocate his time to engage in collateral contacts, attend staff meetings, write reports, travel, etc. Depending on these nondirect service demands, the amount of time available for directly influencing wards in individual or group sessions could vary.

In 1966, community agents were asked to keep detailed records over a twenty-day work period. Fourteen agents, working in Sacramento and Stockton, recorded their activities at fifteen-minute intervals, according to precoded categories. The agents reported that they worked an average of nine hours per day. Within this average workday they reported spending their time as follows (*CTP No. 8*, part 1, pp. 50–53):

(a) *Direct Ward Contact—38 percent* (this category included individual treatment, diagnostic interviews, prerelease planning, informal activities, school and job-related activities, placement-related activities, driving individuals, group treatment, group informal activities, and group driving).

(b) *Direct Family Contact—7 percent* (this category included initial home visit, placement planning, family treatment, family informal activities, and similar contacts with foster or group home parents).

(c) *Collateral Case Contact—4 percent* (this category included nonagency and agency contacts).

(d) *Case Planning—16 percent* (this category included agent alone with supervisor, research and other CTP staff, group staffing, and meeting with consultant).

(e) *Agency Relations—3 percent* (this category included various contacts with visitors that were non-case related, supervising students, and training others).

(f) *Professional Development—6 percent* (this category included attending seminars or consultant lectures, and discussions with CTP staff).

(g) *Research—2 percent.*

(h) *Administrative—15 percent.*

(i) *Miscellaneous—9 percent.*

This time study indicates that 38 percent of an agent's time was spent in direct work with wards. The figure may be a generous one; of the varied activities coded as "direct ward contact" only 20 percent were classified by agents as consisting of "individual treatment" or "group treatment." However, if all reported activities that involved service to wards were included, then the maximum amount of time would be 45 percent (i.e., direct ward and family contact). This agent-reported figure can be used to compute the operational intensiveness of services available to each ward and his family.

At the outset of the project, agents had an average of eight wards. By 1966 the average appeared to fluctuate between eight and twelve wards per agent:probably in response to pressures to increase the size of the experimental treatment group. If the agents worked about 9 hours a day, then in a 45-hour work week they would have a maximum of 20.25 hours (45 percent of 45 hours) available for direct services to individuals and families. For a caseload of ten wards (mid-way between eight and twelve wards per agent) this would amount to about 2.0 hours per week of direct service time available to each case. In a quantitative sense, then, it is possible to define intensive treatment in 1966 as consisting of a worker's devoting, on the average, two hours a week to direct service to each ward and family when his caseload has a median of ten cases. While this method of measuring intensity is our own and not CTP's, it appears to flow logically from a reanalysis of the original data. Besides specifying the actual meaning of "intensive service," this measurement can also be used to provide a basis for estimating the average treatment exposure time for each ward for any time period. Intensive treatment, however, is *not* the sole program element.

Assessing the Balance between Program Elements

In August 1963, nineteen months after initiating the program, CTP issued a progress report (*CTP No. 3*) detailing the use of various elements of the treatment program with 72 experimental cases (62 boys and 10 girls). Table 2 is an adapted reproduction of the data that provides insight into the early use of program elements.

TABLE 2
Use of Program Elements in CTP, as of 1 January 1963 (Total N=72)

	Youth Receiving Element			
Program Elements	Boys	Girls	Total No.	% Receiving Element
Individual counseling	44	10	54	75
Individual psychotherapy	10	1	11	15
Guided group interaction	27	0	27	38
Group psychotherapy	11	0	11	15
Activity group therapy	16	0	16	22
Discussion group therapy	9	10	19	26
Family treatment	20	1	21	29
Foster home / group home placement	39	9	48	67
Foster parent group meetings	13	0	13	18
School tutoring	19	1	20	28
Temporary confinement*	50	7	57	79

*Figures include the use of temporary confinement for all purposes, including control, protective, medical, etc.
Source: *SCYA, 1963, Report No. 3*, p. 28.

At first glance, the table appears to convey an operational categorization and counting of differential treatment. However, the last column provides evidence that the actual program and the ideal program had diverged in the elements of "placement" and "temporary confinement." As originally conceived, only I_2

youth were to live away from their homes, and mainly I_3 youth were to experience occasional weekend lockups (see table 1). Instead, community treatment had begun to mean that 77–79 percent of the youth were removed from their homes during an average community exposure time of eleven months per case. According to other data in the report, only 11 percent of the youth were I_2 cases—but 67 percent of *all* youth were placed in group or foster homes. And 51 percent of the youth were I_3 cases—but 79 percent of *all* youth were placed in temporary confinement in county detention centers or in the CYA's Northern Reception Center Clinic.

By 1968 the experimental caseload had increased to 276 youth, with an average community exposure time of 22.5 months. By this time the proportion of youth classified as I_2 was only 4 percent, while I_3 and I_4 represented 33 percent and 64 percent respectively. By this time 89 percent of *all* experimentals had experienced temporary detention at least once as CTP wards (*CTP No. 9*, part 3, pp. 4 and 14). The use of deprivation of liberty had become an operational policy for the life of the project, for virtually all wards, regardless of I-Level classification. How this major policy shift occurred is reflected in early progress reports:

Original planning for the overall treatment-control program allowed for the fact that some wards on occasion would have to be placed under restraint as a control measure. Arrangements were made for using the Youth Authority Reception Center and the county juvenile halls as places for temporary detention. In practice, the use of detention has emerged as an important intervention strategy, useful under a variety of circumstances. [*CTP No. 1*, p. 12]

The necessity for the project to enforce controls for acting-out behavior and to provide temporary shelter for experimental wards led to an arrangement whereby cases could be placed . . . for brief periods of time as needed. As the Project has developed, such temporary confinement has become an important treatment and control tool. Of the 72 experimental cases in the Project during the 19 month period of analysis, 57 cases have been placed in temporary confinement for a total of 183 times, or an average of three times each with an average length of stay in confinement of 12 days per confinement. Prorated on a yearly basis, experimental cases have a yearly average of two confinements per case.

The reasons for confinement, in descending order of frequency, are: car theft, 26 times (16 boys, 1 girl); misbehavior at school, 24 times (10 boys); uncooperative attitude toward the program, 18 times (10 boys); truancy, 17 times (10 boys); trouble in home or foster home, 15 times (11 boys, 3 girls); runaway, 12 times (7 boys, 3 girls); burglary, 11 times (8 boys); curfew violation, 10 times (9 boys); failure to attend group meetings, 9 times (7 boys); drinking, 8 times (6 boys); prevention of acting-out, 7 times (5 boys, 1 girl); ward's request, 5 times (4 boys, 1 girl); fighting, 4 times (4 boys); petty theft, 4 times (3 boys); possession of knife, 2 times (2 boys); glue sniffing, 2 times (1 boy); malicious mischief, 1 time (1 boy). As can be observed, the same wards may appear in more than one of the above instances and categories. [*CTP No. 3*, p. 38]

By 1966 the number of youth in CTP had increased, but the frequency and the broad array of reasons for many detentions had not appreciably changed. Comparisons with the control parolees highlight the existence of differential practices regarding CTP wards:

Information relating to parole suspension behavior will be presented for the 243 experimentals and 220 controls who had been released to parole between 10-31-61 and 3-31-66. The mean time spent in the community for the experimental subjects was 16.4 months, and it was 17.9 months for the controls.

... Of the 243 experimentals studied in connection with parole suspension behavior, 180 (74 percent) had one or more suspensions. Of the 220 control subjects, 157 (71 percent) had one or more suspensions. Experimental subjects had a total of 678 suspensions—*an average of 2.8 per ward* (or an average of one suspension for every 5.9 months of community exposure)—while controls had a total of 355 suspensions—*an average of 1.6 per ward* (or an average of one suspension for every 11.9 months of community exposure).

... *A great deal of use is made of temporary confinement* as a treatment-control device in the Community Treatment Project, and since temporary confinement may *only* be used with a warrant of arrest, arrests are frequently made, in the experimental group, for such *relatively nondelinquent offenses as missing a group meeting, "sassing" a teacher, showing an unco-operative attitude, or a threat of an emotional explosion at home* (protective custody).

... Related to this is the finding that *54* percent (365) of all experimental suspensions had been initiated by community agents, while *21* percent (176) of all control suspensions had been initiated by regular parole agents. [*CTP No. 7*, pp. 64–65; italics added]

This kind of evidence indicates that CTP agents used control measures more than regular CYA parole agents. They formally arrested and detained youth for noncriminal offenses more frequently. They also engaged in discretionary decision making more frequently, since judicial orders by a judge were not required; nor were orders from CYA board representatives required *prior* to placing youth in a lockup. The occasional weekend lockup, as envisioned in the original treatment design, had grown to 2.8 suspensions per youth with 1.75 suspensions per youth attributable to either juvenile status offenses or technical parole violations (see table 3 for sources used in this computation). The average length of stay in 1966 had also increased to twenty days per confinement, as disclosed by a special report by a Task Force evaluation team (SCYA, June 1966, *Temporary Detention*).

The evidence that deprivation of liberty was, in practice, used "a great deal" by CTP agents appears indisputable. What is not as evident, without further analysis, is the likelihood that CTP wards actually experienced this program element *more* than they experienced treatment services. This inference concerning the relative balance of social control and treatment is based on the outcome of the type of analysis depicted in table 3.

Table 3 attempts to translate the average available treatment exposure time per week into average days exposure for sixteen months and then compare this exposure to the detention days experienced by youth. Two comparisons are attempted: (1) a comparison of average number of days detained per ward for a sixteen-month period as compared to the average days available for "direct service" per ward for a comparable time period; (2) a second comparison of only the average number of detention days for noncriminal offenses (i.e., juvenile status and technical violations). The table will *not* be found in the CTP research reports. However, all of the facts upon which this analysis is built can be found in the appropriate citations.

The mathematical computations involved in this analysis are rather straightforward. The steps for computing the average number of days in detention lockups is as follows: (a) *CTP Research Report No. 7* disclosed, in 1966, that the average number of detentions forming part of a parole-suspension per ward for a 16-month period was 2.8; (b) the 1966 Task Force evaluation on temporary detention disclosed that the average length of stay for one suspension was approximately 20 days; (c) therefore, if each ward received 2.8 suspensions, and stayed in

---

TABLE 3
Exposure to Detention and Treatment Program Elements

A. *All Detention vs. Maximum Direct Service*
  1. Temporary Detention
    a. Average suspensions/ward in 16-month period   2.8
    b. Average length of stay/detention   20 days
    c. Average no. of days/ward/16 months   56 days
  2. Direct Service
    a. Maximum working hours/week per CTP agent   45 hours
    b. Percent time in direct service (wards and families)   45 percent
    c. Average no. of hours/week available to all wards   20.3 hours
    d. Average no. of hours available/week/ward   2.0 hours
    e. Average no. of hours available/mo./ward   8.6 hours
    f. Average no. of hours available/16 mos./ward   137.6 hours
    g. Average no. of days available/16 mos./ward   5.7 days
  3. Ratio of Detention: Service/16 mos.
    56 days: 5.7 days   9.8:1

B. *Noncriminal Detention Only vs. Maximum Direct Service*
  1. Noncriminal Detention*
    a. No. of suspensions/100 youth
       classifiable as juvenile status offense or
       technical violation   175/100
    b. Average no. of suspensions/ward   1.75
    c. Average length of stay/det.   20 days
    d. Average no. of days/ward/16 months   35 days
  2. Direct Service (as computed above)   5.7 days
  3. Rate of Detention: Service/16 mos.
    35 days: 5.7 days   6.1:1

Sources: A. SCYA, 1966, *Report No. 7*, pp. 117–18, and 92, and *Report No. 8*, part 1, pp. 50–52. B. SCYA, June 1966, *Temporary Detention: A Task Force Evaluation*, p. 11.

*The following types of CTP descriptions of suspension offenses were used to code as juvenile status or technical parole violations: "medical, protection, preventive (ward's request), preventive (agent's request), uncooperative attitude, missed group meeting, home adjustment, poor school adjustment, simple runaway, investigation, loitering near school, curfew, loitering, trespassing, runaway (whereabouts unknown), fighting (no weapons), drinking, possession of alcohol, malicious mischief, disturb the peace (etc.), begging, driving with suspended/revoked license, intoxication (alcohol, glue, etc.)" (see SCYA, 1966, *Report No. 7*, Appendix R, pp. 117–18).

detention an average time of 20 days (per stay), then the average number of days would be 20 days times 2.8, or 56 days. Each CTP ward, on the average, experienced about 56 days of detention during a 16-month period.

The specification of the meaning of intensive treatment was discussed in the preceding part of this chapter. The 1966 community-agent time study disclosed that the maximum working hours that a CTP agent might normally make available is 45 hours per week. The analysis of how parole agents actually spent their time disclosed that only 45 percent of their time was devoted to "direct services"—the time when they were in direct contact with wards and their families. This means that only 20.25 hours per week were maximally available to treat wards. However, since the agent had an average of ten wards to whom he must provide this intensive service, he had about 2.0 hours per week, on the average, that he could spend with each ward. In a month (i.e., 4.3 weeks) this amounts to 8.6 hours, and in 16 months he could have treated, on the average, each ward for 137.6 hours. When these average hours are translated into units of average days, the average available time to provide direct services to wards, in a 16-month period, is about 5.7 days. The ratio of detention exposure days to direct service exposure days is 56 to 5.7 or a ratio of 9.8 days of detention to 1 day of direct service.

Section B of table 3 uses the same kind of logic, except that only *noncriminal* offenses are included. A reanalysis and recomputation of the raw data found in Appendix R, *CTP Research Report No. 7*, disclosed that the rate of juvenile status or technical parole violation suspensions was 175 per 100 youth—or 1.75 suspensions per ward. For these types of noncriminal offenses, CTP youth each spent an average of 35 days in detention during a 16-month period. The ratio of control experiences to treatment experiences is, therefore, 35 days to 5.7 days, or 6.1 to 1.

This assessment of the relative balance between detention and treatment does not take into account the quality of each exposure. Even if all treatment were of the highest quality, it is appropriate to determine whether there is an empirical basis for claiming intensive treatment as the primary element. While treatment may have been primary in intention, the facts clearly indicate that a social control was delivered much more intensively during a given time period. Even if the amount of social control intensiveness was reduced to a 16-hour day instead of a 24-hour day, to eliminate involuntary sleep and nighttime living accommodations, the imbalance would still disclose detention as the primary program element.

If the other two program elements, individual tutoring and foster home placement, were capable of being analyzed, it is unlikely that the amount of treatment exposure would be increased. Table 1 shows that only 28 percent received some form of tutoring, and none of the subsequent reports indicate that tutors were trained or actually delivered treatment. Foster homes and group homes were used extensively by CTP, but these alternative environments and living arrangements were not staffed on a 24-hour basis by treaters. Rather, the CTP agent in charge of a case continued his treatment role and delivery of services wherever youngsters might be assigned. In addition, it is possible that many group home arrangements involve an altered form of social control. Reanalysis of CTP Group Home data indicates that 50 percent of the children placed ran away at least once; this figure indicates that many youth probably perceived this program element as a type of involuntary living arrangement (SCYA, 1968, pp. 119–26).

Taking into account all of the program elements, it appears reasonable to conclude that the CTP parole agent, and not tutors and foster parents, delivered the program's treatment services. There is little reason to doubt that intensive exposure to the CTP agent, in individual and group settings, was considered to be the primary program element.

On the basis of the evidence, we conclude that the primary program element actually experienced by CTP wards (in 1966) was short-term confinement and not intensive-treatment services. Whether this component was ultimately effective in changing youth can only be determined by evidence relating to an *overall* evaluation, since the original research design did not contemplate measuring impact for *each* program element. This overall assessment, however, can be made for the entire CTP program and will be documented in the next chapter.

Assessing the Rationale for Using Temporary Detention

The analysis of the relative balance of program elements actually used by CTP is based on the assumption that *any* correctional program can be conceptualized as an organizational effort that can engage in control and treatment activities. In the Introduction it was suggested that social control activities pertain to types of sanctions or deprivations, while treatment activities pertain to helpful benefits or services. Without this kind of distinction it would be impossible to measure the degree and duration of *distinctive* program elements. Instead of making distinctions we could count everything in a program as consisting of "social control" (as appears to be done by many current critics of traditional institutional programs). Alternatively, we could count everything in a program as consisting of "treatment" (as appears to be done by many current supporters of community treatment programs). If we balk at this either/or approach, and strive to make analytic distinctions, then "social control" and "treatment" must be defined as mutually exclusive—and measured by using *independent* indicators of their usage.

What appeared in the Introduction to be merely a theoretical exposition is, therefore, an analytic perspective that has profound implications for what shall be measured and counted. Besides these research implications, it is also evident that the outcomes of data analyses can pose some fairly basic policy issues. Instead of just being concerned about treatment effectiveness, we could, in addition, evidence concern about the fairness and justice of the activities and decisions of correctional programs.

While these ideas may appear to be reasonable, there are many treatment-oriented correctional administrators and workers who do not distinguish between social control and treatment. It thus appears that the way one conceptualizes correctional programs is a fairly critical policy issue. Fortunately, there is empirical evidence available that permits an assessment of this alternative mode of perceiving the world of corrections.

In 1965, as a result of management interest in evaluating temporary detention, the CYA created a special committee to assess its use by special parole projects. Specifically, the CYA Task Force was requested to assess the use of detention in CTP and the Oakland Community Delinquency Control Project. The committee of five members included Warren, the co-author of the CTP proposal and the principal research investigator (1961–67). Joseph Kleine, a former treatment and operations supervisor of CTP served as the CYA consultant to the Task Force. Loren

Look, the 1965 Administrative Supervisor of CTP, and Edward
Harrington, a former CTP parole agent, served as resource
persons. An unusually frank, but sympathetic, report was issued
in June 1966. The Task Force commented about the problem of
temporary detention as follows:

> The need to alter or influence human behavior through the use
> of sanctions (both positive and negative varieties) is well
> established. Modern rehabilitative agencies have a severely
> restricted range of sanctions. Fewer rewards, if any, can be
> offered clients. Corporal or psychological punishments are for-
> bidden. One of the few sanctions available is to grant or restrict
> personal liberty.
>   Over the years, courts and correctional agencies have restricted
> liberty for a variety of reasons. In recent years the most common
> reason given for the restriction is the 'rehabilitation' of the
> offender. It is within this general framework, that is, a treatment
> technique designed to influence or change behavior in a positive
> direction that temporary detention in Youth Authority programs
> is being used.
>   The Youth Authority is not the first agency to use detention as
> a tool in the rehabilitation process. Other jurisdictions also have
> encountered a need for applying negative sanctions in the form of
> temporary detention. For many years, probation officers, parole
> agents, and other treaters have attempted to use detention in a
> therapeutic manner.
>   The Youth Authority has a mandate to control delinquent
> behavior, and, if possible, change delinquents into non-
> delinquents. Community treatment programs are a serious
> attempt to carry out this mandate. If these programs are to
> continue to function successfully, they must be able to exercise
> control over ward behavior. Temporary detention is one method
> of control which has been effective with many wards. More
> importantly, it is the only method of control which has proven
> effective with some wards. This treatment technique is vital to
> community programs and the further restriction or elimination of
> its use may jeopardize the success and survival of these programs.
> [SCYA, 1966, p. 3]

The argument presented can be broken down into a sequential
statement as follows: (1) there is a need to influence behavior in a
desired direction; (2) sanctions can alter or influence behavior;
(3) restriction of personal liberty is one of the few sanctions we
have; (4) restriction of liberty can be used for a variety of reasons;
(5) *however*, if liberty is restricted for rehabilitative reasons, such
restriction can be redefined as a "treatment technique"; (6) oth-

ers, like ourselves, have done this in the past and are doing it today; (7) temporary detention has already proved its effectiveness with many wards; and (8) if these programs are to continue, agents must be granted the freedom to control their wards. The critical parts of the argument revolve around *intention* (5) and *effectiveness* (7).

Regarding the intention argument (5), what specific rationales did the Task Force discover as they read through case records? They listed the following "ten specific purposes":

1. Adjudicative
   a. To hold in custody pending decisions by Youth Authority Board (e.g., following arrest on a new offense where it is *felt* that the ward constitutes a *threat* to the community, to himself or would flee the jurisdiction of the Youth Authority).
2. Situational
   a. To allow time to *develop placement* in the community.
   b. To accommodate *community reactions* to the ward.
   c. Medical (*psychiatric observation, illness*).
3. Therapeutic
   a. As a means of *controlling behavior*.
   b. To impress ward with his *responsibilities to the program*, e.g., helping other wards, participation, etc.
   c. To establish, emphasize or *refine a treatment relationship*.
   d. To handle in a residential setting, *anxieties arising from therapy*.
   e. To prevent acting out in *reaction to internal stress*.
   f. To prevent acting out in reaction to *external stress*. [SCYA, 1966, p. 2; italics added]

Initially, the rationale for confining youth was to alter delinquent behavior. However, the only specific reason listed related to actual *illegal* behavior is "adjudication" (1a), and this reason refers to a felt community threat and is based on a subjective prediction about future offenses. The list of proposed reasons for confinements refers to violation of treatment expectations, accommodation to community pressures, administrative convenience, diagnostic purposes, and predictions of "acting out," rather than to specific chargeable offenses. A sixteen-month research report (*CTP No. 7*, p. 117) included the following list of more specific reasons:

uncooperative attitudes	53 suspensions
missed group meeting	14 suspensions
home adjustment	67 suspensions
poor school adjustment	78 suspensions

simple runaway	35 suspensions
curfew, loitering, trespassing	31 suspensions
drinking, possession of alcohol	19 suspensions

In reporting on work with I_3 youth, one agent described the need for agent freedom to impose temporary detention as follows:

Temporary detention, particularly in the early phases is absolutely essential, and we need as flexible as possible temporary
detention, meaning we need as much freedom as possible to place
a youngster in detention on a minute's notice and to take him out
on a minute's notice, based on whether or not his response is
genuine.
The ability to work on the basis of intuitive, subjective cues, the
ability to play hunches and make "high stakes" decisions that
may make the difference between success and failure with a kid,
on the basis of a subjective clue or a hunch rather than logical,
concrete information seems to be the other ingredient that a
person must possess. You don't have time to work out the logic
and gather all of the facts. You have to act instantaneously and
part of the role of the community agent is the ability to work
comfortably in making decisions, even when he has only unclear
or subjective clues. [*CTP No. 2*, pp. 24–25]

According to this agent, a "genuine response by wards" and using "subjective clues" are additional factors in determining need for detention. Upon analysis, he appears to claim the right to exercise individual discretion unfettered by the rules of law or organizational constraints. (This agent's ideological stance, of course, may not have been representative of that of other agents.)

The Task Force reached the conclusion that "an element of therapy is present in every detention" (SCYA, June 1966, p. 20). They did so, not only on the grounds that the agent's *aims* were therapeutic, but because the sanctions were effective. However, they did not assess the subsequent behavior of wards upon release from therapeutic detention stays. They recorded impressions from interviewers and CTP agents and made an attitudinal assessment of locked-up wards.

The assessment of ward attitudes toward being locked up included interviews such as the following with wards and evalua-tions of responses by the Task Force team:

When the ward was asked whether or not he wanted to be
locked up, the typical response was, "no, no one likes to be locked
up," but it was the feeling of the interviewers that what was really

being said was, "although I didn't like being locked up, I profited from the experience and in retrospect 'liked' being locked up because it discontinued my antisocial behavior." [Ibid., p. 21]

Wards apparently did not understand why they were being detained, according to the same report:

We tried to determine if specific goals or objectives had to be achieved by wards prior to their release from temporary detention. We discovered that wards were generally unaware of any predetermined goals. When wards were asked if a specific accomplishment was necessary prior to release, the almost unanimous answer was no. On the other hand, agents and supervisors indicated that they had a specific objective in mind for each ward placed in temporary detention. They stated, however, that these objectives could not always be completely achieved and that detention is terminated when it becomes apparent that further gains cannot be expected from the detention. [Ibid., p. 23]

There is no clear evidence that wards were receiving therapeutic "messages" that agents believed they were transmitting. Yet the Task Force made the following overall assessment:

The Task Force interviews with wards and Youth Authority staff did not indicate overuse of detention or inappropriate length of detention stays. The interviews did indicate that both wards and staff felt detention practices to be appropriate and effective in achieving stated goals. [Ibid., p. 24]

A reasonably fair conclusion from this kind of evidence would be that the CTP agents and the Task Force felt that detention was effective, but lacked objective data. The wards said they didn't like being locked up; they didn't know what the goals were; and they didn't know what to do to get out. Agents and evaluators, however, interpreted these replies with a projection of their own feelings regarding what the wards "really" meant and, therefore, were convinced that the CYA was "achieving stated goals." This kind of bias also raises the possibility that agents misheard and misinterpreted what was occurring in the day-to-day contacts with wards. Regardless of why they engaged in selective communication with their wards, it is apparent that merely knowing "intentions" did not necessarily lead to clarity regarding the correctional activities and decisions of workers and the experiences of wards. In brief, defining treatment as embracing control activities leads to an array of analytic difficulties. The evidence from CTP and the Task Force indicates that temporary detention is a potent form of social control and should not be confused with intensive treatment services.

The Task Force (ibid., p. 17) provides evidence that the locked-up wards did not receive special program services from the detention facility (most CTP wards were detained at the CYA's Northern Reception Center Clinic):

A ward temporarily detained at the Clinic does not normally receive any special attention or clinical services. He is counted as part of the Clinic's average daily population and the only costs that are applicable across the board relate to custody staff salary, feeding, clothing, personal care and housekeeping. We, therefore, submit that the average cost per ward per day in temporary detention is $5.82.

The Task Force did not indicate that youth were doing more than just being kept in solitary confinement for an average of 20 days per stay. It appears that youngsters did not attend academic classes or vocational shops, nor did they receive work assignments. It is unknown whether they could relieve boredom and loneliness by using recreational facilities. The earlier computations on the relative balance between control and treatment services do not appear to require correction for any extra treatment services that wards received in detention.

Operational Problems in the Use of Detention

The CYA Task Force was interested in increasing the "effectiveness" of using detention as a treatment tool and tried to deal with a variety of problems that placed constraints on the use of detention. A description of some of these constraints indicates that external factors also influenced the use of this major program element:

1. Availability of bed space:
One of the persistent problems that has interfered with the establishment of an effective detention program has been uncertainty as to the availability of bed space. If the full potential of this treatment-control technique is to be realized, a fixed number of beds must be reserved for detention purposes. [SCYA, June 1966, p. 95]

2. Time and distance:
Another factor which has reduced effectiveness has been distance from available facilities. The Community Treatment Project Unit

in Sacramento is able to make good use of its proximity to the
Northern Reception Clinic. The Community Treatment
Project Unit in Stockton finds it much less convenient to utilize
the Northern Reception Center Clinic for detention. Finally, the
units in the Bay Area find it very expensive to utilize the Northern
Reception Center Clinic . . . in terms of staff time and transportation resources. When Bay Area units find it necessary
to place a ward in detention at the Northern Reception Center
Clinic they must invest at least one day of parole agent time for
transportation of the ward to and from the Clinic. [Ibid., p. 25]

3. Variable county cooperation:

In Alameda County Youth Authority warrants are not
recognized. Thus, Alameda County Juvenile Halls are not
available for "therapeutic" detention and are available for temporary detention for "adjudicative" and "situational" reasons
only when the ward is detained on a juvenile court petition filed
by the Alameda County Probation Department.

Sacramento County Juvenile Hall is never utilized for
"therapeutic" reasons pending decision by the Youth Authority
Board.

Recently permission was secured from the Chief Juvenile
Probation Officer, San Francisco County, for Youth Authority to
utilize the San Francisco Youth Guidance Center for temporary
detention upon issuance of a Youth Authority warrant.

The Juvenile Hall in San Joaquin County can be used for
temporary detention only in cases of emergencies not to exceed
three days. However, the Chief Probation Officer of San Joaquin
County Probation Department permits Community Treatment
Project staff to define an emergency. [Ibid., p. 15]

4. CYA Board administrative release procedures:

In the early stages of this Program, each release from custody, for
whatever reason, was either approved at a Board hearing or
approved by a member of the Board prior to the Board hearing.
As the number of youngsters in the project increased, . . . the
frequency of temporary detentions for therapeutic reasons also
increased. Finally, the volume of requests to Board hearings
became so great that an informal arrangement was approved,
which permitted the Supervisor of Community Treatment to use
his authority as a Director's Representative to release wards
pending a report to the Youth Authority Board.

This procedure which was in operation for approximately three
years has recently been questioned and the above procedure
discontinued. . . . If a Community Treatment ward is to be
released prior to the Board hearing on his case, authority for this

release must be obtained directly from a Board member. [Ibid., pp. 17–18]

Also on release procedures:

Agents, supervisors, and Board members usually prefer to wait for a Board hearing to arrange release.

Since prior Board approval must be obtained before release, wards frequently must remain in custody for several additional days. In some cases, this does not significantly affect the course of treatment, but in other cases it may provide a ward with a reason, opportunity, or excuse to change his mind about the proposed placement, the sincerity of the agent, the wisdom of trusting authority, etc.

Entirely aside from the impact on the course of treatment a delay in release may have, there is yet another inevitable result; this is to increase both the average number of days per detention as well as the total number of temporary detention days per unit. [Ibid., p. 27]

Of the four types of constraints influencing detention decision making, it is apparent that the first three affect getting *into* a lockup. Apparently the availability of beds, time and distance to the available beds, and county cooperation in making extra beds available can have an impact on the relative ease of "signing" a youngster into a facility. There were no major procedural obstacles for putting youngsters into detention, since facilities were available. However, there could be administrative obstacles in getting wards out.

A comparison with a contemporary CYA Community Project—the Oakland Community Delinquency Control Project—highlights the fact that CTP had fewer constraints in initiating temporary detention. For the Sacramento CTP wards there existed a ready access to the Northern Reception Center Clinic (NRCC) on the outskirts of the city. For the Stockton CTP wards there existed the San Joaquin juvenile county facilities and, as a lockup facility, the NRCC, about an hour's drive from Stockton. For the San Francisco CTP wards there existed the county facilities made accessible by the agreement with the Chief Probation Officer. In contrast, Oakland, located in Alameda County, had to contend with a county court system that would not recognize CYA warrants in cases of temporary detention. In addition, Oakland agents had to expend a work day to transport youngsters to and from the nearest CYA facility—the NRCC near Sacramento.

In the six-month period studied by the Task Force, the following data concerning the Oakland Project emerged: the percentage of youth detained was 32, and the average number of detention stays per ward was 0.43. In contrast, for the same period of time, 48 percent of the CTP wards were detained, and there was an average number of 1.49 detention stays per ward. Ease of access appears to have had a strong impact on a CTP ward's chances of being locked up more frequently.

From a sociological perspective, an agency of formal social control like CTP could initiate sanctions much more readily than it could limit the duration of the sanctions. This imbalance in sanctioning power is in part attributable to the fact that CTP was a subunit of a larger system of social control. All subunits of the CYA had to contend with the CYA board's discretionary release procedures, which limited their ability to control the duration of sanctions associated with the suspension of wards. However, not all subunits possessed the ideology, manpower, and available resources to test the larger system's relative receptivity to initiating sanctions. For the average CTP ward, this peculiar imbalance in turning sanctions on and off meant that it was easier to lose personal liberty than to regain one's freedom.

Summary: What Did CTP Actually Demonstrate?

On the basis of the analyses presented in earlier sections, it is possible to assess the extent to which CTP fulfilled its first stated aim—the demonstrating of operational feasibility. However, just as the program design shifted in practice, so, too, did its mode of presenting this initial aim. Regarding its aim of demonstrating feasibility, three types of wording were used. The initial statement of aim (SCYA, 1961a; italics added) was:

To determine the feasibility of releasing selected California Youth Authority wards directly from the reception center to a *treatment program* in the community; to see whether communities are willing to accept the return under treatment conditions of members who have just been "banished" as no longer tolerable.

A later statement (*CTP No. 1*, p. 2; italics added):

To determine the feasibility of releasing selected Youth Authority wards directly from a reception center to a *treatment-control program* in the community.

A recent description of focus (Palmer, 1971, p. 75; italics added):

Phase One of CTP (1961–1964) was focused around questions concerning (1) the overall operational feasibility of a community-based approach to the *handling* of delinquent youth.

According to these wordings, the first aim was either to operate a *"treatment* program in the community," or to operate a *"treatment-control* program in the community," or to operate a "community-based approach to the *handling* of youth."

Regarding the earliest stated aim, it is clear that CTP did not demonstrate the feasibility of setting up and operating solely a *treatment* program. By the end of the first year, detention had "emerged as an important intervention strategy, useful under a variety of circumstances"; to accommodate this program usage, the report referred to a *treatment-control* program. However, CTP did not demonstrate the feasibility of this program aim either, which implies that there is *more* treatment than control. Wards spent more time receiving sanctions (i.e., detention) than they did intensive treatment services (i.e., direct ward and family services by CTP agents). The third description (Palmer, 1971) generalized the aim to be the "handling" of youth in a "community-based approach," which can imply either treatment *or* control.

What, then, did CTP demonstrate in practice? The descriptive data show quite clearly that CTP was an organization that did not place youth in CYA's traditional programs but instead imposed other living arrangements. These other living arrangements included foster homes, group homes, county detention facilities, the lockup facilities of a "reception clinic," and a youth's own home. In *CTP Research Report No. 3,* reporting on an average exposure time of one year, CTP demonstrated rather early that it could avoid traditional CYA facilities if it used foster homes for 67 percent of the wards and detention for 79 percent of the wards. It is misleading to term involuntary living arrangements as merely treatment; and it is also misleading to term living at the "clinic" as either being "in the community" or being "community based." Rather it appears that when youth were removed from their homes, they lived varying distances from their own home neighborhoods.

CTP demonstrated that alternate modes of social control could be substituted for the traditional form of social control—incarceration in a CYA facility on a 24-hour basis for an average period of eight months. In effect, CTP demonstrated that the type, degree, or duration of social control could be altered, either separately or in combination. Regarding detention only the *duration* appears to have altered—since type and degree do not appear to have altered too appreciably from traditional incarceration. In using foster homes (either individual or group), the *type* and *degree* of control probably altered—while the duration may have been the same in some cases. (However, little data are provided regarding this substitute for traditional incarceration.)

As to intensive treatment services, CTP also demonstrated clearly that it delivered much less of this program element than it delivered social control to its wards. Whether wards perceived this program element as another form of coercion is unknown—since there are no independent studies of their perceptions toward this part of the program. In summary, it appears most accurate to describe CTP according to the following dimensions: (1) CTP demonstrated, from 1961 to 1969, that it could operate a special parole program that substituted alternate modes of social control that could vary by type, degree, or duration from the traditional program of incarceration; (2) while providing these alternate modes of social control as the primary program elements, the parole agents also attempted to deliver treatment services to wards and their families; (3) these direct services were delivered to wherever wards were permitted to reside by their parole agents; and (4) most wards, at different times, actually lived at varying distances from the homes they lived in prior to their contact with CTP.

This summary differs from the descriptions found in CTP research reports or journal articles (Palmer, 1971). While the above description is a more accurate rendering of the program in operation (and not of the program as intended), it should be noted that the summary includes the fact that CTP was able to operate as a modified "in lieu" program. During the first eight months of parole (after a four-week stay at the Reception Center Clinic), CTP youth experienced less of the traditional institutional program. During this in lieu period the average number of detention stays for juvenile status offenses or technical violations was probably about 88 per 100 youth (about half of the 175 suspensions for 100 youth noted in table 3); however, the average number of institutional days for all CTP youth was about 18 (20 days times 0.88), and not the average 240 days experienced by all control youth. During the in lieu period, the amount of institutionalization experienced by CTP youth was not reduced to zero, but it was reduced by a substantial amount if youth were able to avoid being defined as noncriminal violators (viz., from 240 to 18 days).

The second eight months constituted the normal period for control youth. During this *post in lieu period* experimentals also averaged about 18 days of detention for noncriminal behaviors or attitudes. However, control youth were far less likely to be detained for juvenile status offenses or technical violations; the same sources that yielded a noncriminal violation rate for CTP youth produce a control rate of 60 per 100 youth for a 17.4-month period (*CTP No. 7*, pp. 119–20). During an eight-month parole period the rate would be approximately 30 per 100 youth; and if the average length of stay were comparable to CTP detentions, the number of institutional days would average about 6 days for control youth. It is evident that during the post in lieu period the control youth are exposed to far less control for noncriminal violations than CTP youth (about 18 to 6 days of detention). As a parole unit per se, CTP delivered more social control than the regular parole organization. However, as a parole unit substituting for an institutional program, CTP delivered far less control than the traditional institutional organization. These dual trends must be taken into account in assessing the overall impact of CTP on the operations of the California Youth Authority.

The general conclusion that CTP functioned as a control/treatment program during the in lieu and post in lieu periods, and not as a treatment/control endeavor, is based on a reasonable analytic scheme and available empirical data. The available data about detentions and the use of agent time in delivering direct services are not really in dispute, since they are based on the official reports of the CTP and the CYA Task Force on Detention. According to the analytic scheme used in this study, "lockup" is not included in the same category as "direct service to wards and families." Nor is *intent* confused with the actual descriptions of program operations. The analytic scheme and the empirical data are quite distinguishable. If CTP had engaged in fewer detention activities, then the balance between control and treatment elements would have been altered because the data would have been coded accordingly.

This analytic scheme seems more reasonable, because it is more reliable and valid than that employed by CTP participant-researchers. (The Task Force on Detention did not indicate that it had made any check of reliability or validity of the reasons for detention.) It is more reliable, because guesses aren't made about what constitutes a "therapeutic" intention from a "nontherapeutic" intention; independent observers would have less difficulty with codifying activities—regardless of intention. This scheme is more valid because it has a "face validity"; detention is perceived in accord with customary sociological, political, and everyday usage. In addition, the approach can be applied to other criterion groups more easily; youngsters and adults in other programs, both past and present, who have been locked up and deprived of liberty have been, and can be, classified in a comparable manner. And, lastly, this analytic scheme predicts that youngsters who are locked up will dislike their loss of liberty. The data from CTP appear quite clear that the scheme has predictive validity.

Therefore, this description of the CTP program package appears to be reasonably accurate and valid. Whether or not outsiders approve of this control/treatment program is, of course, a separate issue; whether or not this complex package proved to be effective in changing the behavior of the official delinquents in a desired direction is also a separate issue. In the next chapter the evidence regarding effectiveness will be reviewed. As noted earlier, this evaluative analysis will not assess the impact of each major program element. Unfortunately, because it departed from its original program design, the range of potential analyses of CTP was also limited.

Assessing the Impact of CTP

In the original proposal, the designers of CTP suggested that they would assess the impact in three ways: (1) the general community adjustment of wards as they functioned in school, on jobs, at home, and in the community with peers; (2) the change in attitudes as indicated by test scores; and (3) the extent to which delinquent behavior had been discontinued. Of the three modes of assessment it is clear that the delinquent-behavior criterion is the most critical. Ostensibly, this is the major criterion by which *any* correctional program is expected to demonstrate impact. Major attention will therefore be addressed to this assessment of impact. In addition, the relative costs and savings associated with CTP will be assessed as well as its potential impact on CYA parole programs.

Assessing Impact via Community Adjustment

In *CTP Research Report No. 6*, readers were informed that the following data gathering procedures were taking place:

An extensive analysis of the community adjustment of experimental and control wards is now under way as a further method of assessing the comparative effectiveness of the two programs. Areas relating to employment, school, family, and peers

are among those included in this investigation. Each area is
studied exhaustively. In order to allow for comparable time
periods for all wards who are studied, parole experience is divided
into six-month blocks. [*CTP No. 6*, p. 29]

As of December 1973, the results of that analysis had not been
reported in any publication. Thus we have no data regarding the
potential side benefits of an early release program in lieu of traditional incarceration.

Assessing Attitudinal Change

Two types of instruments were used to assess attitudinal
change: the California Psychological Inventory (CPI) and the
Jesness Inventory. Of the two instruments, the CPI is most widely
known and used. This instrument attempts to measure youngsters
according to distinctive attitudinal dimensions or scales. Tests
were administered at entry into the project and at a "post" date.
Two post dates are most comprehensively documented in the
reports: (1) as of April 1966 (*CTP No. 7*); and (2) as of fall 1969
(*CTP No. 10*).

Regarding the April 1966 cohort, the results are based on only
85 experimentals and 189 controls. As indicated in the earlier
chapter, the comparability of the two samples at this level of disparity is uncertain. Fourteen CPI scales were used in the analysis.
Both groups showed positive changes on 7 of the 14 scales from
pre- to post-testing. In terms of *degree* of positive change, pre-test
versus post-test scores, the following results were reported:

On the CPI, the *control* group—as compared with
experimentals—showed a greater degree of positive change
(favorable gain) from pre- to post-testing on *none* of the 14 scales.
The *experimentals*, as compared with controls, showed a greater
degree of positive change on *3* of the 14 scales—capacity for
status, dominance, and tolerance. [*CTP No. 7*, p. 79; italics
added]

According to the report the three scales that exhibited a greater
degree of change by the experimentals refer to the following
psychological meanings:

Scale 1: *Dominance*. This scale attempts to assess factors related
to social initiative and leadership ability.
Scale 2: *Capacity for Status*. This scale attempts to measure
certain personal qualities and attributes which are hypothesized

as underlying and leading to social recognition and status. It attempts to measure an individual's capacity for—as opposed to actual or achieved—social status and recognition.
Scale 10: *Tolerance*. This scale attempts to identify the extent to which an individual is non-judgmental and/or accepting with respect to the social beliefs and attitudes of others. [*CTP No. 7*, p. 124]

While these three scales may refer to personal growth, they do not appear to have a substantive bearing on psychological orientations to deviance. Three other scales that did *not* exhibit any experimental-control differences appear to have a greater conceptual link to delinquency:

Scale 7: *Responsibility*. This scale attempts to identify persons of conscientious, responsible and dependable disposition and temperament.
Scale 8: *Socialization*. This scale attempts to assess the extent of an individual's integrity in social contexts, his social maturity, and/or his honesty of intent.
Scale 9: *Self-Control*. This scale attempts to assess the degree of an individual's freedom from general impulsivity in his approach to tasks and to interpersonal situations and/or from seemingly self-centered forms of excitability. [Ibid.]

It seems reasonable to propose that treatment programs might like to have an impact on "honesty of intent" (socialization scale), "conscientious disposition" (responsibility scale), and "general impulsivity" (self-control scale). There is one group of widely known studies on delinquent self-concepts that relied on one of these CPI scales as the critical measurement—the socialization scale. This scale was perceived by the researchers, Walter Reckless and his associates, as measuring the extent of an individual's "delinquent vulnerability." As a matter of fact the socialization scale was formerly called by that term in the 1950s (Reckless et al., 1956 and 1957; Scarpitti, et al., 1960).

In the second report dealing with attitudinal data, the following results were reported:

For the first time since 1966, a re-analysis of psychological test data has been done. Relative to the present, 1969 analysis, all subjects who had completed their pre-post testing subsequent to the 1966 cutoff, and prior to the Fall of 1969, were added on to the earlier sample. The 1969 analysis relates to blind Q-sorts of California Psychological Inventory Profiles. These Q-sorts were done by Dr. H. Gough, the author of the test, on all 299 Project boys and 55 girls from the Sacramento-Stockton area. The same procedures and definitions were used as in the 1969 analysis.

Results: All in all, the findings are quite similar to those presented in CTP's 7th Research Report with reference to scale-by-scale analyses. [*CTP No. 10*, pp. 35–36]

On the basis of the most consistently reported indicator of psychological change, the CPI, it appears that there is some evidence of greater degree of change by the experimentals. However, the findings do not appear striking—nor do they seem to bear any significant relationship to scales that are likely to be related to delinquent behavior.

Did the CTP Change Youth Behavior or Agent Behavior?

If we assume that a major criterion of any correctional program's effectiveness is a reduction in illegal behaviors, then a major problem of evaluational research is to define and objectively measure these activities. Illegal behavior is not as easy to define as is often assumed. Consider the following sequence of minimum events and decisions that can occur before an uncomplicated act by a youth can become an official statistic: (1) a youthful act (either alone or in concert with others) must *occur*; (2) it must be *noticed* by an observer (either a citizen or a law enforcement officer); (3) the noticed act must be defined as worth making a *complaint* about; (4) the complaint must be defined as worthy of a *written record* by a law enforcement agent; (5) the enforcement agent must decide whether the written record should become an *arrest record*; (6) a court intake worker or a prosecutor must decide if the arrest is worth transforming into a *formal petition*; (7) an adjudicatory hearing must decide whether the facts contained in the formal petition's charge constitute a *fact-finding* "beyond a reasonable doubt" (or "by a preponderance of evidence"); and (8) if the youth is found guilty, a formal *disposition* must be entered into the record. While all of these decisional activities are occurring, a youth may or may not be placed in "protective custody." This is usually initiated by a law enforcement officer but with the compliance of court representatives (either probation or parole officers, formal judges, CYA board members or their representatives).

It is well known to serious scholars of criminal justice agencies, as well as to students of civil regulatory agencies, commissions, and boards, that at each stage of an official labeling process there exists an enormous amount of discretionary decision making that occurs as part of the day-to-day tasks of the norm enforcers. As Kenneth Culp Davis, one of the nation's leading scholars of administrative law, has noted, "A public officer has discretion whenever the effective limits on his power leave him free to make a choice among possible courses of action or inaction" (Davis, 1967, p. 4). Criminologists, legal scholars, and even political scientists have known for some time that policemen, probation officers, prosecutors, judges, parole officers, and parole board representatives make many, many decisions that are not publicly visible and that are not constrained by "effective limits" on their power to act or not to act. The few legal scholars that have contrasted civil regulatory organizations with criminal control organizations have reached the conclusion that "there is more recognizable discretion in the field of crime control, including that part of its broad sweep which lawyers call 'criminal law,' than in any other field in which law regulates conduct" (Davis, 1967, p. 18, n. 21).

This kind of perspective means that *any* statistics that are based on official data are complex measures of both *adult decisions* and *youth behavior*. The further we proceed in the discretionary labeling process in order to obtain violational data, the greater is the likelihood that we shall be measuring *official* behavior rather than *youth* behavior. The ideal solution, of course, is to obtain indications of "pure" behavior that are not tainted by the decision to complain, the decision to record, the decision to arrest, the decision to revoke or suspend parole or probation. Unfortunately, social scientists have not produced an ideal solution that is applicable on a large scale and that accords with scientific standards of reliability and validity.

Researchers must do the best they can in such circumstances. But this does not mean that they are free to ignore the important distinctions between official behavior and youthful behaviors. Nor are they free to ignore the possibility that one group of norm enforcers (e.g., CTP agents) might make different kinds of decisions for comparable suspected offenses than another group of norm enforcers (e.g., regular, "control group," parole agents). There is ample evidence that CTP researchers made both kinds of

TABLE 4

CTP Experimentals and Controls Released to Sacramento and Stockton
(Based on reanalysis of primary data)

A. Reported Offenses	As of June 1965 (Rates/100 youth)		As of April 1966 (Rates/100 youth)	
	Exp.	Cont.	Exp.	Cont.
1. Offense against person	14	12	12	16
2. Major offenses against property	30	20	35	33
3. Auto theft offenses	27	31	29	32
4. Petty theft	14	12	12	11
5. All other offenses	7	5	12	9
6. Status offenses/technical violations	172	56	175	60
7. No offenses reported	27	33	25	29
N =	(177)	(199)	(241)	(220)

B. Parole Revocations by Offense	June 1965 (Revocations/ 100 Offenses)		April 1966 (Revocations/ 100 Offenses)	
	Exp.	Cont.	Exp.	Cont.
1-2. Personal/major offenses revoked	23	DNA*	35	42
3. Auto only offense revoked	21	DNA	13	51
4-5. Petty/AO criminal offenses revoked	3	DNA	6	34
6. Status and technical violations to revoke	2	DNA	2	17

C. Formal Agency Recommending Revocation	June 1965		April 1966	
	Exp.	Cont.	Exp.	Cont.
% of revocation decisions by parole agent/CYA Bd.	DNA	DNA	40	73
% of revocation decisions by local courts	DNA	DNA	51	23
% of unclassified revocations	DNA	DNA	9	4

D. Official Revocation Rates by Months in Community	36 Month Cohort (April 1968) (cumulative percentage)	
	Experimental	Control
Less than 8 months	17.7	33.5
Less than 16 months	29.1	53.4
Less than 24 months	39.9	60.2
Less than 36 months	46.2	62.5

Sources: *CTP Research Reports Nos. 6, 7, and 9* (pt. 1). (See my text for definitions of categories)
*DNA means data not available

mistakes in interpreting their data. However, the data are sufficiently detailed that they can be reanalyzed to produce reasonable conclusions. Table 4 attempts to summarize some of the data that emerges from a reanalysis of the primary data reported in publicly distributed CTP research reports.

There are four distinct types of measurements contained in table 4: (a) *reported offenses*—as measured by recording of parole suspensions for *alleged* violations of wards for activities deemed to be in violation of juvenile statutes, penal statutes, parole organization rules, and individual agent control-treatment norms; (b) *parole revocations by offense*—as measured by the proportion of confirmed decisions to revoke parole for the alleged criminal offenses, juvenile status offenses, and parole norm-violations; (c) *formal agency recommending revocation*—as measured by the percentage of revocation decisions that were due to recommendations by CYA officials or local court officials; and (d) *official rates of parole revocation*—as measured by the percentage of youth that were committed to a CYA facility or received a dishonorable discharge.

Until *Research Report No. 9*, published in 1968, the primary researchers emphasized comparisons between experimentals and controls on the basis of D-type measurements (official parole revocation rates). In October 1968, CTP began to take official cognizance of the impact of "differential and treatment-relevant decision making" in explaining why experimentals yielded a lower "failure rate" than the controls. The principal investigator noted that they did so because of outside criticism (SCYA, 1968, *CTP No. 9*, part 2, p. 13).

However, CTP documents still do not emphasize the measurement that comes closest to assessing the behavior of youth rather than the behavior of CYA agents and CYA board members. In 1971 an article by the chief researcher (Palmer, 1971) implies that behavioral rates were changed. In actuality, CTP can only demonstrate that rates of official decision making changed. The program influenced the labeling and social control process, and not the rates of behavioral input that presumably triggers the discretionary reactions to youth. Table 4 is an attempt to analyze the CTP data even further than was attempted in the first published criticism of CTP's claim of effectiveness (Lerman, 1968). The table tries to provide some of the measurements that illuminate both youth behavior and adult behavior.

Part A of table 4 compares the offense rates per 100 youth of both the experimental and the control groups, at two distinct time periods. Rates per 100 youth are used because the original data refers to numbers of offenses—not numbers of youth committing offenses. We have attempted to code the reported reasons for parole suspensions in a manner that makes a distinction between offenses against property and offenses against persons, as well as other distinctions. The codes use the CTP lists of reasons for suspension. They are as follows:

1. *Offenses against persons* refers to the following types of alleged activities: attempted murder; assault to commit grand theft, robbery, or rape; armed robbery; assault with a deadly weapon; battery; purse snatching; hitting a teacher; statutory rape; and abnormal sex act with minor. (Some of these, on closer inspection, could be viewed as misdemeanors—rather than felonies—but we have been guided by the aim of making as broad an estimate of harms against persons [i.e., indication of violence] as possible.)

2. *Major offenses against property* (excluding auto) refers to: grand theft; burglary, both 1st and 2d degree; check passing; attempted felony offense without threat or force; theft other than petty or auto; possession of burglary tools; arson; and illegal-forcible entry. (Again, we have ignored misdemeanor-felony distinctions, and attempted to include the highest estimate of possible major property offenses.)

3. *Auto theft offenses* refers to: grand theft, auto; auto theft; and riding in stolen car.

4. *Petty theft offenses* refers to: petty theft and receiving stolen property.

5. *All other offenses* refers to: escape; attempted suicide; homosexual acts; prostitution; resisting arrest; possession of marijuana; possession of concealed weapon; possession of fictitious identification; interfering with peace officer; prowling; and child harassment.

6. *Juvenile status offenses and technical violations* refers to: medical; protection; preventive detention; uncooperative attitude; missed group meeting; poor home adjustment; poor school adjustment; simple runaway; investigation; loitering near school; curfew; loitering; trespassing; whereabouts unknown; fighting, no weapons; drinking; possession of alcohol; malicious mischief;

disturbing the peace, etc.; begging; driving with suspended-revoked license; intoxication on alcohol, glue, etc.

7. *No offense reported* refers to the number of youth (rather than offenses) who did not experience a suspension of parole for any of the above categories of alleged offenses or norm violations.

Part A of table 4 reveals that as of June 1965, after an average community exposure of approximately 15 months for the experimentals and 16.2 months for the controls, there were minimal differences between the two groups except for the category of status offenses and technical violations (172 versus 56 per 100 youth). There is also an absence of a large difference in the category of no offenses reported. The same pattern of differences occurs for another time period, as of April 1966. At this time, experimentals averaged 16.4 months in the community, while controls averaged 17.9 months.

From other data appearing in the research reports, there is ample evidence that criminal offenses (part A, 1–5) are primarily brought about by police officers. In fact, both experimentals and controls experienced approximately the same total number of arrests by non-CYA law enforcement officers. Each group actually averaged 1.2 arrests per ward by a non-CYA law enforcement agent between 31 October 1961 and 31 March 1966 (*CTP No. 7*, p. 65). The criminal offenses associated with suspension (part A of table 4) reflect this comparability.

Status offenses and technical violations are primarily the result of parole agents acting as peace officers. Given our paradigm of the labeling process, it is clear that the potential noticers of criminal acts are more likely to complain to a police officer than to a parole officer (particularly if they are unaware of the legal status of the alleged offender). While we do not have any information on complaints received about youth regardless of the arrest decision, the offenses associated with the police are a more valid indicator of probable illegal behavior. It is not a "pure" indicator of youth behavior—but it is certainly superior to parole officer arrests; this is particularly true when police do not know the status of offenders. If the data had originally been broken down by source of arrest, as well as suspension for a specific offense or violation, there would definitely have been a preference to isolate reported offenses based on police arrests.

On the basis of these empirical facts, it appears reasonable to conclude that CTP probably did not have an impact on the commission of those offenses deemed to be criminal. If we had not engaged in the prior analyses of the control activities associated with temporary detention, we might have erroneously concluded that the CTP had *increased* the misbehaving propensities of wards under their jurisdiction. However, this is unlikely to be true, since agents relied mainly on their own observations and "hunches," rather than on explicit complaints, to lock youth up for status offenses and technical violations. CTP agents had more time and resources to engage in surveillance activities, establish "control networks," and act according to their treatment ideology than did the regular parole officers. We conclude that the rate differences for status offenses and technical violations are probably due to the organizational mandates and discretionary behavior of the adults.

This kind of inference fits in with other information about the behavior of other norm enforcers—policemen. The less serious or the vaguer the offense, the greater the amount of discretion that can be exercised to enforce statutes (Pilliavin and Briar, 1964; Wilson, 1968; and Black and Reiss, 1970). Citizens probably act in a similar fashion in the role of complainer. There is little reason for not accepting that parole officers act in a similar fashion. However, discretionary decisions do not always imply leniency—they can also move toward "overenforcement" of vague statutes and rules; they may even engage in nit-picking" in order to gain deference to their authority, to another adult's authority, or to their right to gain compliance with treatment norms. If effective limits on agent discretionary power are minimal—or absent—then suspension rates can vary without any change in the behavior of *youth*.

An alternate explanation might argue that the experimental youths *did* misbehave more in these noncriminal areas (perhaps to retaliate for being so closely watched and controlled) and that the rates reflect this greater output of activities. Perhaps a combination of forces was at work to create a vicious circle of greater control—greater resistance—greater control—resistance via "acting out"—greater control, etc. Regardless of the interpretation preferred, neither one yields support for the "success" of CTP when probable *youth behavior* is used as a criterion.

Part B of table 4 provides comparative data only for the April 1966 measuring point. The comparisons are geared toward asking the following question: Were there any differences in rates of *revocation* actions by offenses, when the two groups are systematically compared? Apparently there were for all offense categories, with the exception of the combined classification of the most serious offenses—offenses against persons or major property offenses. The two groups were *not* revoked to the same extent for comparable categories of offenses. The greatest difference in revocations appears to exist for auto theft and related offenses (13 to 51 revocations per 100 offenses). But the difference between the two groups for the less serious and noncriminal offenses are also rather substantial (6 versus 34 and 2 versus 17). Evidently, discretionary decision making can include a paradoxical combination of higher rates of parole suspension (including detention) with lower rates of parole revocation. Since the two groups are probably not different in their offense rates (part A), this means that revocation rates as well as suspension rates can be influenced, particularly if the offenses are defined as less serious or are vaguely defined.

How this was accomplished can partly be inferred by finding out whether the lower revocation rates shown in part C of table 4 are being influenced by the parole *organizations*. Again, the difference between the two groups is substantial. The CTP agents and the CYA board members (or their representatives) recommend far fewer "revokes" than do regular parole officers (40 to 73 percent). However, local courts do not always agree with the CTP propensity not to revoke, so that a greater percentage of the experimental wards are revoked by court decisions, as compared to the control wards (51 to 23 percent). Within certain limits, CTP was able to influence the return of their wards to the community to a far greater degree than the regular parole officers could influence that of the controls. The inevitable result of this organizational behavior is reflected in part D, regardless of the time picked for comparison.

CTP researchers have not been willing to accept the inevitable conclusion that emerges from this line of analysis: CTP changed adult behavior rather than youth behavior. As late as 1971, the following interpretation of CTP effectiveness was presented by the principal investigator of CTP:

Various indices of effectiveness, together with research observations which extend over several years, point toward the following factors as having made a substantial contribution to the comparative effectiveness of CTP:

(1) *matching* of given types of agents with given types of youth; (2) *level of ability and perceptiveness*; (3) *treatment prescriptions and individualized programming* which may involve intensive and/or extensive intervention by agents relative to several areas of youth's life (e.g., family, school) and which first became operationally feasible within the context of small caseload assignments; (4) *decision-making*—(a) differential decision-making and (b) treatment relevant decision-making as an expression of differential treatment prescriptions . . . ; (5) emphasis upon a *working-through of the agent/youth relationship* as a major vehicle of treatment. [Palmer, 1971, p. 89; italics added]

The indices of "effectiveness" that are referred to by Palmer are: (a) parole suspensions, (b) recidivism, (c) favorable discharge, (d) unfavorable discharge, (e) psychological test scores, (f) post-discharge arrests. Of the five indices of effectiveness cited by Palmer only parole suspensions and post-discharge arrests refer primarily to probable ward behavior. *Recidivism* refers to discretionary decision making of CTP agents and CYA board members and representatives (as depicted in parts C and D of table 4). Receiving a favorable or unfavorable *discharge* refers to the ward status at the end of the parole period, after wards have been successively screened by the parole organizations. Appendix A describes how discharged experimentals and controls differ in population characteristics, indicating that they no longer represent comparable samples drawn from a common pool of eligibles. The discharge status of experimentals and controls cannot be used as an indicator of effectiveness because this indicator also refers to discretionary organizational behavior and not just youth behavior. The psychological *tests* do not, of course, refer to youth behavior; it appears that test differences do not even refer to such deviant-related characteristics as "conscientiousness," "honesty," or "impulsivity" (see earlier discussion of attitude change).

Regarding the only two reasonable indicators of youth behavior—parole suspensions and post-discharge arrests—Palmer does not claim that there exist any significant differences between experimentals and controls. This lack of difference for post-1969 parole and post-discharge groups is interesting, since the post-1969 experimental and control samples are not comparable (see Appendix A).

It appears evident, therefore, that the critical CTP indicator of 1971 effectiveness is still "recidivism." But "recidivism," as table 4 indicates, is also a measure of discretionary revocation decisions by parole agents, board members, and juvenile court judges—not solely a measure of youth behavior. Instead of being called "discretionary decision making," these adult behaviors are called "differential decision making." Regardless of the label, it is clear that changed adult decision making should not be confused with changed youth behavior.

The evidence indicates that when youth behavior is used as the major criterion of effectiveness, CTP researchers do not *empirically* demonstrate significant relationships with *any* of the five factors cited. There is not one example of reliable and valid evidence that youth behavior is related to (1) matching, (2) level of ability and perceptiveness of the agent, (3) treatment prescriptions and individualized programming, (4) decision making, or (5) working through the agent/youth relationship.

We conclude, therefore, that CTP did not have an impact on youth behavior that differed significantly from the impact of the control program.

Assessing the Economic Costs and Savings of CTP

One of the major arguments in favor of the CTP, in comparison to the regular program, is that the community treatment program was less costly. In fiscal 1964-65, for example, the per capita costs for treating a CTP ward was estimated at $178 per month (*CTP No. 5*, p. 23). In the same fiscal year, keeping a ward in an institutional facility cost approximately $375 per month. If CTP had carried out its original plan of withdrawing intensive services after eight months (stage A), then providing a transitional service (stage B), and finally a regular parole service (stage C), the costs per capita would have been less than $178 per month per capita in stages B and C. However, CTP did not adhere to this design. Instead, it kept offering intensive services for an average of two and a half to three years (Palmer, 1971, p. 76). This change in operational strategy cost the CTP program dearly, for it wiped out the original savings and, in fact, transformed it into a more costly program than that of the control group. Table 5 documents this conclusion.

TABLE 5
Costs of Original CTP Design, Actual CTP Program, and Control Group, Assuming a Successful Career (1964-1965) Costs

		CTP	
	Control Program	As Proposed	Actual
8 Months			
Institutional period (stage A)[a]	$3,000	$1,424	$1,424
4 Months			
Transitional period (stage B)[b]	75	356	712
24 Months			
Regular parole (stage C)[c]	600	600	4,272
Total program costs	3,675	2,380	6,408
Prorated capital outlay/ admission[d]	400	None	None
Total—all costs	4,075	2,380	6,408

Source: CTP costs—*CTP Research Report No. 5*, p. 23. Control costs—Robert L. Smith, "Probation Supervision: A Plan for Action," *California Youth Authority Quarterly*, 18, 2 (Summer, 1965), p. 3.

[a]Institutional costs were $4,500 in fiscal 1964-65 or $375 per month per capita. CTP costs were $178 per month per capita.

[b]Regular parole cost $300 per year in 1964-65; Stage B "proposed" is computed on the basis of one-half the annual CTP cost, prorated by one-third of a year.

[c]Regular parole costs are computed for 2 years at $300 per year; CTP actual costs are based on $2,136 per year, for two years.

[d]Prorated capital costs are taken from Smith article.

A "successful" control career cost $4,075, but the *proposed* CTP career cost was only $2,380 or a per capital saving of $1,695. The *actual* CTP program was less costly during the first year of operation, but when compared to the relatively low cost of the regular parole supervision program, the savings vanished. The actual CTP career cost was about $6,400, as compared to the proposed cost of $2,380—almost three times as much. Compared to the control program, a CTP ward in 1964-65 would cost the funding sources $2,333 more per career. This run-up in costs appears to be primarily related to the decision to substitute intensive services for regular parole during stage C ($4,272 versus $600).

If CTP had proved effective in changing the behavior of wards, we might have considered how much that changed behavior was worth in cost. However, it did not prove effective by the criterion of behavior, and so the extra $2,333 is really an extravagance. CTP research reports did demonstrate some changes in attitude tests on pre- and post-scores. However, policy makers would probably not approve an expenditure of $2,333 to change *attitudes* when change in behavior cannot be demonstrated.

Other Assessments of the CTP Strategy

Since 1961, other units in the California correctional system have attempted to use aspects of I-Level theory. An early release parole project in Los Angeles, the Community Delinquency Control Project, attempted to utilize I-Level diagnosis and treatment strategies (CDCP). This project was conducted as an experiment, so that there were random assignments to a control and experiment group. The results were summarized in 1970 by Esther Pond (SCYA, 1970c, p. iii), as follows:

Perhaps the most outstanding finding was that there were no significant differences between the experimental and regular parole programs in either project area on any of the parole performance criterion measures.

The results are in accord with our reanalysis, although Pond did not delve into the issues of detention and discretionary decision making.

In the middle 1960s, CTP set up a unit in San Francisco to duplicate the I-Level model of treatment, to test its general applicability, and to compare it to a peer-oriented, social-psychological model of treatment. The San Francisco CYA board members did not permit as high a rate of youth to be eligible for this experiment, but there was a sufficient number to conduct the replication. According to data reported by Palmer:

Relative to criterion (1), parole suspensions, the San Francisco boys compared slightly more favorably with the C's than was the case with the former's counterparts within Sacramento-Stockton. Even so, the C boys remained slightly ahead of the E's. [Palmer, 1971, p. 83, n. 24]

Again, I-Level yielded no differences as to the major criterion variable—behavior.

In an unpublished study, conducted by the Alameda County

Probation Department, an attempt at an experimental replication of the CTP model was conducted. Since the probation officers had been trained by highly qualified I-Level practitioners, this test is of some interest. According to Deming, the principal investigator, the results indicated a lack of difference in the arrest rates between probationers receiving I-Level diagnoses and treatment and those receiving a regular probation approach. (Personal interview with Research Director of the Alameda County Probation Department, July 1971; the study is not available as a public document.) The department believes that the results indicate that I-Level is inappropriate with lower-class, black youth, but may work with middle-class youth. However, the evidence concerning its hypothetical worth with middle-class youth is nonexistent at this time. The evidence that is available indicates that in samples of predominantly lower-class, white youth (i.e., Sacramento and Stockton) I-Level programs were ineffective; and in samples of predominantly lower-class, black youth (i.e., San Francisco and Oakland) comparable ineffectiveness occurred.

The evidence indicates that the I-Level strategy associated with CTP has not yielded higher rates of success in special projects in Sacramento, Stockton, San Francisco, Oakland, and Los Angeles. Despite this failure to demonstrate effectiveness, efforts continue to disseminate the theory and practices associated with I-Level theory. In a recent survey of forty-seven California probation departments, nineteen were classified as utilizing I-Level as a system of youth classification (SCYA, 1974, p. 12). Interviews with knowledgeable administrators in several of these counties (conducted in the summer of 1971) indicate that, besides the unpublished Oakland study, additional scientific assessments are unlikely to be forthcoming as a result of the diffusion of I-Level theory and practices.

The large counties that are using I-Level classifications are not attempting to replicate the model in a pure, exact fashion. The practical reasons why I-Level ideas and practices are extremely difficult to incorporate into an ongoing correctional organization have been noted by one probation department. In 1970, the Los Angeles County Probation Department, after considering the possibility of incorporating I-Level theory and practices within its program, rejected it for the following administrative reasons:

a. *Excessive staff training investment*—80 hours would be required to train DPO's in the application of I-Level diagnosis and treatment strategies. The number of trainers would be excessive *and* would require that a major training and re-training program be maintained indefinitely.
b. *Impractical caseload size*—Many of the CYA I-Level caseloads consist of about 12 juveniles. We cannot afford this.
c. *Inconclusive experimental results* . . .
d. *Staff assignment problems*—Thoroughgoing application of I-Level method requires that the caseworker be "matched" with his clients. In a county as large as Los Angeles with emphatic geographic assignment preferences of staff members, I-Level matching and its accompanying transfer requirements would create significant morale problems.
e. *Differential effectiveness according to race*—I-Level researchers see indications that the method can be more reliably applied to white clients than black clients. Any method with such selective applicability would probably pose more problems than it was worth in Los Angeles County.
f. *Unclear treatment strategies*—The I-Level approach provides a highly refined classification method but the treatment strategies prescribed for these various classifications of clients are not so specific.
g. *Treatment resources*—Youth Authority Community Programs which have used I-Level have also relied upon therapeutic detention. Los Angeles has no room nor program which provides for such an alternative and does not anticipate the development of one. [County of Los Angeles, 1970]

Besides being associated with administrative complexity, I-Level theory contains many methodological difficulties that have not yet been adequately addressed. The reliability and validity of I-Level as a theory of delinquency, and as a diagnostic tool, has been examined by Beker and Heyman (1972) in their recent article "A Critical Appraisal of the California Differential Treatment Typology of Adolescent Offenders." After reviewing the evidence that CTP researchers can reliably reproduce each other's I-Level and subtype diagnoses, Beker and Heyman conclude that the ratings were seriously contaminated by a failure to conduct completely blind ratings. As currently described in the classification manual (SCYA, 1966*b*), it is unclear how or why non-CTP raters reported higher degrees of agreement, since "the diagnostic criteria not only lack behavioral specifics, but also fail to describe the key dimensions in parallel forms to permit comparisons of the same variables for different I-Levels" (Beker and Heyman, 1972, p. 18). Regarding the validity of the model, Beker and Heyman also question its premature acceptance as follows (p. 20):

The authors do not state explicitly how and on what bases the I-Levels and the subtypes were developed. Although the I-Levels are presented as a developmental continuum, their interrelationships and the logic of their progression is not specified, nor is there a clear dimension or dimensions along which successive I-Levels are characterized by systematic change. Therefore, there is little basis on which to generate hypotheses or predictions that would tend to establish even the internal consistency of the system.

I-Level theory, by implication, is a theory of delinquency as well as a personality classification system. According to the logic of the theory, there should be lower delinquency rates as youth progress toward higher maturity levels. This falloff in delinquency should occur independently of any increase in chronological age, since I-Level, and not age, constitutes the focus of the theory. Empirical data to support such an inference are lacking. Despite these difficulties, the CTP strategy might have proved to be pragmatically useful, providing an impact on behavior had actually been demonstrated. Beker and Heyman agree that my own earlier criticisms are valid, and that claims of success are not warranted by the evidence.

Potential Impact of CTP on CYA Parole Work

While CTP had no demonstrated impact on the behavior of youth, it is quite probable that it has had an impact on its sponsoring organization—the CYA. Its major impact appears to be in the use of temporary detention as a parole strategy in work with youth. The reasons for suggesting this possibility will become clear in the ensuing discussion.

Beginning in 1965, four years after the initiation of CTP and one year prior to the report issued by the Task Force on Detention, the Information Section of the CYA began routinely to collect statistics on the use of parole detention in CYA parole work. Previously, this type of data had been placed in the residual category of "other" receptions to CYA facilities. The 1970 CYA *Annual Report* disclosed the following pattern regarding the use of "Parole Detention" as a reason for admission to a CYA institution (SCYA, 1970a, table 31, p. 42):

1965: 580 Parole Detentions out of 12,437 total admissions
1966: 664 Parole Detentions out of 12,147 total admissions
1967: 767 Parole Detentions out of 12,506 total admissions
1968: 1,627 Parole Detentions out of 13,076 total admissions
1969: 1,757 Parole Detentions out of 13,405 total admissions
1970: 3,346 Parole Detentions out of 13,768 total admissions

The 1970 CYA *Annual Report* commented on these trends as follows:

Another notable point . . . is the marked increase of parole detention cases received and released between 1965 and 1970. This is due to the increasing use by parole agents of short term detention of parolees *in lieu of revocation* or other action. Since 1969, the increase has also been due to procedural changes involved in "due process" regulations which require that a ward *facing parole revocation* must have a hearing in a reception center during which time he is on parole detention status [SCYA, 1970a, table 31, p. 42; italics added]

According to this official interpretation, the sharp rise in the use of detention in 1968 and 1969 is due to the use of temporary detention ("short-term detention"). The next sharp rise, in 1970, is also due to new formal procedures that evidently *require* parole detention status in order to receive "due process" at a suspension/revocation hearing at a reception center.

It is evident that parole detention became a significant enough category (or issue) within CYA circles to begin to be identified and counted separately in 1965. During 1965, 1966, and 1967, these counts referred *primarily* to "special projects" like CTP, the Oakland Community Delinquency Control Project, and perhaps a few others. During 1968 explicit permission was granted by the CYA board to *all* parole agents to utilize temporary detention. This permission was explained to "all holders of Youth Authority Parole Manuals" as follows:

Following is a restatement of policies and procedures concerning the arrest and detention of Youth Authority wards.
I. *Reasons for Detention*
Detention may be used for any of the following reasons:
A. Secure custody is required to control behavior because a ward:
1. Is an immediate danger to the person or property of another, or
2. Is an immediate danger to himself, or

3. Is in immediate danger of leaving the jurisdiction of the
   Youth Authority.
B. There is no other placement resource immediately available.
   Comment
   Occasionally it may be necessary to place a ward in
   detention temporarily when there is no other placement
   resource available, e.g. failure of a foster home, etc. This
   action may be taken in *emergencies only*. Every effort must
   be made to find an appropriate placement at the earliest
   opportunity.
C. Confinement is required for treatment purposes and to
   redefine conditions of release from custody.
   Comment
   Note that this policy has been changed to allow regular
   parole staff to use detention for this purpose, *as well as the
   special programs*. [Italics added.]

(These extracts are from a memorandum written by Thomas A.
McGee, Acting Chief, Division of Parole. As "Administrative
Bulletin No. 7 [revised 1 August 1968]," it superseded "Administrative Bulletin No. 7," dated 1 March 1967, and can be found
in CTP files.)

Evidently, many agents took advantage of this new *regular
parole policy*, as indicated by the 1968 and 1969 counts of parole
detention. It is important to note that the writer of the memo,
Thomas A. McGee, functioned as the former Operations Supervisor of CTP, according to *CTP Research Report No. 5* (February
1964). The change probably occurred in 1968 and not in 1966
because of the new availability of bed space. This availability of
bed space will be discussed in chapter 9, in relation to Probation
Subsidy. At this point it is sufficient to note that the average daily
population on 31 December 1968 reflected the biggest one-year
drop since 1956 (SCYA, 1970a, p. 42). This notable drop in
average daily population continued further in 1969, and at a
less-accelerated pace in 1970.

The available bed space *facilitated* the use of temporary
detention, but it did not *invent* its broad use as part of parole
"treatment." This was performed by the "special programs." The
CTP and other "special programs" helped to teach *and* legitimate
the "treatment" uses of detention to CYA board members and
CYA agents and officials. The 1968 comment by McGee indicates
this special link by the special programs in regard to temporary

detention. What had begun, in 1961, as a possible treatment method to be used on occasional weekends—and only for special subtypes—had become a legitimated treatment method that was now applicable to *all* CYA parolees. In 1969 the CYA board spelled out in even greater detail the administrative rules that were to guide its use.

It will be recalled that in the early 1960s, and as late as 1966, CTP parole agents and supervisors as well as agents associated with the Oakland Community Project were complaining about the cumbersome procedures that were required before temporary detention could be used. In order to detain a youth, CYA officers had formally to suspend wards from parole and, before releasing, had to appear before a suspension hearing, as required by CYA board policy. CTP attempted to change some of these requirements. The Task Force on Detention, strongly influenced by current and ex-CTP personnel, made a variety of recommendations to the CYA administration regarding changes in release procedures. In the period between the report and 1969, the release procedures continued to require a suspension hearing. In 1969 the procedures for initiating and releasing wards were officially changed, as noted in an administrative memo of 22 September 1969. The CYA board seems to have made other changes that affected the use of detention. But the applicable 1971 procedures (which were also in force in late 1969) agree essentially with the viewpoint of the 1966 Task Force on Detention. The *CYA Board Policy Manual* (1971*d*) contains the following provisions (pp. 29–30):

Section 29 *Temporary Detention Defined*

Temporary detention authorized under W.I.C. 1768, is recognized as a treatment method, as distinguished from parole suspension or parole revocation. Temporary detention is the confinement of a ward for 30 days or less for treatment purposes and/or to redefine the conditions of release from custody and when there is no other placement resource available. It shall be used when revocation of parole is not contemplated.

Section 29.1 *Temporary Detention—How Initiated*

Temporary detention may be initiated as follows:

1. A Youth Authority parole agent may detain a Youth Authority ward for not to exceed 48 hours (excluding Saturdays, Sundays and legal holidays) at his own discretion. Before the end of the 48-hour period, the parole agent must proceed as follows:

   a. Release the ward, or
   b. Immediately present the case to the Board (panel or
      referee) for a detaining order or other action, or
   c. Secure detaining order from a Director's representative or
      referee (sec. 61.2) and calendar the case within 7 days with
a temporary detention report to the Board.

   2. Temporary detention of not to exceed 30 days may be
ordered by the Board when the written report indicates that the
ward is in need of confinement for training or treatment purposes
and/or to redefine the conditions of parole. The parole agent
shall list the specific reasons for requesting temporary detention.
The Board Order shall then read: "Detain temporarily for 30
days or less."
   No more than thirty (30) total days are authorized under such
an order. the detention days do not necessarily need to be con-
secutive days. When a ward is in need of temporary detention
in excess of the thirty (30) days, the case must be presented to the
Board with justification on request for a new Board Order. When
more than 30 days of temporary detention are requested within a
6-month period, a revocation proceeding will be initiated at which
time the Board will revoke or restore to parole, or order additional
temporary detention.

   29.2 *Where to be Detained*
   Wards may be detained temporarily only in places approved by
the Director.

   29.3 *Release from Temporary Detention*
   Inasmuch as Board Orders specifying "temporary detention"
already read "30 days or less," another Board Order is not
necessary and the parole agent must arrange the release within
the 30-day period. Excessive use of temporary detention shall be
controlled administratively.

   It is quite evident that placing parolees in detention for the
purposes of "treatment" or "placement" has been made much
easier. The definitional boundaries for triggering agent discretion
have been broadened to include reasons that had been advocated
by the 1966 Task Force Report (SCYA, 1966). Youth can first be
locked up for forty-eight hours (as contemplated in the original
CTP proposal)—excluding Saturdays, Sundays, and legal holidays. This means that in practice youth can be detained for four
days, at the agent's discretion.

   In addition, parole agents can detain a ward for any *number* of
detentions during a six-month period, providing the *total time*
does not exceed thirty days within that six-month period; the
mandate to exercise this discretion is officially renewable every

six months. Other than available space, time and distance, and cooperative counties, the only organizational restraint mentioned is the recommendation that the detention power of agents be "controlled" by parole administrators.

In 1960, when CTP was first being proposed, there appeared to be no intention of increasing the amount of social control that the CYA parole organization would exercise over wards. An unintended byproduct of CTP and other "special programs" was to teach and legitimate the multipurpose uses of temporary detention. In practice, temporary detention can be now used by any CYA parole agent, without any special reference to I-Level theory or practice. It is the legacy of special social control practices, and not the special I-Level treatment classifications and prescriptions, that can be found in section 29 of the *CYA Board Policy Manual* and the annual detention statistics. The legacy of section 29 and the daily practices of regular parole agents appear to constitute evidence of a potent impact on the parent organization. There are few visible signs that this legacy of the 1960s will not be transmitted to the parole agents of the 1980s. In contrast, there are many visible signs that the treatment classifications and practices associated with CTP will not be part of this transmitted legacy.

5   CTP and Issues for
        Correctional Policy

The assessments of the CTP program design, activities, and impact have revealed that supervisory and line personnel engaged in a great deal of discretionary decision making. The major aim of this chapter is to assess the relative advantages and disadvantages of the discretionary choices that evolved into CTP policies. It is important to recognize that the use of discretion per se is not unique to CTP or even to the field of juvenile or criminal justice. Discretionary decision making, as a mode of policy development and implementation, occurs in all areas of public regulation, benefit, and welfare programs (Davis, 1967). However, it appears highly probable that policemen, prosecutors, judges, and correctional workers engage in more policy making by virtue of their discretionary power than do personnel in other public programs.

The discussion of discretion proceeds on the assumption that the execution of any ideal policy or program design is rarely an automatic one—but requires administrative decisions and individual choices to transform the ideal into the practical. The exercise of discretion can offer advantages that are often highly prized. Some of the advantages are nondoctrinaire flexibility, tailor-made individualization, pragmatic efficiency, occupational autonomy and expertise, and creative problem solving. These advantages can help to operationalize a complex policy, modify and even create new policy directions, adapt laws and rules to fit individual circumstances, and provide program priorities by selective emphasis (Davis, 1967).

While discretionary decision making can possess these advantages, it is also possible that the absence of limits on the power of officials to act or not act, as they distinguish among possible choices, can give rise to a variety of disadvantages. Power that is not reasonably confined, structured, and checked by public rules, procedures, and legal constraints can produce arbitrary decisions that are unjust to individuals. These undesirable consequences can occur despite the intentions of officials to realize the advantages associated with flexibility, individualization, and expertise. A major task of policy analysis is to determine how any particular correctional strategy practices its discretionary power, and whether authority has been exercised fairly and reasonably.

Specifying the types of choices and the CTP responses is a first step in assessing the use of discretion. Discretionary choices can involve a definition of what constitutes delinquency, whether distinctions will be made between degrees of deviance, and deciding who will interpret the definitions of renewed deviance. Discretion can also be exercised regarding the standards, procedures, and limits used in conducting hearings and imposing sanctions. In addition, discretion can be directed toward organizational choices that influence fiscal costs and evaluation. The varied types of decisions that were made will be assessed, and possible alternative choice srategies will be posed for consideration.

Choosing a Definition of Delinquency

Theoretically, the juvenile laws of a state govern the correctional agency's definition of delinquency. These laws, however, can be interpreted by the correctional organization either in a limited or in a broad manner. In the earliest reports there is evidence that CTP defined delinquency much more broadly than did the control organization. For CTP, uncooperative attitudes as well as "sassing" teachers constituted grounds for parole suspension; not only were many behaviors included that might not be considered grounds for suspension by the control organizations, but CTP grounds for suspension included an unfavorable assessment of ward attitudes and potential "acting-out."

This broad policy was perceived as advantageous by CTP personnel, since it provided them with legitimate authority to monitor and treat *any* aspect of the personal functioning of wards—verbal and nonverbal. In effect, it gave CTP a great deal of freedom to execute diagnostic and treatment plans. To impose any limits on a broad definition of delinquency would have meant that the agent's freedom to treat would have been curtailed. The right to define delinquency broadly was associated with a broad, individualized right to treat. In this view, narrowing definitional boundaries should be secondary to the treatment needs of the wards.

One disadvantage of this broad approach to defining delinquency is that wards will be assessed by what they *think*, by what they *might do*, and by what they *say*. Arresting youngsters for their ideas and thoughts, as well as for their possible behaviors, raises serious legal issues. Traditionally, *actual* harmful deeds are perceived to comprise a basis for approving a societal right to interfere with the behavior of individuals. If correctional agencies move away from a standard of *actual* behavior, what legal basis will the society utilize to interfere with the rights and liberties of individuals? Illegal thoughts? Everybody is capable of having illegal thoughts. Potential misdeeds? Everybody is capable of committing bad acts. If there are no reasonable boundaries regarding the charges against individuals, then there is apt to be an absence of legal reasons for abrogating the rights and liberties of individuals vis-à-vis the state.

Besides this legal concern, there are the pragmatic considerations of defining a task that has no limits—since for correctional personnel the appropriate bases for action would be virtually anything a youngster might think, say, or do. By setting no limits on the definition, there are, in effect, no boundaries on the job tasks of the correctional personnel. A job definition without specific boundaries runs the risk of obtaining diffuse task performances, diffuse task-assessment criteria, and diffuse supervision.

It appears that a much narrower definition of delinquency, particularly excluding thoughts, ideas, and potential deeds, would not have precluded CTP's goal of influencing delinquency.

Given the range of actual criminal misdeeds covered in the delinquency statute, CTP would still have had an enormous array of youth functioning to address in the role of treater. The control organization used a narrower definition, but it does not appear to have been any less effective in reducing actual misdeeds. CTP appears to have compromised legality and efficiency without any obvious benefits.

Distinctions Regarding Degrees of Delinquency

Since 1961 the California Welfare and Institution Code has made a distinction between adult criminal behavior (sec. 602) and juvenile status offenses (sec. 601). Implicit in this distinction is a moral judgment regarding types of behaviors. It is generally accepted that citizens, including many policemen, also make distinctions between the harms associated with felony-type offenses and misdemeanors (President's Commission, 1967c, pp. 85–95). Criminal codes usually reflect this moral judgment by sharply limiting the penalties that can be imposed for less offensive behaviors. From the perspective of private and public morality, it appears these distinctions should be made, once the behavioral boundaries are agreed to.

In practice, correctional organizations exercise an option to make distinctions between offenses, thereby varying the responses of their agents. It is clear that CTP did not choose to make this distinction regarding *suspensions of parole.* Youth were as likely to be arrested by CYA agents for displaying uncooperative attitudes as they were for truancy, minor theft, or a suspected rape.

With respect to *revocation of parole*, CTP experimental wards were dealt with as if there were a distinction between major personal and/or property offenses (see table 4) and all other types of offenses. In fact, for serious offenses, the rates of parole revocations appeared to be similar to the control wards. However, since these revocation rates were also influenced by the CYA board and juvenile judges, it is uncertain to what extent CTP agents made distinctions after suspending parole.

In the area where CYA agents could exercise a higher degree of discretion—namely, parole suspensions—the data as well as CTP statements indicate that degrees of delinquency were not considered a significant criterion for making decisions. CYA agents were not usually in a position to notice many clearly defined criminal acts, and therefore they initiated few suspensions for these offenses. They were able to notice the noncriminal "offenses" and appeared to have acted as if nonserious and serious offenses were to be dealt with on a similar level.

By failing to make a distinction by degree of offense, CTP appeared to be unconcerned about the degree of personal or property harm associated with the parole suspension charge. However, this assessment of relative harm seems to be a basic criterion for judging varying deviant activities along a continuum of seriousness. Adherence to a policy followed by CTP ran the risk of dealing with nonserious social harms much too seriously— and of dealing with serious social harms much too *non*seriously. In practice, this could mean that one ward was locked up for twenty days for sassing a teacher, while another was locked up for twenty days for carrying out a theft. It is questionable whether upholding the right to be taken seriously as an agency of authority can justify this kind of unreasonable outcome. This conclusion is buttressed by the fact that there is no evidence that undifferentiated adult responses had any impact on the future activities of youth. It appears likely that CTP's failure to make elementary legal and ethical distinctions could lead to a variety of unreasonable outcomes without any compensating benefits.

Interpreting Definitions of Delinquency

The ideal design of CTP encouraged maximum individualization of treatment planning and activities. As a corollary to this policy, it was assumed that agents would also be permitted to individualize their roles vis-à-vis wards. In practice, discretion was not only permitted but was actively encouraged. Agents could "play hunches" or even make snap judgments on very little evidence (see chapter 4). In effect, agents were free to continually impose their own standards regarding what constituted delinquency. The high rates of parole suspensions for juvenile statute and technical violations as compared to the rates for controls indicates that these discretionary decisions were made quite frequently.

It seems reasonable to infer that in many cases the discretionary determination of the broad and vague boundaries could be quite arbitrary. Not every agent would have the same hunches, spot the same cues, or even perceive the same attitudes. To the extent that different agents might reach different conclusions, the decisions might be veiwed as arbitrary. To the extent that outsiders might have difficulty in making similar assessments, the decisions might again be viewed as arbitrary. In the absence of clear-cut, written guidelines concerning the definitional boundaries, each agent was free to determine whether a ward's thoughts, stated ideas, expected behaviors, or actual behaviors constituted grounds for a parole suspension.

If the consequences of these decisions were not so significant for each youngster, then it might be argued that the discretion to define treatment should also include the discretion to define renewed delinquency. Since the consequences were not benign, the two types of discretion should not be confused. The risks of making a broad array of decisions, on arbitrary grounds, appear too great to grant the amount of unlimited discretion as existed in the CTP.

Distinguishing between Negative Sanctions and Treatment

In the introduction and in subsequent chapters the conceptual and research advantages of distinguishing social control from treatment was discussed. As practiced by CTP, treatment was found to be a vague concept that eluded intellectual clarity. In addition, distinguishing between therapeutic detention and other forms of detention led to coding problems. From a policy perspective, advocating anything done by agents *for* and *to* wards is a type of treatment that permits a correctional organization to evade responsibility for social-control activities. If agents are not administering negative sanctions, then there is little reason to be concerned about broad and vague definitions of delinquency, degrees of social harm and degrees of deprivation of liberty, and arbitrary criteria for making decisions. It is extremely difficult to hold correctional organizations accountable for the manner in which they execute the police powers of the state when they verbally deny that they are involved in a coercive social institution.

The issue is not whether, on reasonable grounds, wards should ever be locked up. The issue is whether a correctional agency like CTP can accept the responsibility for depriving youth of rights and privileges—and can then forthrightly address the issues associated with the administration of sanctions. If the conceptual distinction between social control and treatment is not made, then the responsibility for organizing a nonarbitrary administration of sanctions is not likely to occur.

Imposing Sanctions

Even if a correctional organization restricts jurisdictional boundaries, assesses degree of social harms, and minimizes arbitrary charges of misbehavior, it may still face the problem of how to process charges and arrive at a disposition of the charges. Whether a ward should receive considerations of due process or whether the agent has discretionary decision-making power to impose sanctions is a major policy issue.

The evidence appears rather clear-cut that the CTP agent could "sign in" a youth to detention without considering whether he was entitled to any or all of the following minimum elements of due process:

Clear, written notice of the exact charges prior to parole suspension;

A formal hearing of the charges by someone other than the accusing agent prior to the suspension;

A right to try to rebut the charges by cross-examination;

The right to have counsel of his own choosing;

A right not to testify against his own interest;

Exclusion of irrelevant detail in determining the facts of the charge.

The advantages favoring due process in handling *juvenile court* cases were summarized in 1967 by the U.S. Supreme Court in the Gault decision (*In re. Gault*, 1967). Even prior to the Gault decison, California had amended its Welfare and Institution Code, in 1961, to afford juveniles legal safeguards in juvenile court hearings. However, it is clear that the statute, administrative rules, and CTP operations did not require procedures for insuring fairness in the handling of *parole suspensions*. Apparently, in the late 1960s, formal hearings with elements of due process, did occur at the *parole revocation hearing* conducted by the CYA board. The question is whether elements of due process should have been introduced *prior to* a parole suspension and informal sentence to a detention facility.

The legal and moral advantages of protecting the rights of wards prior to being suspended and detained appears rather evident. Elements of due process might have helped confine and check arbitrary decision making by CTP agents. However, implementing due process would involve transforming the parole suspension act into a process of semi-litigation. The simple procedure of "signing in" would have been made more complex and cumbersome and might have been more costly in time, effort, and funds. These are, of course, potent costs to endure for the benefits associated with insuring fairness in handling temporary detention decisions. On the other hand, it could be argued that without due process the costs in individual rights and privileges are rather high. The state (represented by the correctional organization) should bear the high costs required to insure that individual liberty will not be treated lightly. If lockup procedures for CTP wards had been more cumbersome, perhaps fewer arbitrary and unfair decisions might have been made.

Whether any state is willing to pay the price of insuring fairness to juveniles at *any* decisional point where incarceration is a likely disposition appears uncertain at this time. Whether correctional agents would be desirous of having their power to make incarceration decisions confined and checked is also uncertain. In CTP it is clear that due process was not considered an issue.

Checking Detention Decisions

Related to the discussion of the due process element is the consideration of conducting formal hearings and of delineating the roles played by correctional agents.

In practice, the CTP agent could play all of the following roles vis-à-vis wards he suspended: (1) he *noticed* the thought, stated idea, behavioral expectancy, or the actual misdeed; (2) he *complained* about the "offense"; (3) he *charged* the youth with the offense; (4) he *determined the facts* of the charge; (5) he *ascertained the disposition* of the charge; (6) he *made the only written record* of the proceedings; and (7) he *transported* the ward to detention. In effect, the CTP agent played roles commonly associated with citizens, police, court intake workers, judges, and court clerks.

If fairness is an appropriate aspect of correctional policy, consideration must be given to reducing the power of the agent to complain, police, judge, and enforce his own orders. Fairness, in brief, appears to require a separation of powers.

Limiting the scope of the agent's role would mean that outsiders would weigh his charges and the evidence, examine witnesses, conduct the hearing, and finally reach a fact-finding decision prior to determining a disposition.

For the CTP, these outside reviews were not conducted *prior to* suspensions. In restoring parole or making a revocation decision the CYA board could function as an outside reviewer. While the CYA board is separate from the parole organization, it is questionable whether the two organizations are actually autonomous. Legally, the CYA organization operates under the policies of the CYA board. The board is expected to act as a policy supervisor of the activities of all of its personnel. In practice, there is no outside, impartial agency that confines or checks the discretionary decisions of the CYA personnel. The CYA board, in effect, performs this review function for its own employees.

CTP reports and the Task Force evaluation reveal that there existed a close degree of cooperation between the regional CYA boards and the CTP agents. For a while, the CTP program director was actually defined as a CYA board representative, and thereby empowered to judge cases of parole restoration and detention release (see chapter 3). During this period (probably 1962 to 1965), independent review by the CYA board was virtually eliminated as a technical possibility. Even after this practice ended (for reasons that are not clear in the CTP documents), there did not appear to be any questioning of the suspension-detention practices of the CTP agents. Evidently the CYA board cooperated in keeping revocation decisions below the norm for all offenses other than major personal and/or property offenses.

In portraying the CYA board as partial to the CTP there is no intention of implying that there was any conspiracy or collusion to keep revocation decisions below the norm of the control group. It is more likely that the CYA board members and representatives believed in the worth of the program and acted accordingly. However, this diminished the technical possibility the the CYA board might function as an independent review body regarding discretionary decision making.

As noted in the description of detention practices in the late 1960s (see chapter 4), the CYA board formulated section 29 to guide temporary detention. This rule permitted detention stays for forty-eight hours (exclusive of weekends and/or holidays) without prior review. It also provided for continuing detention (for treatment purposes) if the CYA parole agent intended to request a temporary detention order for a six-month period. The agent had seven days to make the request. After being in detention for a minimum of nine days, a ward might receive his/her first independent review—based on the agent's written report. How much time usually elapses before a CYA board hearing on the request for a six-month order is not known, but could well be longer than nine days. If a legal order to detain at the agent's discretion is granted, then the ward can be detained any number of times, for any length of time, providing that during the six-month period the maximum number of days does not exceed thirty (probably exclusive of the initial stay preceding the order). The order is renewable, on request, for another six-month period.

It appears that it is still quite easy to sign a ward into a lockup facility before obtaining a legal review and an order to detain. Given the broadness of the definition of the reasons for detention, and the past experiences with CTP, it is unlikely that many requests for temporary detention orders are turned down. The major external check provided by the rule appears to be the thirty-day limit within a six-month period. The CTP detention data (see chapter 3) indicate that CTP agents could have functioned quite easily within these rules. In 1966, during a six-month period, the CYA Task Force on Detention reported that CTP wards averaged 1.49 stays per ward—for an average stay of twenty days. This amounts to an average of thirty days' detention per ward during a six-month period. Discretion could have continued in CTP under section 29.

The problem of obtaining an independent review of discretionary decisions was an issue between 1961–69. There is little reason to doubt that it remains an issue today.

Checking Treatment Decisions

The discussion of the varied policy issues associated with CTP indicates that its operations were predicated on a major conception—the right to treat. Virtually every issue discussed is related to this value position. Proponents of this position seem much less concerned about the rights of those being treated than about their own right to treat—the right to treat has priority over the rights of individuals. In the potential conflict between concern over legal and human rights and treatment rights, the individual is presumed to be "better off" if treatment needs are attended to as the highest priority. According to this position, the experts should have the primary power in defining and prescribing the type, degree, and duration of the treatment, once the judicial process delivers wards to the correctional system.

Analysis of the CTP in operation provides insight into what is likely to occur when the right to treat is accorded primacy as a correctional value. Youngsters can be "placed" with minimum external checks. Thoughts, stated ideas, and potential behavior can be defined as legitimate indicators of a "need" to be "therapeutically" detained. Arbitrary decisions to "sign in" wards into detention can be viewed as "treatment-relevant decision making." And controls on wards' "acting out" can be a "tool" of treatment. In practice, granting to treaters the right to define the type, degree, and duration of treatment can be equivalent to granting them the right to define the type, degree, and duration of sanctions.

The CTP treatment position did not contain any internal check for placing limits on dealing with individuals. Restrictions on what could be done emanated from external sources: cost limits, legal restrictions on age or release procedures, organizational efficiency in dealing with supply and demand of beds, loss of time in traveling, etc. As the CYA Task Force made clear, the major considerations, indigenous to the right-to-treat value position, related to intention and technical effectiveness. But intention merely set forth the verbal aims of their activities, not the limits; and the technical considerations were related to an extension of "intensive treatment" beyond the period in lieu of traditional institutionalization. Theoretically, the procedures could provide limits, but these would be guided by efficiency, not by ethical concern for the rights of individuals. Technical efficiency cannot be the sole criterion upon which to base a policy that involves the reality of coercion.

An alternative policy could emphasize that the rights of individuals have precedence over the rights of treaters. For corrections, this would mean that the rights and privileges associated with liberty can only be interfered with when a fair and legal case can be made that a clear, actual, social harm has occurred. The right to sanction, and the corollary right to treat, can only be legitimated after the facts have been properly adjudicated. Moreover, since a restriction on liberty can occur as part of the disposition, limits on the type, degree, and duration of the sanctions must also occur before related treatment plans are decided upon.

Unless a just disposition is decided upon first, there is a danger that involuntary "treatment" plans will generate disproportionate sanctions. Sentencing a youth to twenty days' detention for sassing a teacher is an unjust sentence when compared to a twenty-day sentence for stealing a car; and sentencing a youth to twenty days' detention for sassing a teacher, when an adult is not even liable for a similar offense, is of itself an unjust sentence. These two examples appear unjust (even though the decisions may have been arrived at by fair procedures) because they violate two important elements of justice: (1) persons below majority age should not be sanctioned more severely than adults for a comparable criminal offense; and (2) sanctions should be appropriate to the degree of social harm that has occurred, regardless of age.

Such an alternative policy would posit that unless attention is paid to just sanctions, there is a likelihood that unjust treatment will occur. The right to treat, therefore, is secondary to the right to receive justice. In corrections, treatment is usually involuntary and takes place within a coercive context of social control. In order for treatment efforts not to *add* to the existing deprivation of liberty, fairness and justice must be attended to first.

In practice, the chances of CTP wards being locked up for technical violations of organizational or agent standards appear to have been higher than for control wards. Treatment in the community can, in practice, have outcomes similar to what might occur in a traditional institutional program. The primacy of the right to treat is potentially capable of leading to unintended, as well as unjust, outcomes.

A reasonable alternative policy would suggest that correctional agencies supervise their wards by using fair methods and administering just sanctions. Presumably these activities would be carried out with a concern for the human, as well as legal, rights of youth. Given this set of priorities, it is still possible to experiment with new forms of treatment, to gain future compliance with clear societal standards that refer to actual social harms. This kind of policy involves regulating the regulators and treaters *before* they engage in involuntary treatment activities.

The imbalance between control and treatment activities in CTP indicates that the policy of the right to treat can, in practice, yield more control than treatment experiences for youth. Without an alternative policy to confine and check the dominant aspects of correctional programs, there is no assurance that community treatment programs will diminish the social costs to individuals, nor is there any assurance that the current policy of unregulated treatment will automatically be associated with social benefits for society.

Measuring Program Effectiveness

Nonresearchers may be unaware that initial research choices of social indicators may not be based solely on technical criteria. In deciding upon indicators to be used in measurements, researchers may rely on theory, conceptual judgments, availability of data sources, time pressures, resources, or even social customs. Program personnel can hardly be held accountable for measurement deficiencies, since this is not their area of discretion. In deciding to use parole revocation as an indicator of effectiveness, CTP researchers were following a time-honored custom within correctional research (Lerman, 1968; Sellin, 1962; Davis, 1964). Recidivism had traditionally been conceived to be an appropriate indicator of effectiveness; parole revocation, in turn, was considered to be a good indicator of recidivism.

Researchers, however, are also expected to guide their work by the use of technical criteria to assess the reliability and validity of their measurements. These relatively neutral criteria are intended to guard against the potential biases that might influence the choice of indicators, the use of indicators in making measurements, or the coding of the measurements.

The reanalysis of CTP data clearly reveals that parole revocation rates may provide an inadequate basis for the measurement of youth behavior. In addition, reliance on these rates may lead to a biased assessment of program effectiveness, provided youth behavior is the primary target. If CTP had desired to change the decision-making patterns of CYA agents and board members, then shifts in parole revocation rates (controlling for types of offenses) could have been used as appropriate indicators of this aim. Clarity about the intended aims of a program makes it easier to select appropriate indicators for gauging the effectiveness of the program.

Furthermore, parole revocations per se technically could yield reliable measurements if decision makers, using common criteria, reached similar revocation/nonrevocation judgments, regardless of CTP or control status. However, both CTP agents and CYA board members knew which boys were experimentals—and they judged youth differently for comparable offenses. The judges (or primary coders) used different criteria for controls and experimentals, except for the most serious personal and/or property offenses. This coding bias undermined the use of revocation as a reliable instrument of effectiveness.

In addition, these same measurements have a low validity since they do not tend to measure what they purport to measure, that is, youth behavior. For example, among control youth, out of 100 major property and/or personal offenses only 42 are revoked (see table 4, part B). This means, of course, that 58 of these alleged 100 offenses will be "missed," using revocation as an indicator of illegal behavior. Similarly, 49 will be missed out of 100 auto thefts; 66 will be missed out of 100 petty theft and other minor criminal offenses; and 83 will be missed out of 100 juvenile status and/or technical violations. While it is possible that some of these "misses" are due to erroneous allegations, it seems unlikely that most of them are of this type. It appears evident that applying revocation as a measure of illegal behavior to a *known criterion group*—suspended parole violators—yields a great number of misclassified youth; many youth will be counted as nondelinquent even though they probably have committed another offense. In research terminology, the measure performs poorly on one critical test of validity.

Parole suspensions appear to be a more valid indicator of youth behavior. Data are lacking to apply a specific validity test to ascertain to what degree parole suspensions for specific offenses reflect the offenses that appear on police "rap" sheets. Yet evidence of an indirect type does exist that permits an analyst to have greater confidence in certain types of suspension data than in the revocation rates. First, police rates of arresting CTP and control youth are virtually identical; since the police are independent of the project (and have no connection with the experiment), their indications of illegal behavior are apt to be less biased. Second, more serious offenses are likely to be complained about by victims; but victims, as citizens, tend to think of the police and not the parole agents as the enforcers to complain to, according to victim self-report studies (President's Commission, 1967c, p. 93). Third, there is one offense in the data that is particularly well reported—auto theft. Suspension data can be presumed to be quite accurate regarding this indicator of illegal behavior; victim surveys and insurance data are the bases of this confidence (ibid., p. 24).

If we compare the CTP choice of parole revocation as the primary indicator with our own choice of certain types of suspension data, it is evident that the CTP researchers made the poorer choice. Regarding the best indicator, auto theft, CTP researchers missed over three-quarters of the known suspensions for the experimental group and almost one-half of the control group. There is no reason for other studies to emulate their errors. The fact is, of course, that the rates of auto theft per 100 youth on parole are quite similar for the two cohorts at sixteen months' community exposure.

Another reason for seeking better indicators of illegal behavior lies in the assessment of the probable social risks associated with alternative programs of corrections, for varied time periods. From a policy perspective, we can shift from a comparison of the *relative* differences in illegal behavior rates between two cohorts to a comparison of the probable *absolute* rates of illegal behavior associated with alternative programs. For example, we might be interested in knowing how many probable auto thefts will occur for every 100 youth released to a CTP-type program in lieu of institutionalization. Of particular interest is the time period, in this case eight months, when a cohort of youth might have been institutionalized. Analysts might ask, for example, what levels of social risk are posed by the experimental and controls groups for eight-month time periods.

Unfortunately, the available data are not reported in a manner that permits an exact answer. But, using table 4, part A, let us *assume* that one-half of the offenses occurred during the first eight months of community exposure—for each cohort—and the other half occurred during the next eight months. The CTP youth could be perceived as engaging in varied types of behavior that the controls might engage in if they were released. This seems to be a reasonable assumption since, at sixteen months' exposure, the rates for each type of offense are quite comparable, with the exception of the least reliable and valid suspension—juvenile status and/or technical violations.

Using this line of reasoning, there is a risk that about 15 auto theft incidents per 100 CTP youth will occur during the eight-month period. Is this an unusually high risk to take? The fact is, we don't really know, since we lack a *baseline* regarding what *might* be the "normal" or average output of auto thefts among *non-CTP youth* of comparable backgrounds, living in similar communities. It is conceivable that a random sample of comparable non-CTP youth could produce similar, lower, or even higher rates of auto theft during a comparable eight-month period. It is unlikely that the rate would be zero or even similar to a statewide average. We know too much about "high delinquency" areas to make such a naïve assumption (President's Commission, 1967c, pp. 60-77). However, if we could obtain precise data about the "normal" rates of auto theft, by time periods, there would certainly be a more reasonable basis for assessing the social risks associated with a new correctional program.

Shifting attention to the control group, we would expect a cohort of 100 youth to be involved in about sixteen auto thefts in their first eight months of community exposure. This means that at eight months' exposure, after being institutionalized for eight months, the control cohort probably produced a rate quite comparable to that produced in the CTP youth's in lieu time period. If this were so, then it could be inferred that the eight months' institutionalization merely delayed the risk of auto theft incidents occurring at a rate of 16/100 youth. However, interpreting whether the rate was indicative of a high social risk would be uncertain, for reasons similar to those discussed with reference to the CTP experimentals. If the normal, baseline rates were lower, we might infer that the controls had not been *deterred* by institutionalization, but merely *delayed* in their behavior.

It appears evident that obtaining data to engage in these lines of analyses would be extremely useful, both theoretically and practically. Continued reliance on customary research policy, as practiced in CTP, will probably not provide the information base necessary to assess program decisions. Some correctional organizations erroneously assume that they already possess indications of individual and group risk by using "base expectancy rates." In California, base expectancy scores are computed by using background variables associated with parole revocations (Beverly, 1965; Molof, 1967). On the basis of our analysis of parole revocation as an indicator of illegal behavior by youth, it is unlikely that base-expectancy scores are very powerful indicators of risk to the community. In addition, by using parole revocation there is no way of assessing the "normal" risk that exists in a community or among varied population groups that have not been in contact with CYA.

An alternative research policy would end excessive reliance on recidivism measures, and begin work on obtaining the best indicators of *youth* behavior for varied population groups. By ending a parochial emphasis on measures associated with *adult* decisions about youth behavior, an alternative research policy would begin to attempt a specification of the degree of social risk, by offense and time period, associated with new experiments in corrections. This alternative research policy is just as applicable to local, county, and federal innovations as it is to state experiments.

If reliance on the old research policy of using "recidivism" continues, we can expect inappropriate assessments of correctional programs to continue. For example, in a recent CYA report, a statewide drop in the fifteen-month revocation rate occurred for the first time in a decade (SCYA, 1971a, table 26, p. 38). Given our knowledge of the potential influence of discretionary decision making on these rates, it is certainly possible that this shift could merely reflect a change in adult behavior, provided that the wards of 1960 are comparable to those of 1970. Under the old research policy, adults could continue to measure shifts in adult decision-making behavior and program spokesmen could continue to claim "more success" than in the past. Meanwhile, the actual levels of social risk, over a sixteen-month period, could remain just as stable as in the comparison of CTP and control youth.

The alternative research policy would not necessarily be easy to implement, since many harmful acts can escape detection, can be treated as not worthy of complaint, or can be handled in a discretionary fashion by local police. Past studies indicate that the more harmful offenses (the most "serious") are those least likely to be treated in a discretionary fashion by citizens or police (President's Commission, 1967c, p. 65). From a research perspective, these offenses are the potential social risks that are currently most amenable to measurement, even to the extent of specifying degree of harmfulness through use of the Sellin-Wolfgang (1964) index. In practice, researchers lack reliable and valid instruments to assess noncriminal offenses (juvenile status and technical violations) among youth populations.

For these noncriminal offenses (delinquency without crime) the best that researchers can currently do is to measure how adults expand, or narrow, the boundaries of their power to define deviance. This appears to be a poor research policy, if the aim is to accurately assess illegal youth behavior—independent of correctional responses. Given the earlier discussion of definitional boundaries used by CTP, to attempt to correct delinquents without crimes as if they were actually socially harmful "true" delinquents may also be a poor correctional policy. Perhaps both correctional researchers and correctional workers should be held accountable for the manner in which they treat delinquents without crimes. Holding both groups accountable for their approach to delinquents without crimes may not increase program effectiveness, but it might increase the accuracy with which social risks are counted and the fairness with which they are locked up.

Assuming Correctional Ineffectiveness

The reanalysis of CTP data provides rather clear evidence that CTP did not have any measurable impact on youth behavior, in comparison to a traditional CYA program. Using this standard of comparison, the program was relatively ineffective. However, this is not a unique finding. Robison and Smith (1971), reviewing over a decade of innovative correctional research, reached a similar conclusion regarding ineffectiveness. Earlier, I had concluded (Lerman, 1968) that admired treatment modalities were ineffective. Other careful reviews of the correctional literature have reached similar conclusions, after taking into account the lack, or biases, of research design, differences in population at risk, or the adequacy of measurements (Bailey, 1966; Hood and Sparks, 1970). There is an array of evidence that current correctional "packages," regardless of their contents, are relatively ineffective in changing youth behavior.

This is a difficult overall conclusion to accept. The responses of CTP researchers and agents yield evidence of the difficulty in accepting the null hypothesis that their program was indeed ineffective. Even after published criticism had questioned their use of revocation as an indicator of "success," the CTP researchers and agents continued to claim success (Palmer, 1971). On a humanistic level, this is quite understandable. Very few dedicated people care to be associated with a program they do not believe to be effective to some degree. The founders of the first juvenile correctional program believed they would be effective in setting up the House of Refuge (1824) (Bremner et al., 1971, pp. 674-96); the founder of the "placing out" of juveniles, Charles Loring Brace, believed in his program (1853) (ibid., pp. 742-47); the administrators of the early juvenile asylums and reformatories held a similar belief (1830-90) (ibid., pp. 696-726); and so, too, did the child savers that founded America's juvenile court system (1895) (Platt, 1969). More recently, the participants in the Cambridge-Somerville study (Powers and Witmer, 1951), as well as those operating the program at Vocational High (Meyer, Borgatta, Jones, 1965), believed in what they were doing to and for youth. Historically, each generation of correctional reformers has criticized the effectiveness of their predecessors—and then proceeded to behave as if *their* program or approach was effective in saving youth. In this respect, CTP spokesmen are similar to the child savers of past eras in American history.

The policy recommendation that can be advanced, based on available empirical evidence and logic, is as follows: assume the null hypothesis that *all* programs are ineffective, until competent researchers provide public and acceptable scientific evidence that this assumption is unwarranted. This policy alternative is obviously at odds with the policy of the past and the present. Its aim is to address realistically what *is* reasonably true in corrections—not what corrections *wants to be* true.

It is important to note that American juvenile corrections

would not grind to a halt if this policy recommendation were accepted by the public and the decision makers. American adults and legislators would still insist that they have a right to set standards for youth, enforce the compliance with standards, and, if necessary, sanction violators to uphold the legitimacy of standards, rule makers, and enforcers. The public regulation of youth activities will continue, regardless of effectiveness; in addition, it will continue to pose policy issues that are generally associated with active social control efforts. The policy recommendation of assuming ineffectiveness can highlight these unstated assumptions about American juvenile justice and corrections.

Even in the future, when we discover the correctional technology that has, until now, eluded us, the problem of constructing— and practicing—a legal and humane correctional policy will remain. As noted earlier in the discussion of the right to treat position, technology per se is incapable of generating standards pertaining to fairness, justice, humaneness, and reasonable boundaries of public regulation. While we may not always adhere to these latter standards, it is unlikely that we would ever deny their worth.

By assuming ineffectiveness, it may be possible to address the other policy issues more consistently and dispassionately— without pretending that effective treatment existed in the past or exists in the present. Correctional workers may thus be free to enlarge their creative search for more effective procedures and programs. Besides encouraging a "strategy of search" (Empey, 1967), we can also encourage researchers continually to assess both intended and unintended accomplishments. As both groups engage in a strategy of search, it will also be necessary to assess the costs and benefits of the new programs and procedures. It is conceivable that, if new recommended procedures and programs are too depriving of legal and human rights, too aversive in character, or too excessive in monetary cost, we may choose *not* to "buy" the proffered technology. Limits may be reached regarding what constitutes a reasonable and humane trade-off in costs and benefits.

While the search continues, it might be prudent to recommend that the experimentation be scientifically regulated by assuming the null hypothesis and ethically regulated by protecting the rights of human subjects. Such regulation is currently attended to in the granting of NIMH funds to demonstration and research projects. However, the examination of the hypothesis and risks to subjects occurs primarily at the stage of grant approval. The CTP experience provides potent evidence that approved projects can change their design in practice, after approval has been granted. As far as can be ascertained, the issues surrounding the disproportionate use of temporary detention were not raised at the federal level—the source of research funds. It could have been raised, however, since being a CTP youth increased the chance of being locked up while on parole, *after* the in lieu period. Perhaps funding sources have to expend a limited, but definite, amount to perform site visits to approved projects. They could then help "enforce" the goal of protecting human rights in practice.

Regulating Fiscal Costs

If one of the implicit aims of CTP was to demonstrate the economic superiority of a community treatment program, then the evidence is rather clear that it failed. In fact, CTP demonstrated that it is possible for a community treatment alternative to be more expensive than a regular program on a per capita basis. Just as it is imprudent to assume program effectiveness, so, too, is it unwise to assume that early release, or in lieu programs, will automatically be cheaper. Ironically, the cost run-up was primarily due to excessive provision of intensive-treatment services during the second and third years of a youth's parole. The high valuing of intensive treatment cost the state of California quite dearly—$2,333 per capita more than if a youth had proceeded through the traditional program. As noted in earlier sections, this high valuing of intensive treatment also had social costs, but these are not as conducive to precise quantification.

Treatment-oriented personnel are unlikely to be aware of the fiscal implications of their program strategies; they may even be unconcerned about them. However, correctional administrators cannot afford to be indifferent to the fiscal costs of a search strategy. The Los Angeles County Probation Department administrators appeared to be aware that the CTP package had economic and social cost implications. Extending their line of reasoning, it is possible to list the components of the CTP package that would increase the fiscal costs of community-based corrections. These components are:

1. Release for training a sufficient number of personnel to learn nomenclature and use of I-Level theory, so they can become in-service trainers;

2. Set up and maintain a training department to teach new workers and resocialize more senior workers;

3. Release workers from regular duties, so they can be adequately trained in diagnostic and treatment strategies;

4. Provide treatment supervisors, as well as administrative supervisors, at a ratio of one supervisor to six workers, to insure quality control;

5. Match worker-personality style to the I-Level of wards, regardless of geographical distance and organizational difficulties in maintaining filled-up caseloads;

6. Set caseload ratios at no more than one worker to twelve wards;

7. Maintain levels of intensive service for as long as treaters deem necessary, thus reducing the rates of case turnover;

8. Permit agents to devote only 45 percent of their time to direct service to wards and their families, thus reducing the opportunity to increase caseload size;

9. Utilize foster home and group home placements for more than two-thirds of an average caseload size, depending on the judgment of the workers and their treatment supervisors;

10. Utilize temporary detention for about 90 percent of the wards, depending on the judgment of the workers and their treatment supervisors;

11. Provide travel expense funds, so workers can visit their wards wherever they might be living: in foster homes, group homes, county detention facilities, or at a state reception unit;

12. Provide auxiliary services, as determined by the workers and their treatment supervisors.

Each one of the components can add to the per capita cost but not necessarily in a proportionate manner. In comparison to a regular institutional package, a correctional organization could sustain this CTP package for a year—and still save money. According to table 5, it cost CTP $2,136 for program expenses the first year, and the regular program $3,075, for a comparable period—a saving of $839 per capita. However, a second year cost the regular program only $300 per capita, but it cost the CTP package $2,136—an imbalance of $1,836. By the end of the second year the program savings had been wiped out—and the

CTP package had now cost the state of California about $1,000 more per capita than the regular program. The inference is quite clear: effectiveness and organizational consequences aside, the CTP package did not save the state money after about fourteen months of sustained operation.

The original design appears to have been aware of the fiscal implications of the CTP package. By tapering off the intensive services after eight months, the expensive part of the package ceased—while still costing less than institutionalization. These savings could be maintained by giving up the package for the regular parole period. On fiscal grounds, it is surprising that administrators would permit the design to be so drastically altered. The project would have had to become an extremely effective strategy in order to justify the extension of a costlier program than CYA had started with at the outset. The available facts indicate that *nobody* was aware that continuing the package for two additional years would have such profound fiscal implications.

This analysis suggests that treaters need to be regulated for fiscal reasons, as well as for legal and humane ones. In order to encourage a reasonable search strategy, two policy recommendations appear to be alternatives to an unlimited treatment strategy:

1. Any *new program* strategy must annually *cost less* (in practice) per capita than the average yearly cost per capita of a traditional program of institutionalization plus parole;

2. In addition, any *traditional program* must *not annually cost more* per capita (in practice) than might occur because of inflationary increases for its customary expenses.

This twofold fiscal alternative assumes, of course, that the existing programs are ineffective. Therefore, there is no justification for increasing the per capita costs for traditional programs. Also, since new strategies of search must be regulated by some standards of fiscal restraint—to prevent costly overruns—the use of the cost of customary programs, as a fiscal ceiling, seems quite reasonable. But traditional programs can increase in per capita cost, over and above inflation, for reasons similar to the CTP cost overrun. If this actually occurred, any fiscal benefits produced by a search strategy could also vanish.

The cost of institutionalization per capita has, in fact, risen sharply in Calfornia, over and above inflation, in the past five years, even though the number of special community treatment programs has also increased (see part 2). To guard against the hazards of unregulated fiscal costs, a baseline for search strategies must be established. Freezing the per capita yearly costs of our most expensive program package—traditional institutionalization—seems quite prudent.

This twofold fiscal policy is compatible with the previous policy recommendations, since we have suggested that control and treatment activities also be regulated by prudent standards of proved social harm, fairness, justice, and humaneness. It may appear odd to some readers that the regulation of youth is inexorably linked to regulatory policies concerning adults. But a policy of active social control cannot be executed without attention to the social and economic costs to the society sponsoring the policy. The regulation of others must include the regulation of the regulators unless we are unconcerned about the cost run-ups in cherished values.

An economic perspective, besides being useful in and of itself, helps us perceive more acutely that we cannot have the presumed benefits of upholding standards of youthful conduct without also paying some costs. We can evade consideration of these costs, as was apparently done in the case of CTP cost overruns, or we can try consciously to address a critical question faced by corrections: How much are we willing to pay, economically and socially, for the benefits of regulating and treating youthful behavior? How we cope with this question, wittingly or unwittingly, may tell us more about American adults than about our youth. On the basis of the CTP experience, it appears that we are willing to pay a high price—probably much higher than the facts or our values warrant.

Summary and Conclusions

The CTP did not set out to demonstrate that temporary detention could become an important tool in treatment, "useful under a variety of circumstances." Nor did CTP set out deliberately to influence the CYA board to adopt Section 29 as part of its *Policy Manual* (SCYA, 1971*d*), explicitly authorizing temporary detention as a "recognized method of treatment." These unintended consequences emerged out of attempts to utilize discretionary authority on behalf of a broad correctional mandate. In the process of monitoring compliance with treatment norms and special organizational rules, as well as legal codes, social control emerged as the dominant program element. The empirical reality of the CTP operation indicates that simple adherence to a community treatment strategy does not automatically produce less costly responses to the traditional correctional dilemma: whether to provide correctional treatment or to provide authoritative control.

Historically, American juvenile correctional policy has tried to avoid that dilemma by claiming that its aims were not punitive, so that it never used social control. CTP, as an expression of this tradition, argued that society's harshest sanction for youth—deprivation of liberty—need not be perceived as a social control measure as long as its use was guided by a rehabilitative intent. The rationale provided by the CYA Task Force on Detention, as well as the wording of Section 29, indicate that the CTP does not consider anomalous its approach to defining and operationalizing treatment. The rationale appeared to possess widespread support in influential circles of an esteemed correctional establishment.

The rationale for a broad conception of correctional programming is not restricted to the argument that benign intentions are a sufficient criterion for defining the content of methods of treatment. The proponents of therapeutic detention believed that inclusion of this discretionary tool of treatment would produce more effective, as well as less expensive, correctional results. If these beliefs had actually been sustained by empirical evidence, there might be a reluctance to question the fundamental assumption that benign intentions justify a variety of discretionary practices. It is not uncommon to value superior technical achievements and the saving of money. On behalf of these achievements, we might be willing to delegate to professional agents of the state an array of discretionary powers. Short periods of temporary confinement in a Reception Clinic or Juvenile Hall might have proved acceptable, even if the decisions were guided by unreasonable and unfair standards and procedures. It is quite conceivable that a pragmatic argument concerning efficient and effective results might have been persuasive to many critical policy makers—even if the results were achieved by questionable means.

The case for therapeutic detention as a necessary means to accomplish desired goals relies on a demonstration that increased effectiveness and reduced costs have actually been achieved. The fact that the total CTP program package did not yield better results or reduce per capita costs seriously undermines the pragmatic case. In this instance, the benefits that could have offset the social costs associated with an expanded use of detention were not forthcoming. Instead, the costs associated with detention appeared to mount as precipitously as the fiscal increase in program costs. While we have attempted to locate the sources and amount of these unintended costs, it is difficult to quantify social costs as neatly as fiscal costs.

A different argument favoring CTP might acknowledge these excessive social costs and still argue that the total amount of institutionalization was reduced by the program. According to this view, the net social costs would have been reduced by CTP, particularly for the eight-month in lieu period. CTP youth would be at a disadvantage primarily during the normal parole period, since it is during this time that they would have received more short-term lockups for noncriminal reasons than control youth. In addition, CTP demonstrated that parole suspensions and short lockups could be substituted for parole revocations and longer institutional stays.

This new argument for assessing CTP more favorably was not explicitly set forth in the *Research Reports*. Unlike the reports, the argument does not make any claim about increasing benefits. Instead it focuses solely on the issue of reducing social and fiscal costs in comparison to the costs of traditional efforts. This cost-reduction position would probably stop short of insisting that all social costs could be eliminated, since few persons would argue that all types of sanctions should cease. Even a recent Quaker report is unwilling to favor a total abolitionist position regarding the use of institutionalization. Therefore, the argument favoring a reduction of social costs appears to involve proponents in a determination of what social controls are necessary, when sanctions can legitimately be used, and when institutionalization (as one type of sanction) should cease. This reliance on setting social standards is, of course, at variance with the vague legitimation set forth on behalf of temporary detention in CTP or Section 29 of the CYA board *Policy Manual*.

It is possible to make a case for programs like CTP, provided one relies on the value of reducing unnecessary social and fiscal costs. But this positive assessment could be altered if the impact of CTP on regular parole operations were taken into consideration by analysts. The publication and implementation of the CYA board *Policy Manual*, Section 29, is directly traceable to CTP and other special parole programs. While authorizing discretionary temporary detention for noncriminal reasons, the policy change did not link the use of such detention to an expanded early release program. Instead, temporary detention was *added* to the existing system of social control. This means that potentially unfair and unreasonable social costs have been disseminated throughout the entire CYA parole program, since at least 1969. These costs are, of course, accumulating over time, and are likely to continue for the foreseeable future.

It is evident that determining whether CTP actually reduced unnecessary social costs is related to the choice of a particular systemic and temporal frame of reference. As the discretionary use of temporary detention continues to affect the lives of thousands of paroled youth, any short-term reduction of social costs associated with CTP may become increasingly difficult to discern. If attention is focused solely on CTP and the demonstration period, the reduction in costs might appear more promising. From a social policy perspective, the long-run impact appears to offset this limited promise of reducing unnecessary institutionalization.

PART TWO
Probation Subsidy

6   Probation Subsidy: Assumptions and Operating Criteria

In 1965 California enacted legislation empowering the state to provide subsidies to county probation departments if they reduced commitments to state adult and juvenile institutions. By fall 1971, George Saleeby, one of the architects of the program, described the accomplishments of the State Aid for Probation Services as follows:

Like a precocious child, California's fledgling probation subsidy program has knocked existing routines into a cocked hat, challenged time-honored concepts in the handling of juvenile and criminal offenders, and brought utter dismay to the self-annointed patriarchs defending the status quo in California's justice system. How this major bit of boat-rocking could be achieved by a single program in the short span of five years is one of the truly amazing stories of our time. It has prompted Richard McGee, internationally acclaimed penologist, to speak of the program as "having greater impact on California corrections than any program in the last 25 years." It has brought about what my colleague, Robert Smith, has called a "quiet revolution" in the way we provide more public protection through better rehabilitative treatment of offenders. [Saleeby, 1971, p. 3]

By 1972 three other western states—Oregon, Washington, and Nevada—had adopted similar subsidy programs, and administrators from over half of the states of America had expressed sufficient interest to send observers. And at a federal level, Robert J. Gemigani, commissioner of the Youth Development and Delinquency Prevention Administration located in the U. S. Department of Health, Education, and Welfare, has provided an official endorsement of the program:

The Youth Development and Delinquency Prevention Administration endorses the use of probation subsidy as a viable way for states to aid those offenders entrusted to their care. [Smith, 1972, p. iii]

This endorsement, enunciated in such a short span of time, is certainly sufficient to arouse the curiosity of anyone interested in corrections. Saleeby explains the major dimensions of the subsidy program as follows:

The probation subsidy program is a pioneering effort to put California's correctional dollar where the problems are. It is a program that allocates state funds, normally used to incarcerate offenders and treat them while on parole, to the counties for the development of adequate probation services. The theory is that this not only will reduce commitments, but it will also permit offenders to be treated in their home communities where chances for rehabilitation are increased.

The probation subsidy program uses a statutory formula to determine a participating county's "earnings." Participation by the counties is entirely voluntary. Earnings are based on a county's reduction of adult and juvenile commitments to the state.

The benchmark by which a county's earnings are computed is its own past commitment performance over a five-year period beginning in 1959 and continuing through 1963, or the two years 1962–63, whichever is higher. This five-year or two-year average commitment rate becomes a never-changing "base commitment" rate for the county.

Annually, this rate is applied against the county's population to determine its "expected number of commitments." A county is entitled to subvention if its total commitments for any given year are less than its "expected number of commitments." The amount of subvention is dependent upon a formula that provides varied amounts from $2,080 to $4,000 per case, with the larger amounts taking effect as counties increase their percent of reduction. Generally speaking, counties with a relatively low base commitment rate need only reduce commitments by 5 percent to reach $4,000 per case figure, and counties with high base

commitment rates need to reduce by 25 percent to achieve the
$4,000 figure.

A county's earnings are computed annually, and these earnings
are paid by the state as reimbursement for expenses incurred.
Earnings may be spent over a two-year span, e.g., earnings for
1970–71 may be spent in 1970–71 or 1971–72. Counties may
assign anyone who is on probation to special supervision
units. Proposed budgets must be approved by the Youth
Authority, and separate accounting procedures must be
maintained, because field audits are made both by the
Department of the Youth Authority and the State Controller's
office.

The Youth Authority is responsible for the administration of
the program and enforces standards established by the Board of
Corrections. These standards cover caseload size, staff
supervision ratios, staff qualification and training, ancillary or
supporting services on which subvention funds may be spent,
diagnostic and classification systems to be used, and staff-clerical
ratios. [Saleeby, 1972, pp. 4–5]

Using the statutory formula and the administration standards
enunciated by the CYA (and adopted by the Board of Corrections)
the funds actually provided to the participating counties increased
from $1,632,064 in 1966–67 to $18,292,145 in 1972–73 (SCYA,
1974, p. 18). To earn this amount of money, counties will have
reduced adult and youth commitments by about 44 percent from
the "base" period of 1959–63.

In this chapter we will attempt to describe the assumptions,
rationale, and operating criteria associated with this novel community treatment program. Chapters 7 and 8 will examine two
unintended consequences of probation subsidy that have not been
noted by participants or outside observers. These unintended
consequences refer to the sizable increase in CYA institutional
costs and the increase in county rates of institutionalization. This
analysis will be geared primarily to the impact on juvenile
corrections. Chapter 9 will assess the policy issues associated with
probation subsidy.

The Rationale for Pursuing a Subsidy Strategy

The Probation Subsidy Bill was officially signed into law on 12
July 1965—having been introduced into the California legislature
in March 1965. This speedy passage of innovative legislation was
preceded by a great deal of work behind the scenes. Governor

Edmund G. Brown and the legislative sponsors of the bill were certainly influential participants in the political groundwork (Smith, 1965). But the ideas for the bill, and even the writing of the legislation itself, were not the product of legislative deliberation or the governor's staff. The framing of the bill and the explanation of its provisions were primarily the work of two California Youth Authority employees, George Saleeby and Robert L. Smith. Smith was the chief study director of the 1964 *Probation Study* (State of California Board of Corrections, 1964) that provided the rationale and the evidence for strengthening county probation programs. Saleeby is credited (by Smith) as being the author of the idea to connect a subsidy with county performance in reducing state commitments (*Probation Study*, 1964, p. 178, n. 1).

Historically, the founders of probation subsidy may be viewed as representatives of professional corrections in California; for in earlier studies of 1948 and 1957, a strong case for obtaining state funds to support county probation had been documented (State of California Special Study Commission, 1957). These earlier attempts at obtaining state aid had not been successful. The 1964 study was an attempt on the part of key leaders in state corrections, as symbolized by the Board of Corrections, to revive interest in this idea and, if possible, to devise an "offset" formula, whereby the state legislature would not appear to be authorizing additional funds to help county probation departments. Saleeby is frank in his appraisal of the reasons for passage of the bill:

The 1964 study clearly indicated that things probably would not change very much unless the state provided the funds to strengthen county probation services. This hardly qualified as news for those who had been working in California corrections for any period of time; but it was patently and manifestly true. Several times in the prior decade, efforts had been made to establish subsidy programs, but each time the legislature rejected these efforts because of the heavy costs involved.

Those of us who played a part in getting the 1965 legislature to enact the present probation subsidy program into law are convinced that the primary reason we succeeded where others failed was because we built into the program a performance principle that provided subventions only when there were guaranteed savings to the state. In other words, counties that produced (reduced commitments to the state) got subventions;

those that didn't got nothing. In convincing the legislature that
the program be adopted, effective use was made of arguments
that state institutions were overcrowded and were receiving as
many as 25 percent of total admissions who might more
profitably benefit from probationary supervision. However valid
these arguments were, they were forensic in nature, designed to
make the program palatable to a legislature that had traditionally
been cool to the idea of subvention.

The primary purpose of the subsidy program was then, and is
today, *to provide state funds for the strengthening of probation
services*. The resultant reduction in state commitments is a
fortuitous spin-off or by-product; it is not the primary reason we
have a subsidy program. The primary reason for the program, as
spelled out in the law, is to *increase public protection through
better supervision* of a large number of offenders who formerly
were committed to prison. [Saleeby, 1971, pp. 4–5. Italics in
original]

Saleeby's assessment is interesting, since he indicates that the
state leaders of California corrections were primarily interested in
"strengthening probation"—and not in reducing institutionalization per se. The reduction of state commitments was a means to
the end that had been sought since at least 1947. If the state
legislature, at an earlier date, had been willing to provide
subvention funds to counties, there would have been no need to
devise a performance principle based on reduced commitments.
Prior to 1964, the problem had appeared to merely consist of
helping probation achieve "its great promise as one of the
greatest social advances in the twentieth century" (Smith, 1965,
p. 1). To Smith, the author of the 1964 report, the problem
appeared to call for a more complex approach:

The riddle facing California has been how to help probation
services, and to reduce the rate of commitments to state
institutions, while reducing the costs to the taxpayer for a rapidly
expanding service. [Ibid.]

By posing the riddle in this more "palatable" manner, Smith
and his collaborators were able to accomplish their major goal—
the diversion of state funds to county probation departments. In
the course of reaching this goal, they also assisted in the
development of a new correctional policy that could affect some
of the critical decision points in the criminal justice system. The
formulators of the new policy were aware of some of these
decision points. In fact, it was acute awareness of the discretion

attached to critical decision points that helped suggest the
initiation of a subsidy program that might *increase* the granting
of probation, in both the adult and juvenile systems—in lieu of
state institutionalization.

According to Smith (1972, p. 17), there were nine basic
assumptions underlying the idea which, together with the fiscal
offset formula, influenced the legislature:

1. The most effective correctional services are provided in the
local communities where the problems are, where they must be
resolved, and where both the offender and the correctional
agency are subject to local influences and control.
2. Probation has a greater total responsibility for the
supervision of offenders than any other local correctional service.
3. Straight probation (without jail conditions) is the least costly
correctional service available.
4. Probation is as effective, if not more effective, than most
institutional forms of care.
5. Probation grants can be safely increased without increasing
the rate of violation by probationers.
6. The actual rate of probation grants is determined by the
decisions of probation officers and not the final dispositions
made by the courts.
7. Organizational or institutional change can be achieved by
rewarding probation departments for engaging in approved
behavior, providing that behavior is clearly defined.
8. At least 25 percent of the new admissions to state
correctional agencies can safely be retained in the local
communities with good probation supervision.
9. The cost for improved probation supervision can be offset by
savings made at the state level.

The first four assumptions have been an implicit part of
correctional philosophy for many years. They include beliefs and
facts that underlay the 1949 and 1957 reports requesting state aid
for local probation.

The fifth assumption is based on a study by Davis (1964), which
indicated that *adult* California superior court probationers,
residing in high probation-granting counties, did not have higher
rates of revocation than those residing in low probation-granting
counties. If the fifth assumption is sufficiently broad to include
revocation as an indicator of "violation," and if juvenile as well as
adult rates can be equated, then the Davis study could be used to
support this assumption. However, Davis found that the younger
the probationer, the greater the likelihood of revocation. He

asserted that this finding is consistent with the traditional criminological conclusion that younger wards have higher rates of parole revocation than older wards.

It is still possible, of course, that on a statewide basis, controlling for age, probation violation data would be comparable to that obtained in our earlier analysis of CTP and regular parole groups. If that were the case—and it seems a reasonable assumption—then it would be possible to posit that probation (or parole) is as effective (or ineffective) as institutionalization in changing illegal behavior, provided the groups are comparable in age and background characteristics. It is apparent that the null hypothesis could be substituted for the fourth and fifth assumptions, and a case for pursuing a probation subsidy strategy could still be argued.

The last four assumptions are the interesting ones to consider. The sixth assumption indicates that judges are strongly influenced by the recommendations of probation officers—and evidence is provided that judges concur, to a high degree, with officer recommendations. The seventh assumption indicates that probation officers might increase their recommending behavior if they received sufficient rewards, and this seems reasonable. These two assumptions indicate that a strategy to influence the decision-making behavior of probation officers, and indirectly the judges, could be successful in increasing the granting of probation. This is a novel strategy for changing the correctional behavior of *adults*. It indicates that decisions about offenders are based on considerations other than "the facts of the case," "the needs of the offender," or "just dispositions." If the supply of alternative dispositions can be increased, then it is possible for officers to change decisions and for judges to acquiesce in these decisions.

According to the eighth assumption, decisions could be so altered that the commitments to state institutions could be reduced by 25 percent below the existing county rates. This assumption is based on evidence that suggested that the youth and adults sent to state correctional facilities for diagnostic recommendations were frequently returned to local courts with a probation recommendation; and short, follow-up, evidence indicated that these cases did not soon return to court. In addition, studies that were conducted at state reception centers for juveniles and adults indicated that correctional workers could make a recommendation of early release to parole, provided that supervisory services were available in the community. On the basis of these appraisals, Smith concluded that 40 percent of the juveniles and 10 percent of the adults—a combined rate of 25 percent—could have been maintained in the community under intensive supervision.

The ninth assumption is that the state would save money if the counties made different decisions and reduced their commitments to state institutions. According to Smith, the hypothetical savings could be passed on to the county, where additional services could be provided to take care of these noncommitted cases, plus three or four others from the regular caseload. In the summer of 1965, the following calculations were presented as an example of the potential trade-offs between the county and the state:

If commitments to the Youth Authority and Corrections can be reduced by 25 percent from those projected (and expected) through 1975, then 33,682 men, women, and children will not come into the state correctional system. These 33,682 people who do not need state correctional services, but who at present are coming into the system, will cost the taxpayers $164,780,000 during the next decade if something is not done to change existing practices. If, on the other hand, the state shares the cost of corrections for this highly selected 25 percent, up to a maximum of $4,000 for each uncommitted case, then the state would have to spend only $134,435,508. This means a savings to California taxpayers of $23,532,542. Savings and sufficient money for greatly improved programs of probation supervision for many cases not now receiving it become possible under this plan. [Smith, 1965]

Saleeby claims that this last assumption, with appropriate calculations, finally convinced the legislature to provide the funds for county probation. However, the CYA had evolved a strategy for changing correctional decision making in order to generate the "savings." In gaining the approval of the legislature the offset formula may have been solved prior to the other problems. But, in practice, the counties would first have to perform by altering their decision-making patterns sufficiently to qualify for payments. After the counties had changed, the state would reward their behavior by providing them with subvention funds—based on money that might have been expended if the traditional decision-making rates had not been altered.

To qualify for money, the counties had to have their rate reductions certified by the CYA and the Department of Finance. In addition, they also had to provide "seed money" to start a special program, and then have this intensive program approved by the CYA. In practice, this meant that counties would be reimbursed for *past* accomplishments and programs rather than for a projected reduction or program. In effect, this added a tenth assumption: any risks attached to fluctuating reduction rates, starting up programs, hiring new workers, and administering separate, special units would be assumed by the counties, not by the state.

In fact, the decision to participate in the subsidy program posed an array of problems for the counties. If they decided to participate, county probation officials and judges would have to reach agreement regarding how reductions might occur and whether special decision-making procedures were necessary to insure and maintain levels of stable target reduction. In addition, probation departments would have to enlist the cooperation of county executives in providing "seed money" and budgeting for the special supervision programs. After critical policy discussions with judges and county executives, probation administrators would have to make programmatic decisions concerning caseload size, salary classifications, staffing patterns, and other organizational matters that would be accepted by the state administrators. Their co-policy makers, the judges and the county executives, might also be interested in influencing the allocation of new fiscal resources. These decisions could influence the numerical size of the program, maximum financial reimbursements, the proportion of the regular probation caseload to be included in the special units, the relative speed of the "turnover" of cases, and types of services to be delivered.

At the outset, it was realized that the counties might not be sufficiently persuaded by the first nine assumptions to participate in view of the uncertainties posed by the wording of the initial legislation with its hidden tenth assumption of fiscal risk at the county level.

The CYA staff was aware of this risk and sympathetic to the

county probation departments. As a matter of historical fact, the *1964 Probation Study* (State of California Board of Corrections, 1964) had included in its draft of the proposed legislation a special subsection on advancing "seed money." The CYA draft legislation included the following clause:

(e) To encourage the broadest use of special supervision programs, the Youth Authority may pay, to the extent funds are available for this purpose, up to 33⅓ percent of the estimated payment that would be due the county at the end of the year, if the county so elects, in the first year of participation only. [p. 197]

This subsection had been deleted by the legislature, so that counties could only be reimbursed "upon presentation of a valid claim based on actual performance in reducing the commitment rate from its base rate" (SCYA, 1970*b*, p. 108). Since the legislature was reluctant to put up any new money but rather insisted on beginning to pay out funds 1 July 1967, one year after the first official fiscal year, 1966–67, the counties could also be expected to be reluctant to provide large amounts of seed money. Aware of the reluctance of the counties, CYA administrators initially approved programs that were often based on administrative juggling of accounts. Smith writes about this difficulty as follows:

Initially, counties had to provide seed money for the first year of the program. All participating counties recovered that seed money and have in fact made earnings far in excess of the actual expenditures for their first year programs. Take, for example, one large metropolitan county that reluctantly entered the program in 1966 by increasing its probation budget by $25,000. That $25,000, along with *considerable administrative manipulation*, qualified for $250,000 worth of programs for special supervision. Put differently, $25,000 made the county eligible for a state reimbursement ten times the value of their initial investment. [Smith, 1972, p. 35; italics added]

While administrative discretion, by the CYA administrators, might be of assistance in overcoming the risk of investing seed money to get started, counties were still faced with the problem of handling year-to-year fluctuations. This uncertainty could not be dealt with by administrative discretion alone, particularly if counties were reluctant to get involved in the first place. This reluctance led to an emergency change in the original legislation before the first subsidy fiscal year 1966–67 was even completed

(Smith, 1972, p. 43). An amendment made it possible for a county to use unexpended earnings from one year in the next year's program. By adroit handling, a county could finance *current* programs on the basis of *last year's* earnings. If this new feature were combined with an existing subsection permitting counties to claim last year's earnings in the event of an unusually low commitment year (perhaps due to a riot or other calamity), counties could have two years to "bail out" of subsidy programming if events beyond their control occurred. (Later, in 1969, counties were permitted to use unexpended earnings over a two-year period plus the calamity year.)

There is strong evidence that these fiscal concerns influenced the decision of major counties to enter the program. In order for the new legislation to demonstrate any impact it was deemed imperative that the state's biggest counties participate. It would be difficult to achieve reduced commitments on a statewide basis if a county that contributed over one-third of the commitments, like Los Angeles, refused to participate. Some counties might receive funds on the basis of reduced commitments, but Los Angeles county decisions could more than offset these lower commitments. The state might pay out money for some county savings and still have no *state* savings to show for its efforts. Apparently, the emergency change in permitting deferred payments of unused funds and quarterly installment of these "incumbered funds" proved persuasive to the large counties. This change, with Smith's accompanying comment, indicates the significance of the timing of payments on possible realization of the new correctional policy:

Section 1825 Quarterly Installments of Incumbered Funds.

(b) If the amount received by a county as reimbursement of its expenditures in a fiscal year is less than the maximum amount computed under subdivision (d), the difference may be used in the next succeeding fiscal year and may be paid to the county in quarterly installments during such fiscal year upon preparation of valid claims for reimbursement of its quarterly expenses.

Subsecton (b) was the first emergency change made in the subsidy legislation. It was made prior to the end of the first fiscal year of actual operation. . . . If a county invested $100,000 in a program and operates it for a year but earns $300,000 through reduced commitments, then under the provisions of this section the State will (1) reimburse the county its actual cost of $100,000 and (2) reserve an amount up to $200,000 for the operation of that program in the succeeding year. If the county elects to continue the program at the same program level of $100,000, then, regardless of the number of commitments it makes, the county is guaranteed $100,000. The remaining $100,000, if unused, would revert to the general fund of the State of California.

Under the provisions of this section, a county may also ask for reimbursement on a quarterly basis during their second operating year which also enables the county to limit its appropriations for the program. If the county, in the illustration given above, had elected to continue operation at the $100,000 program level, then, on a quarterly basis, they could have asked the State of California for quarterly reimbursements in the amount of $25,000. Since the county must first appropriate the money, operate the program and then claim a reimbursement, the county could successfully operate the $100,000 program by appropriating only $50,000. This could be accomplished since they would need funds from the county to operate the program through the first quarter. They would then claim reimbursement for $25,000 during the second quarter in which they were operating under county funds, but could then use the first quarter's $25,000 reimbursement to pay the cost for the third quarter, and the second quarter reimbursement to pay for the fourth quarter operation. [Smith, 1972, p. 43]

Given this legal and administrative approach to program development, a county with shrewd management could: start a program with few funds; promote reductions to earn back this seed money; earn extra money for the following year's operation; continue to expand this approach until all of the new, expanded programs were being funded out of last year's operation—all without any sizable input of county funds except the small seed money that got the system started. This complex reimbursement scheme indicates that probation subsidy legislation (as written and administered in California) involved a great deal more than assumptions about the value of community treatment, probation effectiveness, or reduced commitments.

In fiscal 1966-67 the counties spent about $1.6 million in programs, even though they "earned" about $5.7 million in reduction funds. By 1969-70, the counties spent about $13.3 million in programs, fairly close to their reduction earnings of $14.2 million (Saleeby, 1971, p. 7). Not only had subsidy become a multimillion dollar business, but the local administrators had begun to solve *their* twin fiscal puzzles: (1) how to obtain the maximum amount of state funds with the minimum amount of county expenditures, and (2) how to reduce annual uncertainty concerning the steady flow of state dollars to the counties. The tenth assumption, having counties assume the program risks, is still operative; but it has been considerably mitigated by the combination of administrative discretion, legislative amendments, and managerial skill in using seed money and incumbered funds on a quarterly basis.

CYA Administration of Probation Subsidy

The 1965 subsidy law established the California Youth Authority as the administrator of the legislation. Sections 1821 through 1822 read as follows:

From any state moneys made available to it for such purpose, the State of Caifornia, through the Department of Youth Authority, shall ... share in the cost of supervising probationers who could otherwise be committed to the custody of the Director of the Youth Authority or, pursuant to criminal commitment, to the custody of the Director of Corrections; and who are in special supervision programs. The Department of Youth Authority shall adopt and prescribe, subject to approval by the State Board of Corrections, minimum standards for the operation of a special supervision program.... [SCYA, 1970*b*, pp. 105–6]

The Youth Authority was apparently selected to administer a program directed at both adults and youths because it had actually formulated the entire program. In addition, the Youth Authority had an established relationship with the counties, whereas the Adult Authority had few contacts. Since the 1940s the CYA had been the administrator of a state-county program that offered a maintenance subsidy to county probation departments if youth were institutionalized (as part of "local probation") in a juvenile ranch, camp, or home. In 1957 the CYA began administering a subsidy for the construction of new ranches, camps, and homes that housed youth on "probation." It had also been involved in consultation and training functions on the local level. Finally, the Youth Authority had involved key administrators in county programs in the formulation of the subsidy bill.

The Youth Authority's involvement with both adult and youth probation services is legitimated in Article 4 of the Welfare and

Institutions Code, which sets forth the powers and duties of the Youth Authority. Section 1760.7 reads:

The director shall investigate, examine, and make reports upon adult and juvenile probationers. The director may establish standards for the performance of probation duties, and upon request consult with and make investigations and recommendations to probation officers.... [SCYA, 1970b, p. 99]

This article was amended to the Welfare and Institutions Code in 1951. Standards for the performance of probation duties were first developed by the Youth Authority in 1954 and refined and updated in 1961 and 1965. These probation standards became the basis of the state's definition of a "special supervision program."

The original law specified that probationers whose offenses made them eligible to be initially committed to the state were acceptable candidates for special supervision programs. This stipulation excluded dependent children and children with "delinquent tendencies" (involving juvenile status offenses such as incorrigible, runaway, truancy, morals, and curfew violations, as defined in Welfare and Institutions Code, Section 601). On the adult level, misdemeanants were excluded, as were narcotic addicts committed to the state through civil proceedings. In 1969 the law was changed, so that "delinquent tendencies" probationers were defined as eligible for special supervision; however, they were *not* to be counted as figuring in the computation of the subsidy.

The law is also very specific in regard to procedures for the payment of state money. The method of calculating commitment reductions, and a schedule of per capita payment based on the percentage decrease from various ranges of base commitment rates, are included in the legislation. The law also specifies that applications should include a method of certifying that monies received from the state were actually spent for special supervision programs.

Special supervision programs are legally defined in the legislation as programs "embodying a degree of supervision substantially above the usual or the use of new techniques in addition to, or instead of, routine supervision techniques .... *Such standards shall be sufficiently flexible to foster the development of new and improved supervision practices*" (SCYA, 1970b,

p. 106). This provision, by its broad wording, permits discretionary interpretation of the statute's meaning.

In accordance with the law, the Youth Authority set "minimum standards" for "special supervision programs." Standards were set in the areas of personnel, workload for deputies, workload for supervisors, offender classification, stenographic and clerical assistance, and supporting services. These standards were quite similar to those established as acceptable for all probation services, in the published editions of *Standards for the Performance of Probation Duties* (SCYA, 1954, 1961, and 1965). The CYA apparently reasoned that meeting *these* standards would bring a degree of supervision "substantially above the usual." By using these traditional standards, CYA could continue to press for professionalization of probation services in California.

Some standards are quite specific, such as workload for deputies and supervisors and the ratio of stenographic and clerical assistance. Others are more general and transfer a substantial amount of discretion to the county. While a "classification system" and "supporting services" are mentioned as state standards, it is the counties that determine what "classification system" and "supporting services" will be described in their special supervision program applications.

The state standards also focus on strengthening probation services by upgrading probation departments. Money is expendable for training, consultation, the purchase of special equipment, and the rental of adequate office space for special supervision personnel. The counties are also free to hire staff according to needed skills. In the following excerpt from the official CYA *Rules, Regulations and Standards of Performance for Special Supervision Programs* flexibility is encouraged:

In-service training, vocational counseling and testing, contracts for special services, training for foster parents, and *perhaps even the creation of a contractual arrangement for short-term detention* may be required by programs initiated under this act. [SCYA, 1969*b*, p. 15; italics added]

The standards were flexible enough to include temporary detention as one of "the myriad of other things that contribute to the success of a probation case" (ibid.).

"No county shall be entitled to receive any state funds until its application is approved and unless and until the minimum standards prescribed by the Department of the Youth Authority are complied with" according to California law (SCYA, 1970*b*, p. 106). The Youth Authority established an application procedure. County plans for a special supervision program must be submitted in advance of the fiscal year in which it is intended to operate and in which a claim would be made on the state for a reduction in commitments. In these authorization plans, the counties are required to specify: (1) the number of probationers to be included; (2) a description of the classification system to be used; (3) a statement of whether the program will serve adults or juveniles, males or females; (4) the number of deputy probation officers, supervisors, and stenographers planned; (5) the estimated cost for salaries, equipment, and supporting services; (6) an estimate of the maximum sum of money the county will claim for operating the program; (7) the anticipated starting date, a description of various phases, and how they relate to each other and the total program; (8) the name and mailing address of the county official designated to coordinate the special supervision program.

After a program is approved and initiated, the Youth Authority conducts annual on-site inspections of all special supervision programs. It also reserves the right to audit these programs. Particular attention is paid to meeting the requirements of *caseload size* (not to exceed fifty per officer), supervisor *span of control* (one supervisor for each six officers) and clerical support (three clerks per unit of one supervisor and six officers). If a program exceeds the limits in any of these critical areas, the county is warned. In the event of continued violations, the county may be threatened with the withholding of funds (as revealed in personal interviews with staff members in 1971).

As noted, the CYA is quite flexible regarding classification systems. A 1971 study disclosed that twenty-two counties reported using a "case staffing" classification, eighteen used I-Level, fourteen used FIRO-B (Fundamental Interpersonal Relations Orientation Behavior, as developed by W. Schutz), two used the Quay system, and single counties used systems labeled as Seven Ego types, Jesness Inventory, Polk, Work Unit Scoring, Workload Determination by Plan, and Bell Adjustment Inventory (SCYA, 1970–72, *Report No. 2*, table 6, p. 14). Apparently the standards did not require the counties to demonstrate the reliability or validity of classification systems; nor did they require that the typologies be periodically evaluated regarding their contribution to the intensive supervision program.

Summary and Conclusions

Probation subsidy appears to have been launched with the primary aim of strengthening traditional probation services. It qualified as a community treatment program because it attempted to achieve this aim by substituting "intensive supervision" in the community in lieu of institutionalization, for both adults and juveniles. While special supervision units would contain offenders that might otherwise have been initially committed to state-operated correctional facilities, it was assumed that counties would also provide intensive services to a portion of their regular probation caseloads. Neither the legislation nor the CYA standards required that *only* those who were earmarked for commitment were the eligible probationers for this special program. In this respect it differed from an in lieu program like the California Treatment Project, which dealt with only those who had definitely been committed to a state correctional facility. Probation subsidy also differed from CTP by requiring that counties earn their right to obtain state funds and thereby operate the new programs that performed in lieu functions.

The fiscal assumptions and initial mode of reimbursement posed problems for the counties that were significantly different from those encountered by CTP. While counties might readily agree with the aims of subsidy, participation could involve fiscal risks. Evidently, the major counties were not persuaded to participate solely on the basis of ideological convictions, but required emergency legislation within the first fiscal year to ease their fiscal concerns. They were then willing to experiment in a new form of state-county "cooperation" to provide enriched services and "better protection to the community." These rather mundane considerations indicate that any attempt to devise a new correctional policy may have to consider economic trade-offs as well as new and better program ideas.

The sophisticated correctional administrators at the county level were quite aware of this critical aspect of policy development. They benefited, of course, as a result of their knowledge and their willingness to utilize strategic power to influence the potential "success" of the policy of reduced commitments. Given the uncertainties they addressed, their behavior—and the quick response of the legislators—appears eminently reasonable. One consequence of this fiscal compromise was that the state would not automatically "pocket" the unused funds, but would give the counties an extra year (and at a later date, two years) to try to capture up to 100 percent of what they might have earned. In general, adding to the initial subsidy bill the section about deferred payments of incumbered funds and quarterly installments constituted the price the state was compelled to pay to gain the cooperation of critical counties. By changing the ground rules (or the assumptions), it became worthwhile for the counties to experiment.

On a program level, there were no assumptions that entailed new risks or uncertainties. Actually, the effectiveness of traditional programs was assumed to be an empirical fact. Therefore, primary attention was geared to instituting *traditional* probation standards as the normative guidelines for the "new" programs. Enforcement of these standards would strengthen probationary practice and enhance the likelihood that the departments would become increasingly professionalized. It is important to note that neither the legislation nor the CYA standards made any reference to a specific treatment technology; nor did either source of program standards specify how frequently and for what period of time a probationer must be contacted to qualify as an example of "intensive supervision."

Instead, intensive supervision programs were to be defined according to *organizational* criteria that symbolized desirable probation practices. These included: smaller than average caseloads (a maximum of fifty probationers); a short supervisory span of control (one supervisor to six officers); clerical assistance; in-service training of officers; a classification system; and supporting services and equipment. The CYA authors and administrators of the subsidy program believed that initiation and expansion of these program "packages" would improve the existing degree of effectiveness of county probation systems. They appeared not to know that other studies and analytic reassessment of the studies had reached the conclusion that an effective correctional technology did not exist. Further, they appeared unaware that a program like CTP, which *did* contain all of the elements of the package in a concentrated and enriched form, was no more effective than a traditional correctional program (see part 1).

It is still possible to conceive of the program as a search strategy for new correctional approaches to offenders. The innovativeness of the subsidy strategy, however, does *not* lie in its assumptions about the desirable program package or beliefs about probation and community treatment. Rather, it is in the assumption that major shifts in correctional decision making can be accomplished in a short time by using monetary rewards for engaging in changed dispositions of many cases. Even if subsidy programs were to prove no more effective than CTP (and this seems a reasonable assumption), it is still conceivable that this novel correctional strategy could yield more advantages than disadvantages, at a state and/or county level.

In order to determine whether subsidy, *as currently practiced*, is a worthwhile policy, it seems useful to find out whether money has been saved by the state and whether the State of California has reduced its institutionalization. The following chapters detail empirical evidence for concluding that the planners of subsidy may have failed to consider that *other* critical decision makers could modify their correctional choices and thereby modify foundations of their new correctional policy. As a result, potential fiscal benefits were apparently transformed into actual, unintended fiscal costs; and potential benefits in decreased use of institutionalization were apparently transformed into alternative modes of social control. The planners and the administrators of probation subsidy appear unaware of the run-ups in economic and social costs; in this respect they are similar to the planners and administrators of CTP.

The data, findings, and conclusions reported in the following chapters refer primarily to youth; an adult-oriented study was not conducted. From a methodological perspective, similar analyses of available public documents could also be conducted for adults, but the findings and conclusions of the following chapters are not automatically applicable to this older category of offenders.

7   The Social Impact
of Probation Subsidy

Probation subsidy has been presented to the
correctional public and others as a community treatment program, where offenders are treated in local communities in lieu of
institutionalization at the state level. Fewer youth and adults were
institutionalized by the state from 1966 to 1972. Even if it is
difficult to establish absolutely whether this would have occurred
in the absence of subsidy payments, the evidence is fairly
persuasive—particularly at the youth level—that persistent reductions in state commitments in the magnitude of 25 to 44
percent per year was an uncommon occurrence. In the presubsidy
years of 1955–65 the trendlines of youth commitment had been in
an opposite direction. Subsidy legislation did appear to have a
substantial impact not only in reversing this trend but in being
associated with fewer initial commitments to the CYA.

Because of this acknowledged impact on reducing commitments to the state, there is a ready inclination to pay primary
attention to fiscal operations and impact. While understanding
how the subsidy formula operates and whether the State of
California actually saved money is important, it is also useful to
examine whether the subsidy period is associated with any social
costs. Shifts in correctional decision making can produce

unintended, as well as intended, consequences. This chapter is concerned with exploring and assessing the social impacts of post-subsidy operations at three levels of analysis: the impact on the CYA, as well as the youth institutionalized in state facilities; the impact on the county social control/treatment system, as well as the youth subject to local correctional efforts; and the combined impact of state and county changes on institutional rates and practices.

CYA Institutional Policy: Before and after Subsidy

The California Youth Authority was established in 1943 as a correctional reform to bring order, planning, and centralized expertise to the state's handling of offenders under the age of twenty-one. The CYA started with only three institutions. By fiscal 1964-65, it had increased to seven institutions (five for boys, two for girls), *plus* two reception center-clinics in the north and south, *plus* four conservation camps. This progress occurred while counties, with state subsidies, were also building correctional facilities on a large scale. However, the construction of beds at both county and state level never seemed to be able to keep up with the increasing demand. Even in fiscal 1964-65, while a few staff were working on the subsidy study, the CYA planned to add more beds at existing facilities during the year (*State of California Support and Local Assistance Budget*, 1964-65, p. 151).

In 1966-67, after subsidy had begun, the CYA completed the first phase of a twenty- to thirty-year master plan for building up their institutional capacity (ibid., 1965-66, p. 176). This master plan projected the building of twelve institutional facilities, around a single northern site, with each institution housing about four hundred wards. In July 1966, the O. H. Close School for Boys opened near Stockton, California, the site area. In the following year the Karl Holton School for Boys also opened up nearby. De Witt Nelson soon followed. On a single southern site the CYA planned to build nine units, with a capacity of four hundred each. These new institutions, part of the first phase of the master plan, were added to the institutional capability of the CYA after the passage of subsidy legislation in 1965. However, these additions are not noted or discussed in *A Quiet Revolution* (Smith, 1972), the authoritative report prepared for nationwide dissemination.

In chapter 8, evidence will be presented that the number of institutional beds phased in to the CYA institutional system, between 1966 and 1972, outpaced the number of beds phased out. These facts will be used to examine the claim that phasing out of beds should be counted as fiscal savings. Here we are concerned with the assessment of the CYA institutional policy from a nonfiscal, social perspective. Even if probation subsidy had not been passed, did the CYA really have to continue its rather consistent policy of increasing bed capacity and investing in capital plant? The answer is related to assumptions about correctional policy or, more accurately, the philosophy of the CYA's approach to youthful offenders.

The master plan for the 1970s, 1980s, and 1990s was based on the number of commitments to be received in future years. In addition, the plan was also based on *how long wards had to stay* in order to be "corrected." Depending on the assumption concerning expected length of stay, and assuming the population projections to be expected were accurate, the master plan would appear as an inexorable example of rationality. It appears fair to inquire what those assumptions were, whether they were valid, and whether they have changed.

According to the rationale submitted with the submission of the 1966-67 budget, the assumptions concerning length of stay were as follows:

The planned average period of institutionalization is eleven months for wards 14 years of age and younger, eight months for boys and girls in Youth Authority institutions over the age of 14, and eleven months for the older wards in Department of Corrections institutions. [*State of California Support and Local Assistance Budget*, 1966-67, pp. 215-16]

At the time of the *1964 Probation Study* (State of California Board of Corrections, 1964), the report that proposed the subsidy formula, the average length of stay for all CYA institutions was eight months. It is on the basis of this length of stay that the basic maximum cost-figure for the subsidy legislation, $4,000, was derived. In practice, the CYA was violating its own "planned average." There was no evidence forthcoming that parole violation rates, the CYA's traditional measure of recidivism, increased as a result of this reduced length of stay. In fact, surprising as it may appear to many, there is no empirical evidence to support *any* of the CYA standards. Further, given a different philosophy, the average length of stay could have been reduced even more. Every major study of recidivism conducted by the CYA or the Department of Corrections has failed to demonstrate any empirical relationship between length of stay in an institution and post-release conduct. In addition, there is not an acceptable study in the country that indicates that any institutionalization per se improves post-release behavior.

Rather than pay attention to the dominant findings of its own research and the results of other studies, the CYA continued to plan as if its assumptions were "facts." But instead of "facts," the plans relied on "standards" that were actually value preferences of professionals leading the institutional system. If the CYA had reduced its "standards" to comply with less costly assumptions, it could have quite easily accommodated to the population pressures of the projected increase in commitments. The projected savings cited by Smith were the projected fiscal costs of a correctional policy that was not based on empirical evidence or reasonableness.

Consider some of the evidence that the CYA had prior to the opening of Holton and Close in 1966 and 1967. Before the beginning of the Community Treatment Project in 1961, the CYA had initiated the release of youths directly to parole (after a short stay at reception centers). This new policy was primarily due to population pressures and an apparent unwillingness to shorten length of stay beyond a preferred minimum average of eight to nine months. Researchers of this emergency response to correctional problems began to collect data that this program of direct release to parole was acceptable to communities, and that post-release behavior was similar to other cohorts of comparable ages and sex (Beverly, 1965). The CTP experiment fitted in very well as an extension of this improvised policy (see part 1).

In 1961, the CTP began to collect data on early release in a more systematic fashion. Early reports of CTP were carefully noted by the CYA leadership. Even if one was not persuaded by the efficacy of I-Level as a correctional technique, evidence began to accumulate that serious delinquent behavior had a tolerable rate of occurrence in the period "in lieu of institutionalization." Other early release projects were actually launched in Oakland and Los Angeles before 1966. It appears reasonable to infer that evidence had accumulated within its own domain, by fiscal

1966-67, that the standards of the master plan were debatable.

Even before the onset of CTP, a well-publicized and competent demonstration-research project, Highfields, had occurred in New Jersey in the 1950s (Weeks, 1958). The designers of CTP had cited the Highfields study in their review of the literature. Published in 1958 and widely known, Highfields had demonstrated that first-commitment youth, sixteen years and older, had certainly performed no worse after only four months of group home treatment than the comparison group of boys completing the traditional nine months' program at the Annandale Reformatory. The policy implications of this 1958 study were certainly significant for any projections of a master plan for twenty to thirty years.

Studies completed by CYA researchers in 1967 continued to verify the findings of Highfields and direct release to parole. One study concluded that an experiment using a stay of five months was no more risky than a traditional stay of institutionalization (Seckel, 1967). Another study, also using an experimental design, demonstrated that shorter stays (about six months), in open camps, yielded results quite similar to boys institutionalized according to CYA standard terms (SCYA, 1967a).

Empirical evidence indicates that the institutional policies of the CYA have been guided by unreasonable assumptions. If these assumptions had been questioned with the onset of probation subsidy, the cost of these prior building decisions might have been written off as a bad investment. Instead, the assumptions appear to be continuing in the current operating practices of CYA institutions. As a result of this continued adherence to questionable assumptions, the CYA has seriously eroded the amount of social and fiscal savings that the State of California might experience from a reduction of first commitments to state facilities.

An Assessment of the Rationale

At the time of the *1964 Probation Study* the average career cost per occupied bed was $4,000; by 1970-71 the same bed cost $7,292. During that same period the average daily population had remained fairly stable (SCYA, 1972e, p. 27), around 5,000 youth. During this same period a number of institutional-related changes were also occurring. The critical ones appeared to be the following:

1. *Change in Source of Commitment*—The largest reduction of initial commitments has occurred from the juvenile courts. As a result, the number of new commitments from the criminal courts have increased from 24.9 percent of new admissions in 1965 to 48.6 percent in 1971 (SCYA, 1971*a*, p. 19).

2. *Reduced Use of Department of Corrections Facilities*—In the past the CYA relied on the adult system to house its older wards, particularly when population pressures were creating an apparent shortage of beds. As a matter of policy, the number of CYA wards housed in Department of Corrections facilities has decreased from an average daily population of 1,536 in 1965 to 326 in 1971 (ibid., p. 30).

3. *Age of Wards*—The average age of CYA wards admitted to state institutional care has risen from 16.4 in 1965 to 17.5 in 1971 (ibid., p. 21).

4. *Increase in Average Length of Stay*—In 1964 the average length of stay for wards housed in CYA institutions, boys and girls, was approximately *8 months*. The average stay increased to *10.2* in 1970; in 1971 the average stay was *11.2 months* (ibid., p. 30).

5. *Reduction in Ratio of Wards to Staff*—In 1964-65 the average daily population in CYA institutions was 5,146, while the staff numbered 2,220—a ward/staff ratio of 2.3:1. In 1970-71 the population had decreased to 4,907, while the staff had grown to 2,740—a ward/staff ratio of 1.8:1; if the staff had remained at the 1964-65 level, the ratio in 1970-71 would have been 2.2:1 (SCYA, 1972*a*, p. 25).

On the basis of adherence to correctional standards, CYA institutions increased the length of stay and lowered the ward/ staff ratio. In the budget request of 1968-69, the CYA leadership presented the following rationale for its policy of promoting lengthened and intensified institutionalization (*State of California Support and Local Assistance Budget*, 1968-69, p. 202):

What then do the developments, past and current, hold for the years immediately ahead? Some observations can be made with reasonable safety. . . .
The population committed to the Youth Authority will contain, proportionately, a higher percentage of highly delinquent, more disturbed youngsters. As this population is screened further for the Youth Authority's direct and early release program, that portion that is institutionalized will be increasingly composed of difficult, "hard core," youths, who pose greater problems of

control and more acute treatment need. Normally, these
youngsters are seen as requiring longer periods of
institutionalization, and so the period of confinement indicated
should be greater than in the past. This effect is already apparent
as the average period of stay has increased approximately one
month in the past year.

A further strengthening and intensification of institutional
treatment would seem to be clearly indicated.

It is clear that the major official reason for the "strengthening
and intensification of institutional treatment" is attributed to a
change in the population characteristics of wards assigned to the
CYA. The youth are now presented as "highly delinquent" and
"more disturbed." However, lengthening institutional stays is
quite unlikely to make these youth any less "delinquent" or any
less "disturbed." Evidence cited earlier indicates that length of
institutionalization is not related to reducing delinquency.

In addition, CYA reports of post-release behavior of wards
indicates that the newer population mix the CYA has been
receiving is, by the authority's own standards of evidence, a *less*
risky group. Table 6 summarizes the major characteristics
regarding population differences between 1965 and 1970. Table 7
reports the post-release violation rates—the standard CYA
measure of outcome "failure"—of CYA wards for some of these
salient, identified characteristics. ("Disturbed behavior" is not
one of the characteristics because the CYA does not now report
data regarding this characteristic. It is doubtful whether it ever
reported this kind of data.)

Table 6 is divided into two parts, according to the availability
of comparative data. First commitments in 1970 are, in fact,
older and more likely to come from criminal courts than commitments in 1965. However, there is a lack of strong evidence of a
substantial change in the proportion of youth who had been
institutionalized on a county level (47.7 to 45.8 percent). Regarding comparisons of boys living in institutions on census days in
1965 and 1970, there is evidence that the 1970 wards are older. In
addition, there has been a slight rise in the percent committed for
an offense against persons (21.5 to 26.3 percent), but the biggest
changes relate to property and narcotic offenses. In 1965, narcotics was of minor significance in characterizing wards, but in
1970 it is nearly as significant as offenses against persons. The
racial mix, on the other hand, has changed very little.

TABLE 6
CYA Institutional Wards, 1965 and 1970

Characteristic	1965	1970
A. *First commitments*[a]	(N = 6,190)	(N = 3,746)
Percent from criminal court	24.9	41.2
Median age	16.4	17.2
Percent no prior county commitments	47.7	45.8
B. *Boys in institution*[b]	(N = 5,353)	(N = 4,541)
Percent first commitment to CYA	55.7	57.5
Median age	17.9	18.6
Percent offense against persons	21.5	26.3
Percent offense against property	45.2	32.5
Percent narcotic charge	4.5	15.6
Percent white	50.0	48.9

[a]*CYA Annual Report, 1970* (Sacramento: Department of Youth Authority), tables 5, 7, and 12.

[b]*A Comparison of Characteristics of Youth Authority Wards: June 30 each year, 1962-1971* (Sacramento: Department of Youth Authority), table 1, p. 6.

Table 7 presents evidence concerning the parole violations of a 1969 cohort of 6,228 youth, fifteen months after having experienced an institutional program. While a 1969 release cohort is presented, there is adequate evidence from prior cohort studies that the relationships disclosed in this table are not unusual (see Appendix B, table B-1). Youth committed from criminal courts have consistently had lower parole violations in the past, and this is true in the 1969 data (particularly for boys). Boys convicted of violent offenses (homicide, robbery, and assault) are *better* parole risks than property offenders, as are narcotic offenders. The highest violation rates are related to the juvenile status/technical violation offenders. The persistent age differences (which may underlie the other differences) yield potent evidence that younger boys are a much *higher* risk group than older boys. Again, these are differences that have consistently appeared in California research reports such as that by Davis (1964).

While data clearly indicate that older wards and those committed from criminal courts are less likely to violate parole, there still remains the risk that they may commit offenses of a more violent type. Parole violation rates, as usually computed, are insensitive to this issue. While direct comparisons with 1965 are

TABLE 7
Percentage of Parole Violators, by Population Characteristics of 1969 Release Cohort (N=6,228)

Characteristic	Percent Violators after 15 Months' Release			
	Boys (percent)	Total N	*Girls* (percent)	Total N
Court of last commitment				
Juvenile Court	48.7	(3,678)	31.4	(773)
Criminal Court	24.9	(1,770)	24.3	(107)
Commitment offense				
Homicide, robbery, and assault	31.9	(1,007)	29.0	(93)
Burglary, theft, and forgery	42.9	(2,229)	31.6	(117)
Narcotics	30.3	(719)	26.5	(113)
County camp failures, welfare and institution code, and escapes	54.3	(973)	29.5	(463)
All other	40.2	(520)	39.4	(94)
Age at Release				
14 and under	64.9	(265)	42.5	(49)
15	65.7	(356)	42.7	(124)
16	61.2	(662)	30.7	(166)
17	45.3	(976)	22.9	(227)
18	36.5	(1,080)	26.9	(160)
19	29.7	(891)	25.6	(86)
20	26.1	(755)	34.9	(43)
21 and over	26.8	(463)	---	(25)

Source: *Institutional Experience Summary: 1969 Parole Releases* (Sacramento: Department of Youth Authority, September, 1971), Adaptation of table 2, pp. 19–21.

not possible, evidence exists on three years in the early 1960s and a recent year, 1970 (see Appendix B, table B-2). In this analysis, violent offenses included the following types of offenses against persons: homicide, robbery, rape, sex offenses, assaults, and purse snatching. It is apparent that the rate of violent offenses, after rising slightly in 1962, has *not* risen for the current males on parole. This appears to be the case, despite the fact that this group is slightly older and has more males who were originally committed for offenses against persons.

The best available evidence, relying on official CYA data, does not support the contention that the CYA is dealing with a higher parole-risk group. Empirically, there is no basis for lengthening institutionalization because of risk. Perhaps there is another reason for the policy change—the interest of organizational survival. Robert Smith, in *A Quiet Revolution* (1972, p. 71), has admitted that he believes this to be the case:

Prior to 1965, the Department of the Youth Authority and the Department of Corrections were rapidly expanding state agencies adding staff, new institutions, and increased administration each year to take care of growing workloads. Beginning in 1965, and related directly to the drop in new admissions, was the dramatic curtailment of promotional opportunities. Indeed as jobs became more and more important and opportunities for employment less and less available, organizational survival began to evidence itself. As wards became scarce, the institutional time they served began to gradually creep up.

The argument concerning organizational survival as an explanation for length of stay "creeping up" is, however, only partially supported by the evidence. The CYA "standards" for preferred length of stay were formulated prior to subsidy, and do not appear to have been given up as norms of institutional practice. In addition, opportunities for increased employment did not cease in the first five or six years of the post-subsidy period; instead, the rate of growth of new jobs slowed down. Between fiscal 1960-61 and 1964-65, institutional staff grew from 1,625 to 2,220—a gain of 37 percent. Between 1965-66 and 1969-70, the staff increased from 2,275 to 2,715—a gain of 20 percent (SCYA, 1972*e*, p. 25). As noted earlier, this gain in staff was not justified by the changes in average daily population, since the CYA had managed to maintain this figure at a fairly stable level during this period (primarily by receiving older youth in its own institutions, rather than transferring them to the state Department of Corrections facilities).

It is possible, of course, that many CYA institutional personnel were concerned about a slowing down of job opportunities, and may have behaved adaptively. While it is possible to sympathize with the plight of correctional personnel, the social and fiscal costs of permitting "survival" practices must also be addressed.

The evidence is clear that while fewer youth were being committed to the CYA, those that were being committed were staying for longer periods. The length of commitments had increased from an average stay (in CYA institutions) of 8 months to 11.2 months. From a social perspective, fewer youth are being institutionalized in CYA units for longer periods, while some youth will not be institutionalized at the state level. In numbers this means that in fiscal 1970–71 there were 3,173 youth that received a "strengthening and intensification of institutionalization," while 2,542 were hypothetically spared this type, degree, and duration of penal sanction (SCYA 1971a, table 2, p. 16).

The CYA has tried to persuade others that these 3,173 youth represent a greater danger than those committed in 1965—but the evidence, as we have seen, is not very persuasive. In addition, we lack *any* data about the hypothetical 2,542 who were not committed in 1970–71, and so there is not even a basis for comparing the two groups of youthful offenders. We are unable to compare the characteristics of the two groups before, during, or after institutional or noninstitutional exposure, as could be done in the California Treatment Project, or other experimentally designed projects. The legislation, the administrative guidelines, and the discretionary execution of the program at the county level provide no requirements for specifically identifying those who might have been committed but were not.

In order to justify receiving maximum payments, reports on probation subsidy describing caseload characteristics do not distinguish between those who might have been committed and those who have been included in subsidy units. The payments are based on reductions, but they must be for actual programs, containing actual probationers—and not for programs containing only those that might have been committed. For example, on 31 December 1970, a census of regular and subsidy caseloads was conducted by the Bureau of Criminal Statistics (SCYA, 1970–72, *Probation Subsidy Report No. 1*). This census disclosed that 21 percent of the total active juvenile cases on court probation were in subsidy caseloads. Some counties had subsidy caseload proportions that ranged from a low of 4.6 percent of the caseload, while some had 74.2 percent. There is absolutely no way of determining which of the 6,494 subsidy cases from forty-three counties (excluding Los Angeles and Alameda) might have been the offenders included in the juvenile "reduction number." The best evidence we have of the characteristics of the potential reduction group (i.e., those in subsidy caseloads) discloses that their "sustained offense" characteristics are quite comparable to those of a regular probation group (see table 8).

TABLE 8
Sustained Offense of Juvenile Cases in Regular and Subsidy Active Judicial Probation Caseloads on 31 December 1970 (in percentages)

| | Caseload Assignments[a] | |
| | Regular | Subsidy |
Sustained Offenses	(N = 24,862)	(N = 6,494)
Homicide, robbery, and assault	6.1%	7.1%
Burglary, theft, forgery	26.8	31.0
Auto theft	7.9	8.7
Drug law violations	16.5	16.4
Other specific offenses	4.1	3.6
Delinquent tendencies	38.8	33.2

Sources: Data for 43 counties (excluding Los Angeles and Almeda) as reported in *Characteristics of Adults and Juveniles in Regular and Subsidy Caseloads on December 31, 1970* (Sacramento: Bureau of Criminal Statistics), Table 11, p. 51.

[a]Includes data for cases placed on probation for six months on informal status or as formal court wards.

The modest differences between the two groups appear to be primarily for property offenses and delinquent tendencies. Otherwise the distributions of the two probation caseloads seem quite comparable. It seems, therefore, possible that the juvenile court commitments to the CYA could come from either caseload—and the reduced commitments could also be found in both caseloads. We still have no basis for determining what is the justification for choosing 3,173 youth for a "strengthening and intensification of institutionalization" experience, while 2,542 juvenile court cases are selected for a regular or subsidy caseload experience.

The CYA, of course, is not the primary determiner of who is selected to be a state commitment and who will remain in the county correctional system. Nor is the CYA responsible for selecting the county youth that will receive an intensive supervision experience, rather than a regular probation disposition. However, the CYA does have the power to lengthen or shorten the length of institutional stay. The evidence indicates that the policy of strengthening and intensifying institutionalization cannot be justified on the basis of correcting dangerous offenders or increasing effectiveness. The rationale offered by Smith, organizational survival, may provide benefits to adults within the CYA, but this is purchased at the expense of potential fiscal and social savings. The "creeping up" of length of institutional stay is a cost being borne by the youth being committed in the post-subsidy period. Whether this social cost is offset by any social benefits at the county level will be assessed in the following sections.

County Probation and Institutionalization

To outsiders, probation is usually seen as a judicial disposition that does not involve incarceration. It is generally believed that youth on probation are living at home and receiving supervision by officers of the court—probation workers. Youngsters technically on "probation," however, may be living at home or with relatives, or they may be living in a foster home or group home, in a private institution, a county camp, ranch, or school, or even in a detention facility.

Of all the places where youth might be required to live as a condition of receiving probationary treatment, the only residences explicitly linked to subsidy were the county camps, ranches, and schools. These county institutions were already being partially subsidized by the state at the date of the subsidy legislation. As of 1965, counties could receive up to $3,000 per bed for construction costs, and up to $95 per month for maintenance costs (SCYA, 1970*b*, Secs. 887 and 891). The initial probation subsidy legislation prohibited funds from being used to support, develop, or expand new programs in juvenile homes, ranches, or camps established by the earlier construction subvention. As of 1973, the probation subsidy legislation was amended to permit funds to be used by a county that had not established its own camps, ranches, or homes to pay for placements in the facilities of other counties (SCYA, 1974, p. 6). The receiving county cannot receive a double subsidy for out-of-county placements, just as it cannot receive one for its own placements.

It is possible, of course, for counties to maintain special supervision programs and use their camps, ranches, and schools to handle their more difficult probationers. As long as commitments to the state institutions are reduced and approved programs operated, it does not matter technically whether camps are being used more extensively. The major constraint is that while youngsters are placed in camp, the counties cannot receive a double subsidy.

The question has been raised whether alternate modes of social control have increased at the county level during the subsidy period. Leading officials for the California Youth Authority have replied with only one type of evidence—rates of capacity use. For example, Saleeby has dealt with the issue as follows (Saleeby, 1971, p. 7):

Some critics of the program have asserted in strident voices that the heavy financial incentives are providing a cash register type of justice that is inimical to public protection. These critics claim that county jails and juvenile camps are being flooded with offenders who should be in state institutions. The facts do not justify these assertions. In May, 1971, the population in juvenile camps, ranches, and homes was only 67.5 percent of construction capacity. There is no indication that commitment to these camps is merely being substituted for commitment to the Youth Authority.

It is not necessary to be a strident critic in order to question the use of the percentage of beds occupied as the sole indicator of county impact. Average daily population and the utilization of potential capacity does not, however, refer to number of admissions or length of stay. It is possible for capacity to increase and the average daily population to remain relatively stable, while profound changes are occurring regarding the rates of first admission and length of stay. As a matter of fact, data from CYA operations provide evidence that this combination of events occurred during the time period of 1965-70. Evidence has already been noted that the following institution-related events occurred: (1) *Increase in capacity* outstripped the phasing out of older institutional facilities (see table 20 in chapter 8). (2) *The average daily population* in CYA institutions remained relatively stable (5,210 in 1965-66; 5,342 in 1966-67; 5,289 in 1967-68; 5,394 in 1968-69; 5,312 in 1969-70; and 4,907 in 1970-71 (SCYA, 1972e, p. 25). (3) *The rates of first commitments* to the CYA, from all sources, were reduced sharply (175 per 100,000 youth, age 10 to 20 in 1965; 148 in 1966; 130 in 1967; 119 in 1968; 112 in 1969; and 92 in 1970) (ibid., p. 13). (4) *The average length of stay* in CYA facilities increased from 8 months in 1964 to 10.2 months in 1970 (SCYA, 1971a, p. 32).

The average daily population appears to be a poor indicator of CYA institutional trends and policies. It therefore seems unreasonable to use this poor indicator as a statistic for assessing county institutional trends.

The number of youth admissions, average length of stay, or other county institutional data is not provided by Saleeby. The Smith report, *A Quiet Revolution* (1972, p. 51), also fails to include this type of data. Instead Smith reports that the ratio of average daily attendance to capacity fluctuated, during 1963–65, between 84 and 93 percent of capacity; during 1966–70 it fluctuated between 73 and 88 percent. The most recent authoritative CYA report on county institutional data also omits data referring to juvenile admissions or length of stay (SCYA, 1974, p. 30).

The Bureau of Criminal Statistics (BCS) is the official California state agency charged with collecting and disseminating data pertaining to all levels of enforcement, adjudication, and the correction of juvenile and adult offenders. Unfortunately, it did not begin to systematically collect data on admissions to county camps, ranches, schools, and homes until 1 January 1966 (State of California Department of Justice, 1966a, p. 236). Using the best pre-subsidy data available, as well as the BCS information pertaining to the post-subsidy years, it is possible to construct a reasonable estimate concerning the probable increases in county rates of juvenile institutionalization in homes, camps, ranches, and schools. The data in table 9 refer to the number of facilities actually being used in a year and the rates of new admissions (per 100,000 youth, age 10–17, for the population of that year).

The data pertaining to number of facilities indicate that the counties doubled the number of residences between 1943 and 1956, but were able to treble the number for the comparable period 1956 to 1970 (9 to 18 versus 18 to 53). However, the growth in number of institutions experienced the sharpest rise in the period 1956 to 1965, the pre-subsidy years. This is understandable, since the state did not initiate construction subsidies until 1957; after 1965, counties were participating in a subsidy program that was more rewarding. However, between 1965 and 1970, the number of county facilities did increase; it is the rate of increase that appears to have slowed down.

If we use the average rate of admissions for the two recent years, and divide this rate by the average number of institutions, it is possible to estimate what the rate per facility might have been in other years. Using these estimates, it appears that the rate probably increased from 117 to 183 between 1960 and 1965—a gain of 66 per 100,000 youth, or 56 percent. The rate also increased between 1965 and 1970, but the gain was not as sharp. The gain in the post-subsidy period was 43 per 100,000 youth, a gain of 23 percent.

TABLE 9
Number and Admission Rates of County Camps, Ranches, and Schools, 1943-70

Year	Number of County Camps, etc.[a]	New Admission Rates per 100,000 Youth, 10-17[b]
1943	9	42 est.
1956	18	84 est.
1960	25 est.[c]	117 est.
1965	39	183 est.
1968	45	230
1970	53	226

Sources: (1) *Report of the Legislative Analyst*, Fiscal 1964-65; (2) Bureau of Criminal Statistics, *Annual Reports* 1964-1968; (3) Bureau of Criminal Statistics, 1970 *Reference Tables*.

[a]Years 1943 and 1956 are from source 1. All others, except 1960, are based on number of facilities actually providing summary reports to BCS, sources 2 and 3.

[b]Rates for 1968 and 1970 were computed from data in sources 2 and 3. Estimates of admissions were obtained by multiplying average ratio of admission rates per facility for 1968 and 1970 by number of camps in calendar year. The average ration per facility for 1968 and 1969 was 4.69; and this ratio figure was multiplied by 39 in 1965, 25 in 1960, 18 in 1956, and 9 in 1943.

[c]Estimated that increase of homes, 1960 to 1965, were same as 1965 to 1970—14.

It is possible to conclude that the extent to which capacity was being used may have gone downward since 1965, as indicated by Saleeby and Smith. However, the number of facilities being constructed increased and so, too, did the county capacity and the rates of admission. If all of the new capacity had been used, the rates might have been higher. It is conceivable that the counties, like the CYA, were also attempting to strengthen and intensify their local institutional programs. However, they were increasing their rates of building and admissions at a lower rate than in earlier years. The post-subsidy years appear to have slowed down the rising rates of county commitments. The period 1965 to 1970 indicates that *state* institution rates could be reduced, while *county* rates of commitment to local camps, ranches, schools, and homes continued to increase. In order to interpret these divergent trends further, a fuller understanding of county patterns of discretionary decision making must be analyzed and perceived in a statewide context. Of critical importance is an examination of detention, the other source of county institutionalizaion.

Detention and County Patterns of Decision Making: An Overview

Detention, unlike camps, does not pose problems concerning a double subsidy. There are no state subsidies attached to either the construction of juvenile halls or the maintenance of detainees (as of 1974). As a matter of fact, youth can be placed in detention *prior* to formal adjudication, *during* adjudication proceedings, or *after* adjudication. As noted earlier, youth can also be living in detention and still be considered part of a probation subsidy caseload. Presumably this would occur after being declared a ward of the court in a formal proceeding. Table 10 provides data for considering whether detention rates, at any point in the juvenile justice system, have increased at the county level since the inception of probation subsidy. In order to understand its usage, other types of official responses to youth behavior are also included for 1960, 1965, and 1970.

Table 10 is based on official data reported to the Bureau of Criminal Statistics by local police departments or county probation departments. In part A, the raw data found in annual reports has been converted into annual rates per population at risk, youth ten to seventeen years of age, for 1960, 1965, and 1970. Besides detention rates, rates have been computed for arrests, referrals to probation by police, initial referrals received by probation from all sources, filing of new petitions, declaration of wardship, admissions to camps, and commitments to the CYA. Part B attempts to compare the degree of change for all of these indicators of adult responses. This permits an assessment of detention within the context of other responses and provides a historical baseline for the assessment of all of the major indicators of social decisions that are available.

Table 10 discloses that the police *arrest* rate increased by 18

ABLE 10

lifornia Police, Probation, and Court Responses to Youth Behavior for 1960-65 and 1965-70[a] (by rates /100,000 youth d by percent changes in rates)

Response Category	A. *Rates* (per 100,000 youth 10-17 for each year)			B. *Rate Changes* (percent)	
	1960	1965	1970	1960-65	1965-70
)lice arrests	8,631	10,144	12,417	18%	18%
)lice probation referrals[b]	3,612	4,543	6,948	26	53
l new referrals to probation	2,775	3,540	5,204	28	47
l delinquent detention admissions[c]	2,978	3,261	4,866	10	49
itial petitions filed	1,342	1,301	1,725	-03	33
itial declarations for court wardships	918	937	1,040	02	12
w probation admissions to county camps, ranches and schools[d]	117	183	226	56	23
w CYA commitments	158	169	72	07	-57

[a]Unless otherwise noted, all rates for 1960 and 1965 are taken directly from *Crime and Delinquency in California, 1969* acramento: Bureau of Criminal Statistics, 1969), table I-14, p. 44, and table I-15, p. 45. Computations for 1970 (except rest data) are based on data reported in *Juvenile Probation and Detention: Reference Tables, 1970* (Sacramento: Bureau Criminal Statistics, 1970), table 1, p. 5, and table 30, p. 42; data on police obtained from *Crime and Arrests: Reference ables, 1970* (Sacramento: Bureau of Criminal Statistics, 1970), table 5-A, p. 9.

[b]These rates are computed for 1960 and 1970 on the basis of raw data appearing in Bureau of Criminal Statistics annual ıblications, and population figures provided in *Juvenile Probation and Detention, 1970*, p. 5; the rate for 1965 is timated on the basis of the stability of rates of new referrals/all probation referrals. In 1960 the proportion of new ferrals/all referrals was .765, in 1966 it was .749, and in 1970 it was .747. The mid-point proportion of .757 was used for)65 and the following equation (based on 1965 data for new referrals appearing in the 1969 Bureau of Criminal Statistics): $\frac{540}{x} = \frac{757}{100} = 4,543/100,000$ youth population.

[c]See table 12 for sources on independent computations of detention rates. All detention rates in this and subsequent bles *exclude* dependent-neglect cases.

[d]Systematic statewide reporting of new commitments to juvenile county institutions (camps, ranches, and schools) began 1 January 1966, according to *Crime and Delinquency in California, 1966* (Sacramento: Bureau of Criminal Statistics,)66), p. 236; data for 1970 is computed on basis of *Juvenile Probation and Detention: Reference Tables, 1970*, table 1, p. 5, ıd table 32, p. 49. See table 9 for sources of estimates for 1960 and 1965.

percent between 1960 and 1965, but it increased by a comparable amount during the subsidy period 1965-70. However, the rates of *referrals* to probation by the local police departments changed appreciably. The subsidy years are associated with a 53 percent rate increase, while the pre-subsidy period rose 26 percent. The new referrals to probation (from all sources) displayed a comparable trend—up 28 percent in 1960-65, but increasing even more during 1965-70 (47 percent). The rates of *detention admissions* (regardless of court status, and whether the admission was for a new or old referral) rose only 10 percent in 1960-65, or less than the arrest or referral rates. However, the detention rates in the subsidy years rose substantially, and appeared to keep up with the referral rates.

The rate of *initial petitions* filed also changed, dipping slightly in 1960-65, but showing a substantial increase during the subsidy period (33 percent). However, the actual rates of declaring court *wardships* of the new petitions did not keep pace with either the referral, detention, or filing rates in either period. Trend data for *camp admissions* indicate a lower rate of increase for 1965–70. Unlike the other indicators, *CYA commitments* decreased during the subsidy period.

In general, it appears that the police response shifted to directing many more youth to be processed by the courts (via referrals). While during the subsidy years the filing of petitions also increased (perhaps related to decisions by probation officers), the judges did not appear to respond in kind. The rates of court wardship declared rose, but far below the change in rates of police activity, filing decisions, and, significantly, detention.

Looking at the rate figures in part A for each year, it is quite clear that CYA commitments, even in 1960, comprised only a very small part of the decision workload of the probation departments and juvenile courts. There is also a wide disparity in police referral rates and initial filing rates, indicating that there is probably much informal, nonjudicial handling of the cases being processed in the probation system. Whether or not the police would want their referrals to be taken more seriously is unknown, using available data.

What is most striking, however, is the similarity in disparity between detention admission rates and any of the rates of official handling by probation officers or judges. The disparity between rates of detention and rates of filing or declaration of wardship increases over time. Evidently many youth are, in fact, detained *without* even being deemed worthy of having a petition filed regarding their alleged deviance. It is quite likely that detention can be associated with an informal disposition, as well as with formal dispositions. It is noteworthy that rates of detention far exceed those for any other form of correctional response, for all years.

Since the detention data cannot be broken down to indicate whether a petition is filed, whether it is a new or old case, or whether youngsters are currently on probation, we cannot determine precisely how detention is associated with informal handling and official dispositions. Despite these shortcomings in the data, it is apparent that detention has been—and is—the most significant element of the county correctional program. It was growing before 1965, but during the subsidy years it increased appreciably. During both periods it appears quite likely that more youth received detention than received adjudication or formal treatment services. At the county level, the dominant form of official response appears to be detention—not treatment—since the risk of being detained is much higher than the combined risk of being a probation case, a camp commitment, and a CYA ward.

Specifying the Reasons for Arrest and Detention

One of the major reasons for the rise in detention, independent of subsidy influences, might be a rise in the seriousness of the offenses. Perhaps police, together with probation officers, were detaining more youngsters because they were deemed to be posing a greater danger to the community and thus warranted preventive detention to insure protection of the community. Under the California Welfare and Institutions Code (Section 628) this would be permissible, since youth can be detained for the following reasons: (a) the minor is denied "proper and effective parental care"; (b) the minor is destitute or without "a suitable place of abode"; (c) the home of the minor is "unfit"; (d) "Continued detention of the minor is a matter of *immediate and urgent necessity for the protection of the person or property of another*"; (e) the minor is likely to flee the jurisdiction of the court; (f) the minor has violated an order of the juvenile court; or (g) the minor is "*physically dangerous* to the public because of a mental or physical deficiency, disorder, or abnormality" (SCYA, 1970*b*, Section 628; italics added).

Table 11 provides a comparison of reasons for police arrests for 1960, 1965, and 1970. Part A presents the data according to the rate of arrests per 100,000 youth, age 10-17, for each year. Part B again attempts to note the trends in the pre-subsidy period (1960–65) and post-subsidy period (1965–70). "Specific criminal offenses" refer to those offenses that would be a crime if committed by an adult; "delinquent tendencies" refers to arrests for activities that are not specifically criminal, but are juvenile status offenses (e.g., incorrigibility, truancy, running away, curfew, loitering, etc.); and "drugs only" refers to all types of drug-related charges, except for glue sniffing (which is treated by the Bureau of Criminal Statistics as an example of delinquent tendency). The preponderant majority of drug offenses refer to possession or use of marijuana.

TABLE 11
Juvenile Arrest: Specific Rates for 1960, 1965, and 1970a (in rates per 100,000 Youth, ages 10–17, and percent changes in rates)

Arrest Categories	A. Rates Per 100,000 Youth, Age 10–17			B. Percent Changes	
	1960	1965	1970b	1960–65	1965–70
Specific criminal offenses	3,232	3,636	4,214	13%	16%
Drugs only	59	87	1,189	47	1,266
Delinquent tendencies	5,340	6,421	7,014	20	09
Total arrest rates	8,631	10,144	12,417	18%	18%
(Number of arrests)	(182,715)	(277,649)	(382,935)		

aNumbers arrested and computed rates for 1960 and 1965 can be found in *Crime and Delinquency in California, 1969* (Sacramento: Bureau of Criminal Statistics, 1969), table I-2, p. 10, and table I-14, p. 44.
bNumbers arrested used in rate computations can be found in *Crime and Arrests: Reference Tables, 1970* (Sacramento: Bureau of Criminal Statistics, 1970), table VI, p. 61; population figure used in computations can be found in *Juvenile Probation and Detention: Reference Tables, 1970* (Sacramento: Bureau of Criminal Statistics, 1970, table 1, p. 5.

It is readily apparent that while the overall rates are not changing (18 percent for each period), the rate of drug arrests has risen precipitously. As a matter of fact, it is the only type of offense that is increasing significantly during the subsidy years. Specific criminal offenses are rising at about the same rate for both periods. Delinquent tendencies, on the other hand, rose 20 percent in 1960–65, but only 9 percent during the subsidy years. The major change in the reasons for arrests is clearly occurring with drugs. Perhaps the counties are reacting to this sudden upsurge in noticed usage by increasing their rates of preventive detention as a social control measure. Table 12 attempts to provide data to assess this possibility by classifying detentions according to the most serious offense associated with the reason for admission.

The reasons for detention are classified in the same manner as the reasons for arrests, except for the last category, "administrative/other." According to the Bureau of Criminal Statistics, this category refers to youngsters "whose present detention is an outgrowth of some prior situation and not the result of any new acts of delinquency" (see table 12, footnote e). Examples for this category refer to change of placements, courtesy holds for other counties, specific court-mandated commitments for a specified period, and probation violations. It is clear that during the pre-subsidy period (when this type of detention was first classified and tabulated as a separate reason), this latter type of detention was rising at the fastest rate (56 percent).

The post-subsidy years indicate that drugs are *not* the only reason that detention rates are increasing. While drug detentions do, indeed, show the sharpest rise, the rate of dententions for delinquent tendencies is also rising quite sharply (from a 15 percent increase to 48 percent). This is a particularly noteworthy finding, since table 11 disclosed that the rate of police arrests for this category had *not* increased substantially. Detention for clearly criminal offenses rose at the same rate as the administrative/other reasons (21 percent during 1965–70), but these have the lowest rate of increase during the subsidy years.

If drugs were omitted from the calculations, then the total detention rates would be: 1960—2,930; 1965—3,204; and 1970—4,295. The 1960–65 period would have increased about 9 percent, while the 1965–70 period would have risen about 34 percent.

TABLE 12
California Detention: Specific Rates for 1960, 1965, and 1970a (rate per 100,000 youth, 10–17, for each year and percent changes)

Reasons for Detention	A. Rates per 100,000 Youth, Aged 10-17			B. Percent Changes	
	1960	1965	1970	1960-65	1965-70
Specific criminal offenses[b]	1,368	1,317	1,604	-04%	21%
Drug offenses only[c]	48	57	571	19	902
Delinquent tendencies[d]	1,331	1,524	2,253	15	48
Administrative/other[e], [f]	231	363	438	56	21
All reasons—total rates per year	2,978	3,261	4,866	10%	49%
(Number of detentions)	(63,186)	(88,535)	(150,067)		

aFor population figures, *Juvenile Probation and Detention Reference Tables, 1970* (Sacramento: Bureau of Criminal Statistics), table 1, p. 5; for actual numbers detained, by reason, for each year, *Crime and Delinquency in California, 1969* (Sacramento: Bureau of Criminal Statistics), table X-13, p. 174, and table X-14, p. 177; and for 1970 data, *Reference* c1970 criminal offenses are classified according to codes provided by Bureau of Criminal Statistics in *Juvenile Detention Statistical Reporting: A Reference Manual for County Juvenile Halls and Camps, Ranches, and Homes* (Sacramento: BCS, January, 1966). Offenses include: homicide; robbery; aggravated and other assault; burglary; thefts (non-auto and auto); sex offenses (except girls' illicit sex or victims of rape); weapons' laws; drunk driving; hit and run (auto); all other offenses not specified in any of the other categories (e.g., tampering with auto, fish and game violations, etc.).

c1970 drug offenses are also classified according to *Juvenile Detention Statistical Reporting*. They include sale, possession, or use of narcotics, marijuana, or dangerous drugs, but *exclude* glue sniffing.

d1970 delinquent tendencies are classified according to *Juvenile Detention Statistical Reporting*. Behaviors include truancy; runaways (from home, county camp, custody of an officer or from CYA; excluded are forcible escape, to be included in "criminal, all other"); incorrigible; curfew; transients (out-of-state); malicious mischief; disturbing peace; liquor laws and drunk; glue sniffing; other offenses (including arson, vagrancy, loitering, school suspension, etc.).

e1970 administrative reasons are classified according to *Juvenile Detention Statistical Reporting*. It is "used primarily for delinquent youngsters whose present detention is an outgrowth of some prior situation and not the result of any new acts of delinquency" (p. 4). Detention reasons include: change of placement (delinquents only); courtesy holds (delinquent) of youth for other counties or CYA; court commitments for those committed for a specific period of time, even if in detention previous to this disposition; court commitments for work and school programs; "other" pertains primarily to youths detained for violation of probation, parole, camp returns, transfers from county jails, in-custody transfers, detention pending camp acceptance, etc.

fIncludes detention for traffic violations because 1960 and 1965 figure totals included these violations in "other." In 1970 there were 922 traffic detentions and in 1965 there were 1,104, thus indicating that this reason is *not* increasing, or responsible for the changes in the administrative/other rates.

It is possible that the marked rise in the rate of detention admissions would have occurred in the absence of probation subsidy. We will never know for certain what might have occurred, since subsidy was not launched as an experimental project. The few nonsubsidy counties are rural in character; so we lack any type of comparison or control counties. While we cannot be certain that subsidy "caused" this detention increase, the data indicate that there is a clear difference between the detention rates "before" and "after" the introduction of subsidy. This association between detention and the early years of subsidy suggests that there may be unintended but quite real consequences occurring at the county level.

Once we are aware of the association, it is not difficult to think of post hoc reasons for increased use of detention. Two reasons might be the response of the police to reduce commitments and the increased use of informal and formal probation. The opposition of the local police departments to the subsidy program is a well-known fact in California. For example, the Los Angeles city Chief of Police, Edward M. Davis, delivered an open letter to the county Superior Court judges in which he blamed rising crime rates on "being sold on a philosophy that community-based corrections is the most viable method of rehabilitation." Chief Davis, perhaps relying on his own department's records, also claimed that "it is pretty obvious that home or community-based rehabilitation doesn't appear to be any more effective than institutional corrections" (Davis letter, California Probation, 1972, p. 2).

Perhaps increased referrals and detentions were potent means of expressing this resentment. Locking youngsters up would constitute a sanction, regardless of dispositions. While judges review detention decisions within a forty-eight hour period (excluding weekends), it is evident that police are in an advantageous position to initiate detention requests. Acquiescence to this request would be one means by which probation officers (the administrators of detention facilities) and the police accommodated to each other and thus minimized the emergence of open conflict between the two major agencies of local juvenile social control. Direct data is not available concerning this plausible source of increased detention, but a study geared to this line of reasoning might prove valuable. It could illuminate how social control agencies respond when they are not made partners to basic policy changes and when they are not included in new systems of rewards.

It is possible that local police criticism may have been the primary spur to a critical 1972 Subsidy Amendment, authorizing a *supplemental* two million dollar appropriation in fiscal 1972–73. This supplemental fund was to be used only by local law enforcement agencies for the "diagnosis, control, or treatment of offenders or alleged offenders," subject to approval by the CYA (SCYA, 1974, p. 6). The supplementary programs can include, according to CYA standards, crisis intervention programs, training projects, staff exchange programs, jail counseling projects, and early law enforcement intervention programs.

Another source of increased detention may be located within the probation departments. It may not be accidental that one of the sharpest rate increases was for "delinquent tendencies," the vague and diffuse category that can virtually justify any act of social control. (In the Community Treatment Project, as caseloads became smaller, and more activities of wards were noticed, the rates of "suspensions" for vague charges increased sharply.) This phenomenon also has been noted by others (Lohman, Wahl, Carter, Lewis, 1971). Perhaps, increasing the number of overall probation officers, reducing caseloads, and raising expectations about obtaining treatment results had a comparable impact within probation departments. It is possible, too, that use of detention avoided the problem of receiving a double subsidy. Unfortunately, the data do not distinguish what type of "officer" initiated the detention request or for what reason. Research with this focus might prove worthwhile in illuminating the changes in social-control practices that occur when the numbers of agents increase and the ward/agent ratios decrease, across entire departments.

The search for the causes of increased detention is worthwhile, but it is necessary here to deal with the current set of descriptive facts. The subsidy period is not associated with a decreased use of institutionalization at the local level. It appears that while fewer offenders are being committed to spend more time in institutions at a state level, more alleged offenders are being sent to local detention facilities for shorter institutional stays. This dual set of social-control trends appears to be an important descriptive fact associated with the current operation of probation subsidy. In addition, county commitments to camps, ranches, and schools continued to rise, albeit at a less accelerated rate during the 1965-70 period. The next section will attempt to construct a statewide balance sheet to assess these institutional trends.

Assessing Statewide Institutional Impact

There appear to be two useful methods for assessing increases or decreases in the use of institutionalization for specific time periods. The first method relies on computing admission rates per 100,000 youth at risk, thereby assessing the chances of juveniles being locked up in a detention facility, a county camp, ranch, school or home, or a state facility. The calculation of admission rates does not take into account the fact that the average institutional stay varies by the source of social control. According to the best available data, county detention can average 8 days (San Diego and San Francisco County Reports, 1970) or 16 days (Los Angeles County Report, 1970-71). However, county camps, ranches, schools, and homes appear to have averaged about 182.5 days from 1966 to 1970 (BCS *Annual Reports*), while CYA institutions provided about 243 days in 1960, 262 days in 1965, and 310 days in 1970 (CYA *Annual Reports*). Since the average length of institutional stay can vary within a source, as well as between sources, it seems useful to also compute the average institutional stays associated with the specific rates of admission. This second method can provide an estimate of rates of institutional youth days per 100,000 youth at risk for specific time periods. Table 13 uses both methods to yield insights regarding statewide trends for 1960, 1965, and 1970.

Part A conveniently summarizes data that has been presented earlier, so that statewide trends (and their sources) can be assessed. While rates of CYA first admissions have been drastically reduced over the decade, there have been notable increases in county sources of institutionalization. The primary issue is whether the total state rate has actually been reduced since the advent of subsidy. If it has not, as the data clearly indicate, has the rate of institutional risk been slowed down during the subsidy period? Between 1960 and 1965 the total state rate increased 360; between 1965 and 1970 the total state rate increased 1,551. During the pre-subsidy period the total state rate increased about 11 percent, but during the post-subsidy period the increase amounted to about 43 percent. It is clear that the risks of being locked up in California have increased over the

---

TABLE 13
State and County Rates of Admissions and Institutional Youth Days for All Sources, 1960, 1965, and 1970

A. *Rates of Admission Per 100,00 Youth, Aged 10-17 Years*			
Sources	1960	1965	1970
1. Initial juv. court commitments to CYA	158	169	72
2. New admissions to county camps, ranches, etc.	117 est.	183 est.	226
3. All admissions to juvenile halls	2,978	3,261	4,866
Total state rates	3,253	3,613	5,164

B. *Institutional Youth Days Per 100,000 Youth, Aged 10-17 Years*			
Sources	1960	1965	1970
1. Initial CYA[a]	38,457	44,210	22,342
2. New admissions to camps, ranches, etc.[b]	21,353	33,398	41,245
3. All admissions to juvenile halls[c]	29,780	32,610	48,660
Total institutional days	89,590	110,218	112,247

Sources: (1) see Tables 9 and 10 for source of rates; (2) *CYA Annual Report, 1971*; (3) *Crime and Delinquency in California, 1966-69*; (4) *County Annual Reports.*

[a]The average CYA institutional stay was 8.6 months in 1965 and 10.2 months in 1970. The figure of 8.0 months was used for 1960, based on *1964 Probation Study.* Each monthly figure was multiplied by 30.42, the average number of days per month, to obtain an average of institutional youth days. These figures were multiplied by admission rates to produce the total institutional youth days per 100,000 youth.

[b]Average camp stay has appeared to fluctuate around 6 months (or 182.5 days), according to BCS comments in annual reports, and was used for all years.

[c]The figure used for all years is 10 days. While there are no statewide figures for this inportant statistic, inspection of county reports and interviews with county personnel indicates that 10 days is a very conservative estimate. The largest county, Los Angeles, in 1970-71 had an average stay of 16 days; Almeda in 1970 averaged 12 days; San Diego in 1970 averaged about 8 days; San Francisco in 1970 averaged about 8 days; and Orange County in 1970 averaged about 10 days.

decade. Not only has subsidy failed to reduce this risk; but the greatest increase in risk is associated with the payment of the subsidy to counties to provide local correctional "treatment." (It is important to note that the risk of being locked up increased much faster than the risk of being arrested for an alleged act of youthful deviance.)

The data regarding total institutional youth days, in part B of table 13, indicate that the subsidy period has also failed to reduce the amount of institutional time for the youth at risk (110,218 versus 112,247 institutional youth days per 100,000 youth, 10–17 years of age). However, the rate of increase appears to have been slowed down. In the pre-subsidy period the gain was 20,628 days—a gain of about 23 percent. The gain for the post-subsidy period was 2,029 days per 100,000 youth—a gain of only 2 percent. It appears that the decrease in institutional youth days occurring at the state level almost balanced the increases associated with the county increases. If the CYA had maintained the average length of stay at the pre-subsidy levels, the state total would have displayed a decrease; the CYA institutional days would have amounted to 17,525 youth days instead of 22,342—a reduction of 4,817 youth days.

Summary and Conclusions

The evidence appears persuasive that the counties were successful in reducing the rates of first admissions to the CYA. However, the evidence also indicates that focusing attention on only one discretionary point of decision making is an inadequate approach toward understanding the full range of social impacts associated with the introduction of subsidy payments to the counties. Unintended social consequences appeared in the CYA system, the county social control/treatment system, and in the combined, statewide system.

At the state level, the CYA experienced the receipt of a new mixture of adjudicated offenders. By 1970, a greater proportion of male offenders were older, committed by the criminal courts, and convicted for drug and personal offenses. The CYA responded to relieved population pressures by arranging for older youth to be handled within its own institutional complex, rather than being sent to Department of Corrections facilities. The average length of stay increased at all CYA institutions. The influx of older youth and the lengthening of institutionalization permitted the CYA to maintain an average daily population of around 5,000 persons (between 1965 and 1970). This organizational adaptation occurred while more new institutional beds were phased into the system than were phased out, and the ward/staff ratios reduced from 2.3:1 to 1.8:1.

Three arguments were advanced in various official documents to support the program of "strengthening and intensification" of institutional treatment. The first used the concept of correctional "standards" for different age groups; the second proposed that the new population mixture was more delinquent and "disturbed"; the third proposed that the organization was struggling for its "survival" and reacted adaptively. A reassessment of the available evidence indicated that the CYA was now receiving an offender group that was less of a risk than earlier years. The standards expressed occupational preferences and not empirical evidence, since all reliable studies have failed to demonstrate that increased length of stay is related to post-institutional behavior. The survival argument may only be partially true, since staff hiring continued to increase between 1965 and 1970—but at a lower rate of increase than the pre-subsidy period.

The subsidy years were associated with divergent trends as indicated by the decisions of police, probation officers, and judges. While increases in arrests were similar, police initiated referrals in a greater proportion of cases than in the period 1960-65. Probation officers filed more initial petitions in response to this external demand, but judges hardly kept pace with these pressures by declaring youths official wards of the court. Meanwhile, detention rates climbed, camp institutionalization increased, and CYA commitments were reduced.

The facts do not establish that subsidy was directly responsible for increased police referrals, camp and detention admissions, or even CYA commitment reductions. Rather, they document associational differences between the "before" and "after" periods of subsidy. Further studies might unravel the causal relationships, but meanwhile a reasonable assessment of these documented facts is warranted, since policy decisions are being made even without the suggested causal studies.

The evidence indicates that merely focusing on reduced CYA commitments provides an incomplete understanding of state institutionalization patterns. On a statewide basis it appears that more youth are being locked up for shorter stays at a county level, while fewer youth are entering the CYA for lengthier stays. The institutional days for the total state appear to be leveling off, at a mid-1960 level, but the chances of being locked up continue to increase. From a broad, social perspective, it is difficult to discern any social benefits for youth that would offset the greater risk of lockup. The CYA youth experiencing lengthier stays have probably incurred the greatest amount of social cost, compared to other local youth.

It is also difficult to discern any benefits for adults associated with this increased reliance on local social control. Locking youth up at a faster rate than any increase in crimes against property or persons, primarily for nonharmful or noncriminal offenses (drugs and delinquent tendencies), does not seem conducive to promoting ideals of fairness and reasonableness. In addition, a recent study of subsidy cases indicates that gains in a more effective correctional technology have not accrued to the public. Youth placed on smaller, special supervision caseloads appear to produce as much police-noticed delinquency as juveniles receiving regular probationary treatment. *California's Probation Subsidy Program Progress Report to the Legislature, 1966–1973*, prepared by CYA staff (SCYA, 1974), summarizes the effectiveness of local correctional efforts as follows: "Preliminary analysis suggests that Subsidy probation and regular probation are very similar with respect to rehabilitative effectiveness with similar juvenile probationers" (p. 39). It appears that increased local social control/treatment efforts have indeed occurred since 1965—but the total state balance sheets indicate that these efforts should be counted as social costs rather than as social benefits.

8   The Fiscal Impact of Probation Subsidy

In a *Report on State Aid for Probation Services* (State of California Joint Study, 1970), an official CYA and Department of Finance study group concluded that there had been a significant reduction in commitments to state correctional institutions and that these lower commitment rates were largely attributable to the subsidy program. In addition, the study concluded that the program had saved the state over $50 million in operating expenses over a four-year period, even *after* making deductions for payments to the counties. The study also referred to correctional construction savings, but it remained for Smith, in his booklet, *A Quiet Revolution* (1972), to document this potential benefit of probation subsidy: between 1966 and 1972 California "has saved $185,978,820 through canceled construction, closed institutions, and new institutions constructed, but not opened" (Smith, 1972, p. 69). To have one correctional innovation save a state almost a quarter of a billion dollars in operating and construction costs in such a short period of time, would certainly represent a "revolution." In this chapter these fiscal claims regarding probation subsidy will be assessed.

To facilitate the analyses, it is assumed first that all of the reduced commitments to state institutions can be fiscally attri-

buted to probation subsidy. The extent to which the experience of
California, for the period 1966–72, is unique, as compared to
comparable nonsubsidy states during the same period, is not
known at this time. What would have happened in California
without the new law is unknown. However, since the state is
paying subsidy funds to counties for *all* reduced commitments,
we have accepted this *fiscal* policy assumption as a given in the
analyses. Second, the claims regarding savings reflect the
inflation of the dollar, but we have generally assumed that actual
cost figures for any given year should be accepted. The major
explicit exception to this assumption is in the last sections, where
an attempt is made to assess increased institutional and parole
costs while controlling for 1965 dollar costs. Third, we have
assumed that all raw numerical data is essentially accurate, but
that the analyses and interpretation of the data are susceptible to
questioning on the basis of excluded data, logic, or reasonableness. While our conclusions may differ from those presented by
the joint study team and Smith, we are using the same data
sources—the official documents associated with the state of
California.

The Basis for State Savings of Operating Expenses
The original subsidy legislation set forth a specific formula for
computing the reimbursement basis for providing subventions to
the county. Understanding the logic of computing expected
commitments and fiscal savings helps to provide insight into the
economic assumptions of probation subsidy. Table 14 is an
attempt to depict the manner in which the base commitment rate
is used to compute the "reduction numbers" that can theoretically generate potential savings to the state and justify actual
dollar payments to the counties. After analyzing how savings can
be generated theoretically, we can focus attention on whether
these savings actually occurred.

Four fiscal years are covered in table 14. In fiscal 1966–67,
thirty-one counties, with a total population of 14,391,100 persons
(of all ages), participated in the program by claiming reduced
commitments and having programs approved by the CYA.
According to the experience of the base-rate years of 1959–63,
these participating counties could be expected to send 30.1

persons per 100,000 population to the California Youth Authority during the year. If 30.1/100,000 is multiplied by the total population, the expected commitment number would be 4,332. However, the participating counties only sent 3,872 bona fide initial commitments to the Youth Authority in fiscal 1966-67. Therefore, they had a commitment reduction of 460 persons. As illustrated in the table, at $4,000 per CYA career cost, these 460 persons would total a potential savings to the state of $1,840,000. Using a similar logic for the 938 persons who were *not* sent to California Department of Corrections (CDC) institutions, it is also possible to compute a potential savings. Since the career cost for adults is greater—in 1965 it was $5,700 per successful career—the potential savings for the state is 938 times $5,700 or $5,346,000 in a single fiscal year.

Table 14 also discloses that the combined base rate for CYA and CDC in fiscal 1966-67 is 60.9 persons per 100,000 population (30.1 plus 30.8). The total expected commitments could have been 8,757 (multiplying 60.9 by 14,391,100 and dividing by 100,000). The combined actual CYA and CDC commitments amounted to only 7,359 persons, and thereby yielded a reduction number of 1,398 (460 plus 938). The total subsidy payments that the thirty-one counties actually received that year was $1,632,064— even though they had saved the state a potential savings of $7,186,000. The net difference between potential savings and actual subsidy payments could constitute a net savings to the state of California. This saving—after subsidy payments—would derive from the state of California's not paying counties the total savings occurring from these 1,398 reduced commitments.

If each fiscal year is read in a similar fashion, it is possible to ascertain that the youth share of reduced commitments increased from 32.9 percent in 1966-67 to 50.4 percent in 1969-70. Actual payments by the state to the counties also increased from $1,632,064 to $13,292,266. During the same four years the potential savings constituting the hypothetical "offset" dollars to pay the subvention to the counties grew from over $1.6 million to $17,226,800. It is evident that the counties were able to recapture a greater proportion of each year's potential savings; however, the state was still able to come out ahead, even after deducting subsidy payments to the counties. In fiscal 1969-70, this

TABLE 14
Commitment Reductions under the California Probation Subsidy Program, Including State Costs and Potential Savings to State, for Fiscal Years 1966–70a

Comparison Categories	1966–67	1967–68	1968–69	1969–70
Counties in program	31	36	41	46
Total population (in thousands)	14,391.1	15,716.2	18,709.2	19,549.5
Youth Authority				
Base rate/100.000 pop.	30.1	30.5	29.9	30.1
Expected commitments (number)	4,332	4,793	5,594	5,884
Actual commitments (number)	3,872	3,599	4,162	4,091
Commitment reduction (actual)	460	1,194	1,432	1,793
Dept. of Corrections				
Base rate/100,000 pop.	30.8	30.7	30.5	31.2
Expected commitments (number)	4,425	4,827	5,715	6,098
Actual commitments (number)	3,487	3,605	3,828	4,334
Commitment reduction (actual)	938	1,222	1,887	1,764
Total CYA & CDC				
Base rate/100,000 pop.	60.9	61.2	60.4	61.3
Expected commitments	8,757	9,620	11,309	11,982

Actual commitments	7,359	7,204	7,990	8,423
Commitment reductions (actual)	1,398	2,416	3,319	3,557
Percent of reduction attributable to CYA[b]	32.9	49.4	43.1	50.4
Subsidy payments by state[c]	$1,632,064	$4,072,208	$8,766,667	$13,292,266
Potential savings by state[d]				
CYA savings (@$4,000/career cost)	1,840,000	4,776,000	5,728,000	7,172,000
CDC savings (@$5,700/career cost)	5,346,600	6,965,400	11,355,900	10,054,800
Total savings, CYA and CDC	$7,186,600	$11,741,400	$17,083,900	$17,226,800

[a] Unless otherwise noted, all data are taken from *Report on State Aid for Probation Services*, a Joint Study of the Department of Finance, Department of Youth Authority, and County Probation Representatives (Sacramento: Human Relations Agency, Department of Youth Authority, 30 Oct. 1970), Appendix F-1 and F-2.

[b] This figure is computed by dividing *actual* commitment reduction numbers attributable to CYA by total, e.g., for fiscal 1966–67, 460/1,398 equals 32.9 percent.

[c] *Report on State Aid*, Appendix D.

[d] The Board of Corrections, *Probation Study: Final Report* (Sacramento: Board of Corrections, Youth and Adult Corrections Agency, 7 Sept. 1965), table XIV, p. 181, is the source for each career cost for a CYA or a CDC career. For each yearly "potential savings" the *actual* reduction number for CYA or CDC is multiplied by the appropriate career cost (e.g., for fiscal 1966–67, the CDC reduction number of 938 is multiplied by $5,700, for a potential savings of $5,346,600; the CYA total is 460 x $4,000 or $1,840,000). See table 15 for further examples of potential savings computations, using another method of computation, when expected costs and actual costs are *not* equal.

hypothetical net savings to the state, after subsidy payment, was close to $4 million. On paper, the fiscal assumptions appeared quite sound.

Potential Savings and the Problem of Rising Correctional Costs

It is evident from table 14 that in order at least to "break even" the state needed to have reduced commitments and then to pay no more than the CYA and CDC 1965 career costs. While the legislators and designers of the subsidy bill were quite aware that adults cost more per career (primarily because they were institutionalized for a longer period of time—two years as compared to eight months for youths in 1964), they deliberately set a maximum payment of $4,000 per reduction, regardless of the ages of the offenders. By setting this ceiling, the state appeared to be insuring that it, too, could benefit from the reduced commitments, even if the counties were capable of claiming 100 percent of their earnings in approved programs.

In addition to reduced commitments and a maximum payment of $4,000 per reduction, the state needed one other condition to insure that there were offset savings to pay for subsidies—actual *institutional costs had to remain relatively constant. If institutional costs rose, the potential savings from reduced commitments could be more than offset by the increased career costs for those actually committed.*

There is, in fact, no dispute that institutional costs did rise precipitously (about 50 percent) in both institutional systems. The 1970 joint study team noted that in 1969–70 a CYA fiscal career cost $6,000, not $4,000. And a CDC career by 1967–68 had risen to an estimate of at least $8,777, not $5,700 (State of California Joint Study, 1970, pp. 19-20). The joint study group readily conceded that costs had risen as a result of the subsidy program, and they commented as follows:

The resultant smaller state institution population with a larger number of violence prone individuals requires facilities with tighter security, increased staffing, and consequent increased cost to the state per commitment. Thus the state correctional agencies find themselves in a position of having unused capacity within the institutions but having a need for facilities offering greater security and treatment. With this type of program in operation, there is a declining need for minimum security facilities and conservation camp programs and a greater need for such

facilities as medical-psychiatric and maximum security.
Therefore, recognition must be given to the fact that *as a result of the probation subsidy program*, the offenders who require less security, less costly facilities, and shorter length of stay are the ones being retained in the local community with the high violence potential, maximum security type inmate being sent to the state institutions. [State of California Joint Study, 1970; italics added]

This rationale has been assessed in chapter 7. Therefore, setting aside the rationale, it would appear quite critical to determine whether these increased actual costs for institutionalized offenders had more than offset the potential savings associated with those not institutionalized. The joint study did not make this assessment, but the data are readily available to use the logic of projecting costs for actual and expected commitments according to the new cost figures. At this point in our analysis, it is not necessary to reexamine *why* costs rose, but rather to deal with these new costs as fiscal facts. Table 15 is an attempt to make an overall estimate for fiscal 1969-70.

Table 15 uses the official commitment data noted in table 14. In fiscal 1969-70 there were 5,884 youth expected as commitments to CYA institutions; however, only 4,091 were actually committed. In part I of the table, using the figures for the pre-subsidy career cost policy, it is readily apparent that the expected costs would have been $23,536,000 (5,884 times $4,000), while the actual costs would have been only $16,364,000. The savings are $7,172,000, the same figure depicted in table 14 for those reduced commitments attributable to the CYA. For the CYA's post-subsidy career cost policy, the same logic is applied. While the expected costs are similar, the actual per capita costs have risen to $6,000 per career. Instead of yearly potential savings—available for subsidy payments—the state is now paying about a million dollars *more* for CYA operational costs. The total actual costs are now greater than the total expected costs.

Moving to the adults, the computations lead to the conclusion (in part II of table 15) that the pre-subsidy career cost policy saved the state over $10 million. This figure, of course, is similar to the one that appears in table 14. However, increased actual CDC costs for those actually committed have wiped out this potential savings; the state, in 1969-70, paid over $3 million more than had been anticipated. Again the total actual costs are greater than the total expected costs.

TABLE 15
Assessing 1969–70 Fiscal Impact of Subsidy on the State by Two Types of Career Cost Policies[a]

| | Pre-subsidy Career Cost Policy | | Post-subsidy Career Cost Policy | |
	Projected Expected Costs	Projected Actual Costs	Projected Expected Costs	Projected Actual Costs
I. CYA Institutions				
A. 1969–70 commitment data	5,884 youth	4,091 youth	5,884 youth	4,091 youth
B. CYA costs/career[b]	$ 4,000	$ 4,000	$ 4,000	$ 6,000
C. 1969–70 fiscal costs (A x B)	$23,536,000	$16,364,000	$23,536,000	$24,546,000
D. Yearly institutional cost or savings (expected – actual)		$+7,172,000		$-1,010,000
II. CDC				
A. 1969–70 commitment data	6,098 offenders	4,334 offenders	6,098 offenders	4,334 offenders
B. CDC costs/career[c]	$ 5,700	$ 5,700	$ 5,700	$ 8,700
C. 1969–70 fiscal costs (A x B)	$34,758,600	$24,703,800	$34,758,600	$37,805,800
D. Yearly institutional cost or savings (expected–actual)		$+10,054,800		$-3,047,200
III. 1969–70 combined CYA and CDC				
A. Institutional cost or savings (ID and IID)		$+17,226,800		$- 4,057,200
B. Subsidy payments by state (table 14)		- 13,292,266		-13,292,266
C. Net subsidy Impact		$+ 3,934,534		$-17,349,466
D. Policy assessment		Net Savings to State		Cost Run-up to State

[a]All data, unless otherwise noted, are taken from Table 14.

[b]CYA career cost, pre-subsidy, is taken from the *1964 Probation Study*, p. 181; post-subsidy career costs are taken from Joint Study Document, *Report on State Aid for Probation Services*, p. 20.

[c]CDC career costs, pre- and post-subsidy, are also obtained from *1964 Probation Study* and Joint Study Document. The 1969–70 CDC career cost has been rounded to $8,700; the exact figure is $8,777/career.

The last part of the table reaches the inexorable conclusion that the pre-subsidy career cost policy can pay for subsidy payments of over $13 million and still leave the state an extra savings of $3,934,534. However, the new, post-subsidy career cost policy has no potential savings to offset the actual subsidy payments that were made to the counties. According to these calculations, the post-subsidy policy actually cost the state a total of $17,349,466 more than the pre-subsidy policy had cost in 1965. Instead of the anticipated potential extra savings after paying subsidies to the county, there is evidence of a cost run-up to the state. The steep rise in correctional costs by both agencies, the CYA and CDC, that occurred as a result of probation subsidy has produced an ironic outcome: in 1969–70, subsidy policy cost the state all of the costs of paying subsidies to the counties *plus* increased costs per career for institutional corrections, in comparison to the costs of 1964–65.

As noted earlier, the joint study group did not conduct this type of analysis. Neither did an official CYA *Report to the Legislature*, submitted on 7 January 1969 (SCYA, 1969*a*). Both of the reports took note of the marked rise in costs that were already quite evident in the CYA and CDC career costs. Both of these official reports argued that the state of California was now saving more money than had originally been contemplated when career costs were lower. Both reports clearly imply that increased reductions and increased career costs (paid by the state) lead to more potential savings for the state; this savings can be used to pay for the subsidies to the counties (also paid for by the state), and there will still be money left over. Using this perspective, the joint study team calculated that these extra savings amounted to over $50 million—much more than was originally anticipated. According to this approach, if the career costs had increased even further, then the "savings" would have exceeded $50 million.

The notion that savings increase in direct proportion to the increase in costs seems, on its face, to be unusual. The major reason that the joint study group found savings instead of losses is that their mode of calculating potential savings is quite different from that used in table 15. According to the official reports, potential savings is calculated by multiplying the "reduction number" by the *latest* career cost. For example, if commitments had been reduced by 2,000 and the latest CYA career costs were calculated to be $6,000, then the savings would automatically be $12 million. If the cost were to rise to $10,000, then the savings would also rise to $20 million. We conclude that the Department of Finance and the CYA method of calculating potential savings is faulty as it leads to unreasonable outcomes.

It is instructive to compare the official methods of computing savings with the method used in table 15, in order to determine where the differences in outcome were. According to the Department of Finance joint report and the CYA legislative report, potential savings equals expected costs multiplied by the commitment reduction number, or:

Formula 1: Potential Savings = Expected Costs × (Expected Commitments - Actual Commitments)

It is clear that the commitment reduction number (i.e., the reduced commitments) is actually expected commitments minus the actual commitments. Therefore, formula 1 makes this substitution. From high school algebra, formula 1 can easily become transformed into:

Formula 2. Potential Savings = Expected Costs × Expected Commitments - (Expected Costs × Actual Commitments)

This official formula will lead to the same results, in practice, as if the commitment reduction number were being multiplied by the expected costs. If for example, 5,000 offenders were expected and only 3,000 were committed, then at a $6,000 career cost the formula would be solved as follows:

Formula 2. Potential Savings = ($6,000 × 5,000) - ($6,000 × 3,000)
                             = $30 million - $18 million
                             = $12 million

This result is exactly the same as using the commitment reduction number of 2,000 and multiplying by $6,000, as was done earlier. In the same fashion, the results of formula 2 would always lead to the same solution as the official method. Formula 2 and the official method are, in fact, equivalent.

In table 15 we use the following formula to compute potential savings:

Formula 3. Potential Savings = (Expected Costs × Expected Commitments) - (Actual Costs × Actual Commitments)

The major difference between formula 2 and formula 3 is obviously the substitution of actual costs for expected costs. But this difference in the two formulas is meaningful only when expected and actual costs differ. If actual costs are made equal to expected costs, regardless of the real dollar figures, formula 3 can always be used by the officials of CYA and the Department of Finance—and the results will be exactly the same as the ones they have computed by using formula 1. The earlier example, where 5,000 were expected and only 3,000 were committed—at an actual cost of $6,000—will yield a $12 million potential savings, given that actual costs equal expected costs.

It appears that the major difference between the official approach and ours does not reflect only the use of different formulas but results from a difference in what is used for *expected* costs in formula 3. The numbers and the actual costs are not in dispute—since both official reports use them in their actual computations. From our perspective the expected costs are fixed at the pre-subsidy career costs, since the subsidy payments to the county assume that the state will pay no more than $4,000 per year per reduction (the pre-subsidy CYA career cost). Just as the base commitment rate of pre-1965 furnishes a baseline for determining whether there have been more or fewer commitments since 1965, so, too, does the baseline of the fiscal cost of institutionalization furnish a measure of whether the dollar costs are more or less than in 1965.

The official method of solving formula 3 apparently permits the expected costs to slide upward continually by treating the actual as if it were the baseline to be "expected." This seems unreasonable, both logically and fiscally. If expected commitments refers to 1965—not 1970—then so should the costs of those expected commitments refer to 1965 costs—not 1970, 1980, or 1990 costs. Without fixed cost measurement, there is no logical basis for assessing whether a *later* amount is cheaper or more expensive than what occurred prior to subsidy. From a fiscal perspective, the failure to solve formula 3 in a reasonable fashion leads officials to define cost run-ups as examples of increased savings.

In order to demonstrate the profound fiscal outcomes associated with the two approaches toward defining expected cost, actual 1969–70 CYA commitment data are presented in table 16. Three time periods for assessing fiscal consequences are utilized, while the CYA commitment data are held constant. Subsidy payments to the counties are deliberately omitted to simplify the analysis.

The lefthand columns of table 16 posit that the subsidy legislation was conceived on the assumption that the expected cost to the state would be no more than $4,000 per career. Regardless of the actual increased costs used in the table, the expected 1965 career costs will not vary. The expected 1965 career costs will serve as our baseline to assess what happens when *actual costs vary* over time, but commitments remain at a 1969–70 level, for the purpose of simulating future policy outcome. Using formula 3, it is apparent that in fiscal 1969–70 there is a net cost of over $1 million; this outcome is, of course, similar to the earlier outcome reported in table 15 when actual

TABLE 16
Assessing the Fiscal Impact of Subsidy on State by Using Two Assumptions Concerning Rise in CYA Career Costs

| | Post-subsidy CYA Career Cost Policies | | | |
| | Holding Expected Costs at $4,000/Career | | Permitting Expected Costs to Rise | |
	Projected Expected Costs	Projected Actual Costs	Projected Expected Costs	Projected Actual Costs
I. CYA in 1969–70				
A. 1969–70 commitment data	5,884	4,091	5,884	4,09
B. CYA costs/career	$4,000	$6,000	$6,000	$6,00
C. Fiscal costs (A x B)	$23,536,000	$24,546,000	$35,304,000	$24,546,00
D. Annual net cost or saving available for subsidies (expected - actual)	-$1,010,000		+$10,758,000	
II. CYA-hypothetical 1984[b]				
A. 1969–70 commitment data	5,884	4,091	5,884	4,0
B. Hypothetical CYA cost/career	$4,000	$8,000	$8,000	$8,00
C. Fiscal costs (A x B)	$23,536,000	$32,728,000	$47,072,000	$32,728,00
D. Annual net cost or saving available for subsidies (expected - actual)	-$9,192,000		+$14,344,000	
III. CYA-hypothetical 1994[c]				
A. 1969–70 commitment data	5,884	4,091	5,884	4,0
B. Hypothetical CYA costs/career	$4,000	$10,00	$10,000	$10,00
C. Fiscal costs (A x B)	$23,536,000	$40,910,000	$58,840,000	$40,910,0
D. Annual net cost or saving available for subsidies (expected - actual)	-$17,365,000		+$17,930,000	
IV. Policy assessment				
A. Keeping actual costs down	Lowest cost run-up		Lowest saving	
B. Permitting actual costs to rise	Highest run-up		Highest saving	

[a]See table 14 for all cost data, except hypothetical data.
[b]1984 hypothetical *assumes* actual career cost will rise to $8,000/career cost.
[c]1994 hypothetical *assumes* actual career cost will rise to $10,000/career cost.

CYA cost rises to $6,000 per career. The joint study group, on the other hand, assumed that the expected cost should rise to equal the rising actual career costs. As a result, their expected cost is $35,304,000 (and not $23,536,000). This approach to expected costs leads to the conclusion that the state will *save* $10,758,000 when actual costs *increase* to $6,000 per career.

To obtain a better idea of what can happen if career costs are permitted to rise, two hypothetical cost figures are used—$8,000 for hypothetical 1984 and $10,000 for hypothetical 1994. In hypothetical 1984, calculations in the lefthand columns of table 16 indicate a rise in net cost to minus $9,172,000 (before paying any subsidies to the counties). But the joint study approach, shown in righthand columns, concludes that in 1984 we can expect to save plus $14,344,000. Using this method, the fiscal future is even brighter for 1994, when actual costs increase to $10,000 per career and the savings to the state mount even higher—to plus $17,930,000. A diametrically opposite conclusion, concerning the relationship between increased career costs and state savings, is reached on the left for 1994; the loss to the state will mount to over $17 million.

The fiscal logic of the joint study group is: *the lower the rise* in actual costs the *less* will be available for savings. Therefore, with the *highest actual costs* per career, the state of California can be expected to *save the most* money. When the more reasonable assumption in the lefthand columns of table 16 are used, conclusions reached are just the opposite. To keep the cost run-ups from mounting, the actual costs should be as close to $4,000 per career as possible.

Adding Up the Cost Run-ups since 1967-68

Until now the analysis has been concerned with demonstrating that rising correctional costs were undermining the intentions of the designers of subsidy. It is clear that by 1969-70 the state of California was not "earning" money to pay for its new subsidies to the counties. Actually the fiscal soundness of the offset theory was eroded a few years earlier. According to the joint study team's report, CDC career costs had risen to $8,777 per career cost as early as fiscal 1967-68 (*State of California Joint Study*, 1970, pp. 19, 20). Costs did not rise to a 50 percent increase in CYA career costs, according to available data, until 1969-70. The fiscal reasons for this discrepancy in cost run-up will be discussed in the next section. At this point, the analysis will try to locate the specific fiscal consequences of this unusual increase in career costs which occurred in such a short period of time.

If we add up the expected and actual costs associated with the 1967-68 figures, a rather stark conclusion emerges from an analysis of the data: *By the end of 1967-68, the entire cost of subsidy payments to the county was being paid out of general revenues—not from any potential savings.* The reasoning is not difficult to follow, once the fiscal facts are projected in a reasonable fashion. Table 14 shows that the CDC expected to care for 4,827 offenders in 1967-68; this would have cost the state $27,513,900 (using the 1965 career cost of $5,700). Only 3,605 offenders were actually received by CDC—but this smaller group of offenders actually cost the state $31,363,500 (using the new career cost rounded to $8,700, cited by the joint study team). In 1967-68 the state paid $3,859,600 *more* for adult corrections than it would have been paying if no reductions had occurred. This extra cost occurred *before* the state provided subsidies to the counties for sending fewer adult offenders in 1967–68. It is clear that at the adult level, by the end of 1967–68, the entire cost of subsidies to the counties had to be paid out of general funds.

In 1967–68, the cost data for the CYA are not as discrepant as for CDC. According to the *Report to the Legislature* in January, 1969, career costs had risen to $5,626 (or $5,600 for calculation purposes) (SCYA, 1969a, p. 18). In 1967–68, 4,793 youth were expected by the CYA (see table 14), but only 3,599 were actually committed. The expected costs are $19,172,000 ($4,000 per career), but the actual costs are $20,154,400 ($5,600 per career). Instead of a potential savings to pay for CYA reductions there is an increase of about $1 million in correctional costs to the state. The CYA, by 1967–68, had also stopped "earning" its share of reduced youth commitments. The conclusion that was reached earlier remains valid: by the end of 1967–68 the entire cost of the payments to the counties were paid out of general state funds. In addition, the regular correctional programs were costing the state much more than if there had been no reductions (about $5 million).

The joint study team's *Report on State Aid* and the CYA's *Report to the Legislature* could have reached this conclusion in 1970, since all of the facts were readily available by that time. Instead, they chose to make calculations that demonstrated that increased costs meant savings. The costs rose so fast that they even calculated savings after payment of subsidies that amounted to over $50 million.

According to Smith (1972, table 8, p. 68), the state of California, between 1966 and 1972, will have paid out a total of nearly $60 million in subsidy funds to the counties. However, by the end of 1967–68, according to the calculations just presented, the production of potential "offset earnings" had clearly ceased. The payments to the counties from 1966–72 were paid as if there were still earnings being produced by the state correctional agencies. Only the first year of the program can be perceived as constituting a year of savings. It is possible that even this might be an overgenerous estimate, since data about the CDC cost run-up are not readily available for fiscal 1966–67 (or even post-1968). In the first year, subsidy payments amounted to about $1.6 million (see table 14 for exact figures). If we subtract this amount from the $60 million subsidy expenditures, the remainder is about $58 million. This latter figure represents funds paid out of general state revenues, since there were no offset earnings after fiscal 1966-67 ended.

Analysis indicates that by 1969-70, the taxpayers of California were paying at least $4 million per year more (using 1967-68 CDC data) for operating their correctional agencies as a result of cost run-ups since the inception of subsidy. In addition, they were also paying over $13 million per year more for local subsidy programs than in 1965 (see table 15 for exact figures). Both of these annual costs have risen since then. In the CYA, for example, the cost per occupied bed has risen to $7,292 by 1970-71 (SCYA, 1972e, table 8, p. 68). Career costs were even higher for fiscal 1971-72. Subsidy payments to the counties in 1971-72 rose to about $17.7 million (SCYA, 1974, p. 16). The *counties* "earned" these funds by reducing commitments to the state. But the state's correctional agencies still do not have any "earnings" to match the continued rise in costs for those actually committed. Instead of costing the general revenue fund about $17 million per year as in 1969-70, it is conservatively estimated that in 1970-71 the state will be paying out over $20 million more per year for corrections than in 1965. The cost run-up appears to be escalating over time for both subsidy payments and state correctional costs.

The Fiscal Assumptions of the Cost Run-ups

The estimates of cost run-ups have not, until now, taken inflation into account. The counties have continually complained that they were being paid in 1965 dollars, while costs for local corrections had risen as a result of inflation. The joint study team paid a good deal of attention to this problem and considered various subsidy adjustment proposals. One proposal they considered, but rejected, was that the amount of subsidy be similar to the rising career costs for CYA wards. However, the joint study argued that this was too costly a formula. They said it "did not appear reasonable for the state to *absorb these higher costs per commitment* and turn around and reimburse the counties for these added costs" (State of California Joint Study, 1970, p. 48; italics added). The joint study team appeared aware that the state was indeed absorbing higher costs—even though they expressed the opposite contention in the claim of over $50 million extra savings.

Instead of recommending that the state adjust the formula

according to rising correctional costs, the joint study recommended that the rise in the Consumer Price Index be used as an adjustment factor. (Their proposal was finally accepted by the 1972 California State Legislature [SCYA, 1974, p. 6].) Their preference for this fiscal adjustment factor can be used in the correctional cost analysis. Between the time of computing the career costs (fiscal 1963-64) and the time of sharp correctional cost increases (1967-68), the Consumer Price Index was reported to have risen 10.4 percent (State of California Joint Study, 1970). The CYA cost in 1967-68 should have risen 10.4 percent of $4,000—or $416. However, instead of costing $4,416 the CYA career cost had risen to $5,626.

Similarly, it could be reasonably expected that the CDC cost should have risen by $592. In 1967-68 the CDC career cost should have been $6,292—and not $8,777. Clearly the rise in correctional costs included other fiscal assumptions than just a regular inflationary increase of the value of the correctional dollar. An examination of the official computations of the career costs reveals the underlying reasons for the noninflationary increase in correctional costs. Table 17 compares the 1963-64 and 1967-68 career costs of the CYA and CDC, by the specific categories used in the official computations. As the table indicates, the categories are identical. However, some of the correctional values attached to the categories vary, and, therefore, the fiscal values also vary. The correctional value of time to be spent in the institution, in particular, appears to have a profound impact on the fiscal values that appear in the table.

Table 17 depicts the calculation of "successful" career costs by two major dimensions: operational costs and capital outlay costs. Operational costs, for each time period, refer to salaries and wages, program equipment, staff benefits, and other operating expenses for institutions, reception centers, and parole units. The capital outlay costs refer to a prorated costing of construction, according to the cost and "life" of a correctional bed. For both the CYA and CDC, operational costs per occupied bed (computed on an annual basis) were rising faster than the cost of living index; it is about 20 percent for the CYA and about 25 percent for CDC (i.e., $965/4,500 for CYA and $560/2,000 for CDC). At the same time the "time in institution" is also rising—about 22 percent for CYA and 25 percent for CDC.

TABLE 17

Career Costs of CYA and CDC, by Components and Fiscal Years 1963-64 and 1967-68[a]

	CYA		CDC	
	1963-64	1967-68	1963-64	1967-68
Operational cost components				
Institutional cost/year	$ 4,500	$ 5,465	$ 2,050	$ 2,560
Time in institution	8 mos.	9.8 mos.	24 mos.	30 mos.
Institutional cost for time in institution	$ 3,000	$ 4,463	$ 4,100	$ 6,400
Parole costs/year	$ 300	$ 415	$ 300	$ 566
Time on Parole	24 mos.	18 mos.	24 mos.	24 mos.
Parole cost by time on parole	$ 600	$ 623	600	$ 1,132
Total operational cost	$ 3,600	$ 5,086	$ 4,700	$ 7,532
Capital outlay cost per new admission				
Cost/bed for construction	$18,000	$20,000	$15,000	$15,000
"Life" of bed	30 yrs.	30 yrs.	30 yrs.	30 yrs.
Percent of "bed life" used	2.2	2.7	6.7	8.3
Prorated capital outlay cost	$ 400	$ 540	$ 1,000	$ 1,245
Total cost (operational and capital)[b]	$ 4,000	$ 5,626	$ 5,700	$ 8,777

[a]*California's Probation Subsidy: A Report to the Legislature*, 1966-68 (Sacramento: Department of Youth Authority, 7 Jaunary 1968), table 8, p. 18.

[b]According to the source, these computations assume that the career is successful; the figures are deemed, too, to be "conservative estimates" based on a combination of 1967-68 costs.

This increase in length of institutional stay has a profound impact on the institutional cost per stay. For the CYA, the rise in this element is $1,463 more than the earlier $3,000 per stay cost or a rise of nearly 50 percent. The impact is even greater for the CDC costs, since costs per stay have risen $2,300, or nearly 60 percent. The change in the correctional assumption concerning length of stay has a direct impact on the fiscal assumption of what the operational aspects of a 1967-68 successful career will cost. It also has a direct impact on the allocation of construction costs. For the CYA, the capital outlay cost per new admission rises by $140, or about 35 percent (even though construction costs per se have risen only about 11 percent—similar to the increase in the Consumer Price Index). The CDC calculation assumes no increase in construction costs per se but estimates that the capital outlay cost per new admission will now increase by $245, or about 25 percent.

It appears evident that a potent contributor to the cost run-up in the early years of subsidy, in addition to the fact that operating costs were rising faster than the cost of living, was the lengthening of institutional stay. If the correctional assumptions concerning length of stay had remained constant, the career costs would not have risen as sharply.

It is possible, of course, that this rise in career costs is not a unique event; it might have been occurring in the pre-subsidy years as well. If this were so, then the fiscal cost run-up would have been a "normal" expectation for California corrections. Historical data for the pre-subsidy years is available for the CYA; so this line of inquiry can be pursued for young offenders.

Table 18 presents CYA data, by fiscal years that are two years apart from 1955 to 1971 (with the 1969–71 periods being the only exceptions to the time interval). The table represents an indirect approach toward obtaining historical data on career costs, since direct evidence is not available in published documents. Instead of calculating costs according to the extended career cost method, two methods of estimating institutional costs are presented, using official data. The first method is the cost per occupied bed for an average daily population for an annual period of time. The second method is based on the costs per ward paroled from the institution. This latter approach takes into account length of stay by costing operating expenses on the basis of the average number of youth *leaving*, not living in, the institutions during a year. According to the interpreters of *Some Statistical Facts on the California Youth Authority* (SCYA, 1972e, p. 27) the source of the data, the two methods of calculating cost yield the following result: "The two different methods vary according to the average length of stay of wards in institutions. Hence, when the length of stay is exactly one year, both per capita figures will be the same."

Table 18 discloses that during the pre-subsidy years the operating costs are rising on the basis of occupied beds. Over a decade, costs increased about $870 per occupied bed—from $3,131 to $4,000. This is an increase of about 27 percent for an entire decade and could quite reasonably be due to persistent inflation (the Consumer Price Index rose about 10.4 percent for only a four-year period of 1963–67).

TABLE 18
Historical Data on Average Operating Institutional Costs According to Average Cost per Bed and Average Cost per Ward Paroled[a] (in actual dollars for fiscal years)

Fiscal Periods	Average Institutional Costs	
	Costs/Occupied Bed	Costs/Ward Paroled
A. Pre-subsidy years		
1955–56	$3,131	$2,429
1957–58	$3,487	$2,387
1959–60	$3,838	$2,662
1961–62	$3,836	$2,667
1963–64	$4,001	$2,690
B. Baseline year[b]		
1965–66	$4,510	$2,714
C. Subsidy years		
1967–68	$5,465	$3,879
1969–70	$6,380	$4,879
1970–71	$7,292	$5,854

[a]Adapted from *Some Statistical Facts on the California Youth Authority* (Sacramento: Department of Youth Authority, January, 1972), table 14, p. 27.

[b]This is the last fiscal year preceeding subsidy. Careful readers will note that the cost/occupied bed is quite similar to the figure used in Table 17, even though it is supposed to represent the 1963–64 cost figure. It is also virtually similar to the cost used in the *1964 Probation Study.* Therefore, it is highly probable that the computation of a CYA career cost at $4,000/career is based on *this* fiscal year and not the 1963–64 fiscal year used by the *Report to the Legislature.*

If the baseline year is also included, the costs per occupied bed increased (from 1955 through 1966) about 44 percent for an eleven-year pre-subsidy period. In contrast, the rise for the shorter subsidy period, 1965–66 through 1970–71 (a six-year period) is $2,782, or about 62 percent. Correctional costs for operating institutions appear to be rising in both periods, but at a faster rate during the subsidy years. In the pre-subsidy years, however, costs appear to be rising at or below the rate of inflation for the eleven-year period.

Moving to the data concerning cost per ward paroled, which take into account length of stay, the trends are quite different. For the eleven-year period of 1955–56 through 1965–66, the rise in cost is only $285, or about 12 percent, probably below the rate of inflation for the same period of time. In effect, the career cost, using this indirect approach, appears to be remaining quite stable for over a decade. In the period preceding subsidy, 1959–60 through 1965–66, the cost per ward paroled varies by only $52, compared to the cost increase occurring in the cost per occupied bed for the same pre-subsidy period of seven years (about $672).

This image of stable career costs is in sharp contrast to what appears to be occurring during the six subsidy years, 1965–66 through 1970–71. The cost per ward paroled (as an indirect indicator of career costs) has risen quite sharply from $2,714 to $5,854—a difference of more than $3,000. By the end of 1971, it appears that career costs have more than doubled—an increase certainly far above any that might be ascribed to inflation or even to the rise in costs per occupied bed. The career costs during the subsidy years are, in fact, distinctly different from those during the period 1955–66.

One of the underlying fiscal assumptions of a viable subsidy program that used an offset formula would have had to include stability in career costs. Apparently, the historical experience of 1955–65 provided cogent evidence that career costs could be kept fairly stable, even though operating expenses were increasing (as indicated by the rise in cost per occupied bed). Whether the designers of probation subsidy engaged in these calculations or made these assumptions is unknown, since none of the published accounts dealing with subsidy per se discuss this issue. But, wittingly or not, the historical record indicates that career costs *could* have remained sufficiently stable, at least within the CYA correctional institutions and reception centers, provided that attention was paid to average length of stay. By not addressing this correctional assumption, the fiscal assumptions of stable career costs were drastically changed. The fiscal consequences, as we have demonstrated, have not only been historically unique, but they have been quite costly to the state.

The Fiscal Consequences of Post-subsidy Correctional Policies

Table 19 provides insight into the relative cost of pursuing three correctional policies, by directly controlling for inflation *and* other sources of increased costs (e.g., cost increases due to decreasing ward/staff ratios to 1.8:1, instead of 2.3:1). The costs of pre-subsidy and post-subsidy correctional policies, 1965, 1970, and 1971, are compared.

TABLE 19

Per Capita Career Costs for Successful CYA Careers for Three Correctional Policies (in 1965 dollars)

	1965 Policy	1970 Policy	1971 Policy
Type of costs operations			
Inst. cost/year/ward[a]	$4,500	$4,500	$4,500
Time in institution[b]	8 mos.	9.2 mos.	11.2 mos.
Institutional cost	$3,000	$3,825	$4,185
Parole costs/year/ward	$300	$300	$300
Time on parole[c]	24 mos.	27.9 mos.	28.4 mos.
Parole costs	$600	$698	$710
Total operational cost	$3,600	$4,523	$4,895
Capital outlay/admission			
Cost/bed	$18,000	$18,000	$18,000
"Life" of bed	30 years	30 years	30 years
Percent of bed life used by inmate	2.2	2.8	3.1
Prorated outlay cost/admission	$400	$504	$558
Total cost/nonrepeating new admission	$4,000	$5,027	$5,453
Cost of policy changes/career cost	-----	+$1,027	+$1,453

[a]The Board of Corrections, *1964 Probation Study* (Sacramento: Youth and Adult Corrections Agency, 7 September 1965), p. 181. All other 1965 costs are derived from this source.

[b]*CYA Annual Report, 1971* (Sacramento: Department of the Youth Authority), table 19, p. 32.

[c]Ibid., table 23, p. 35.

In reading table 19 it is important to note that the increase in per capita career costs is noninflationary, because the *costs are based on 1965 prices for all categories*. The costs rise dramatically because there are policy changes in time spent in institution, time on parole, and percentage of bed-life used by an inmate. If these values had not shifted, the per capita career costs would not have risen by $1,027 in 1970 and $1,453 in 1971.

The claim made by state officials that reduced commitments have led to operational savings for the state is, therefore, not supported by either short-run or long-run data. However, savings of operational dollars is not the only claim made regarding fiscal benefits to the state. Claims were also made regarding savings due to the closing of institutional units, the deferred use of new units, and construction of new institutions. The following analyses deal with these claims.

Assessing Savings Due to Closing of CYA Institutions

Of the total $185,978,820 savings that Smith (1972, pp. 68-70) claims are attributable to the subsidy program, two types of savings are related to facilities that actually existed during 1966-72: (1) existing institutional units that were closed; and (2) new institutional units that were completed but never used. The other savings cited by Smith refer to deferred *hypothetical* construction and operational costs. While we will deal with these hypothetical savings in a subsequent section, it is useful to point out that actual savings bear the closest relationship to the annual budgetary savings of the operating agencies. Hypothetical savings refer to future budgets and future policy choices that are implicit in the future projections about "necessary" building programs. These future policy choices have to be examined before accepting the claim that "hypothetical" buildings *had* to be built and staffed. For the existing institutional units, the empirical issue is much clearer: given that they in fact exist, is there any savings associated with closing units or deferring the use of new units?

According to Smith, over $9 million in savings can be attributed to closing institutional units for the period 1966-72; the annual actual savings are over $5 million indicating that most of the savings claimed for "closing" accrued in the last two years. The accumulated savings for institutional units built but never opened amounts to $13.8 million. The annual actual savings are $4.7 million, indicating that these savings accrued over the past three to four years.

Regarding the savings due to institutional units closed, analysis will focus exclusively on CYA operations. According to Smith's data, the CYA closed nine types of living units for a total of 720 beds during 1966-72. However, Smith neglects to mention the addition of two new unit openings that occurred during this same period. These new units added at least 762 beds to the existing operations of the CYA. The precise units that were opened and closed during this period are depicted in table 20.

The "closed out" beds listed in table 20 are taken directly from

TABLE 20
Institutional Beds Closed and Opened in CYA Institutions, 1966-72

| | Number of Beds | |
CYA Units	Closed Out[a]	Opened[b]
Fricot	220	
Spike Camps (3, with 60 beds each)	180	
Fred C. Nelles	60	
Ventura	50	
Los Guilucos	40	
Preston	90	
Paso Robles	80	
O. H. Close		379
Karl Holton		383
Totals for Each	720 beds	762 beds

[a]Figures on *closing* are taken directly from Robert L. Smith, *A Quiet Revolution: Probation Subsidy* (U.S. Government Printing Office: U.S. Department of Health, Education and Welfare, Social Rehabilitation Service, Youth Development and Delinquency Prevention Administration, DHEW Publication No. [SRS] 72-26011), table IX, p. 69.

[b]The data on *openings* are based on the following quote: "The fiscal 379-boy institution, O. H. Close School for Boys was opened in July 1966, while the second institution, Karl Holton School for Boys, is scheduled to open May 1967" (see Request by Department of Youth Authority in *State of California Support and Local Assistance Budget: For the Fiscal Year July 1, 1967 to June 30, 1968*, p. 146). The exact capacity of Holton is not indicated, but in 1970 the average daily population was 383, according to *1970 Annual Report* (State of California: Human Relations Agency, Department of Youth Authority), table 19, p. 30. According to this latter source, Holton officially opened in July 1967—not May 1967, as planned. The capacity of Holton may be 400, but the most precise figure available, 383, has been used in the assessment of closings and openings.

A third facility, DeWitt Nelson, opened in December 1971, but is not included in this calculation because it is discussed in the following section on "Deferred Openings." This facility houses at least 289 wards, and would have raised the total openings to 1,051—rather than 762 (see text).

Smith's data. However, the "opened" beds—on the righthand
side of the table—are derived from the separate official sources
listed. The first new unit, O. H. Close, opened on the starting date
of the subsidy program, 1 July 1966. The second, Karl Holton,
was scheduled to open in May 1967 but did not begin operation
until July 1967. Karl Holton housed an average daily population
of 383 wards in 1970 and 378 in 1971; O. H. Close housed an
average of 359 wards in 1970 and 344 in 1971 (SCYA, 1972*a*).
Apparently both units were being used up to 90 percent of their
full capacities in 1970 and 1971 (using the figures in table 20 as
the capacity figures).

However, there exists evidence that the Karl Holton School for
Boys was opened prematurely, thus increasing the start-up costs
of this new facility. In fiscal 1968–69 the legislative analyst
reported to the California Joint Legislative Budget Committee the
following:

The Karl Holton School for Boys, six months after opening, is
operating at approximately one-half capacity and is projected to
continue at this level for the remainder of the fiscal year.
Based on prior operating experience, the agency could
conceivably have delayed opening this facility for the entire fiscal
year 1967–68. Therefore, a substantial sum has and will be
expended to operate the Karl Holton School because of the
overprojection of population and other administrative decisions
regarding the housing of wards. [California Joint Legislative
Budget Committee, 1968–69, p. 139]

Cost problems continued to plague the new school. In fiscal
1969–70, the legislative analyst commented:

It is noted that the population report for January 17, 1969,
reflects that the agency has opened a fifth cottage at the Karl
Holton School. At that time this 50-boy unit was housing
approximately 22 wards, assuming the other four cottages were at
capacity. At this same time, there was ample capacity at other
facilities to handle this population. [Ibid., 1969–70, p. 170]

In reporting savings due to closing institutions, Smith omitted
any reference to either O. H. Close or Karl Holton; in addition, he
omitted the suggestion that the CYA was experiencing fiscal
difficulties in adapting to reduced initial commitments. As a
result, budgetary critics, like the legislative analyst to the Joint
Legislative Budget Committee, could point out opportunities for

savings that were missed. It appears quite evident that the addition of at least 762 beds, plus extended start-up costs for at least two fiscal years (1967 and 1968) at one new unit, more than offset the potential savings associated with the 720 closings cited by Smith. The analysis of "closings" indicates a net *gain* of at least 42 beds between 1966 and 1972. In addition, these 762 new beds appeared to have been added prior to the closings cited by Smith.

Savings Due to Deferred Openings

According to Smith, two new facilities had been constructed by the CYA but had never been opened as of fiscal 1971–72. One facility, an older boys' reception center, was designed to house wards who had previously been processed at a Department of Correction institution. The annual saving for not operating this reception center-clinic at the existing Southern California Youth Center, in Ontario, was cited by Smith as $2.5 million. The accumulated savings, up to 1971–72, was $5 million, indicating it had been closed for two years. (It is quite likely that this figure follows the practice of using post-subsidy costs rather than 1965 costs. The basis for projecting the costs is not cited by Smith.) There is evidence in the 1971 and 1972 CYA *Annual Reports* that Department of Correction Reception Centers were being phased out for use by CYA wards. It is therefore likely that in 1971–72 some use was being made of the Ontario Reception Center Clinic. However, the data on the Southern Reception Center Clinic (SRCC) are not broken down by living units, so that we cannot directly document this hypothesis.

The evidence is much firmer regarding the second facility cited by Smith (1972, p. 69), the De Witt Nelson School at Stockton, designed to "train older youths for camp placement." According to the legislative analyst, De Witt Nelson was scheduled to open in fiscal 1969–70, but its opening was delayed. Smith indicates that the annual savings for De Witt Nelson is $2.2 million and the accumulated savings is $8.8 million (through fiscal 1971–72). However, according to a CYA report, *Characteristics of California Youth Authority Wards, December 31, 1971*, De Witt Nelson had, on this date, housed 36 youth (SCYA, 1971*b*, p. 6). In the following year's report, *Characteristics of California Youth Authority Wards, June 30, 1972*, De Witt Nelson is listed as housing, on this date, *289* wards (SCYA, 1972*b*, p. 5). Instead of four years of accumulated savings, it is clear that only 1968–69 and 1969–70 can be counted as potential years of savings. But if these presumed savings are balanced by the 1966 and 1967 opening of Close and Holton, the savings attributable to deferred use appear to vanish, for the 720 "closed out" beds were mainly phased out *after* 1969–70.

On balance, it also appears that in 1971–72 there were probably no current savings that could be attributed to deferred use. De Witt Nelson was operating, and probably offset any savings that might be occurring due to deferred use of the Ontario Reception Center Clinic. Meanwhile, of course, the state of California has increased the number of CYA institutional beds since 1965. Close and Holton's openings netted at least 42 operational beds; and De Witt Nelson apparently has at least 289 beds. This represents a net gain of at least 331 operational CYA beds now operating at higher costs than the costs of the pre-subsidy beds phased out by the CYA.

Assessing Hypothetical New Construction Savings

Smith claims that $160 million of the hypothetical savings can be attributed to the delay and slowdown in fulfilling the master plan (see chapter 7), wherein projections were based on population growth and "standards" about length of stay. As was suggested in chapter 7, the master plan lacked a sound empirical basis. It could have been eliminated without a subsidy program, and there is scant justification for considering its deferral as savings attributable to subsidy. The master plan was an untenable policy in 1960. To project 1972 savings for abandoning a policy that was ill-founded in 1960 is an unreasonable approach to assessing costs and benefits.

Fiscal Consequences of Increased Detention

This chapter has focused primarily on the increased fiscal costs incurred at the state level of youth corrections. However, increased costs probably occurred at the county level, too, but for different reasons. Counties, as discussed in chapter 7, had increased their rates of institutionalization, while simultaneously reducing their commitments to state facilities. The increased use of detention was particularly noteworthy, since it rose by nearly 50 percent from the pre-subsidy year of 1965. This rise had fiscal consequences for the county, as well as providing an increased chance of lockup for local youth.

In 1970 the rate of institutional youth days had increased by 16,050 days per 100,000 youth aged ten to seventeen. In 1967 it is conservatively estimated that detention cost at least $15 per youth day (National Council, 1970, p. 100). Projecting these figures for a youth population at risk of 3,084,000 (State of California Department of Justice, 1970*a*, p. 5), the excess detention cost would have been about $7.4 million (i.e., 494,982 youth days multiplied by $15 per day). In 1970 counties received about $14.5 million (SCYA, 1974, p. 18). For the counties these calculations lead to the conclusion that about one-half of their "earnings" were being used to subsidize increased detention. The rise in local social control had fiscal, as well as social, consequences.

Summary and Conclusions

Major attention in this chapter has been given to the claims of fiscal savings due to probation subsidy. State officials claim that over $50 million has been saved in operating expenses, that millions of additional dollars were saved by closing down institutions and not using recently built units, and that the biggest savings had been realized because of deferred construction. Upon close and detailed analysis, none of these claims were substantiated. Instead, it was concluded that cost run-ups in operating state correctional institutions had eroded the offset formula by the beginning of fiscal 1967–68. Beginning in fiscal 1967–68 the state had ceased to "earn" money to pay for county subsidies, and all payments from that date were undoubtedly coming from general state revenues. Officials were unable to reach this reasonable conclusion, partly because of a faulty methodology in computing state "earnings." Instead of calculating a cost run-up of over $50 million, they claimed savings of that amount.

Regarding the closing of institutional units, available official data clearly indicated that the CYA more than offset these losses by adding two large, new institutions to their correctional complex. In addition, new units that were reported to be empty in 1972 were undoubtedly in operation by the end of 1971. The CYA entered 1972 with a minimum of 331 more institutional beds than were in existence in 1965, the last pre-subsidy year.

The hypothetical savings of deferred construction proved to

be based on correctional assumptions that were not sustained by empirical evidence or reasonableness. The hypothetical need for continuing an ill-founded master plan was found to be based on a philosophy of strengthening and intensifying institutionalization—even though neither the CYA nor any other American correctional organization has ever been able to demonstrate that this type of correctional policy has ever been effective in reducing delinquency (see chapter 7 for documentation).

Interspersed in various CYA documents are three types of reasons for strengthening and intensifying the correctional programs and thereby justifying higher fiscal expenditures. The reasons advanced pertain to a need to adhere to correctional standards, the problem of correcting a population that is more delinquent and disturbed, and the interest of pursuing organization survival. The discretionary choices that were made on behalf of these reasons yielded fiscal as well as social consequences.

One critical standard reflected in the CYA master plan referred to the ideal length of stay for older wards housed in Department of Correction facilities. According to this standard, older youth required about eleven months of institutional treatment. With the advent of subsidy and the reduction of juvenile court commitments, older youth were deliberately diverted back into the CYA program. With reduced pressure on bed space, these older youth could be institutionalized according to the ideal length of stay—approximately eleven months. By 1971 the average length of stay for all CYA wards had increased from 8 to 11.2 months. Holding 1965 dollars constant, this increase in length of stay is capable of accounting for about a 35 percent rise in per capita career costs.

The second reason advanced for strengthening and intensifying CYA corrections is based on a belief that the newer population mix constituted a higher-risk group than those received in pre-subsidy years. It was argued that this group required a lengthier period of institutional treatment. This argument appears to buttress the idea of a standard concerning older offenders, since the newer population mix had a higher proportion of youth sentenced from the criminal courts. It is of interest to note that empirical evidence fails to sustain that length of institutional stay is associated with correctional effectiveness. In addition, the high risk argument also fails to be supported by empirical evidence; the post-subsidy population mix does not appear to constitute a higher-risk group. In fact, there are indications that the group might constitute a lower-risk group. It is evident, too, that whether youth are institutionalized for longer stays because of a belief in dangerousness or because of adherence to an ideal standard, the fiscal consequences may be quite similar.

The third reason for intensifying CYA corrections is based on organizational needs, rather than on presumed offender needs or characteristics. According to Smith, reduced commitments posed a threat to organizational survival. It is not unreasonable to hypothesize that, threatened with the loss of their jobs, personnel might make correctional choices that were influenced by their own interests, rather than public or youth interests. If survival rather than expansion of interests were at stake then the data should reflect a stability or shrinking of organizational resources. The evidence indicates that some expansion occurred in the post-subsidy period, and that the survival argument may not be an adequate explanation of what occurred.

It is an interesting fact that the average daily population was quite stable between 1965 and 1970—fluctuating between approximately 5,100 and 5,400. Even in fiscal 1970-71 the figure was about 4,900—only 200 below fiscal 1964-65. These figures indicate that the CYA was able to adapt to reduced commitments by increasing its share of older youth (who were formerly placed in the Department of Correction facilities). If the number of staff had remained at 1965 levels, then the ward-staff ratio would have been virtually identical in the fiscal years 1964-65 and 1970-71. However, the number of staff increased, thereby reducing the ward-staff ratio to a historic low of 1.8:1. While the rate of staff increase was 20 percent in the post-subsidy period as compared to a pre-subsidy rate of 37 percent, the fact remains that a substantial increase did occur. In addition to this expansion of a correctional resource, the CYA also phased into operation 331 more beds than were phased out. The increase in staff and beds are signs of organizational expansion rather than indications of an organization struggling for survival.

The expansion of organizational resources contributed to the increase in aggregate and per capita costs. It is difficult to understand why these increased costs were necessary if survival had been the primary concern. It appears that the organization could have continued to survive if staff and beds had remained as stable as the average daily population. Perhaps an organization that had experienced a steady rise in organizational resources, over an extended period of time, could only think of the future in terms of expansion rather than survival.

The fact that the run-up in fiscal and social costs fails to be supported by empirical evidence does not mean that the correctional rationales are unimportant. These rationales provided the legitimation for making critical discretionary choices. The evidence suggests that occupational preferences and the promotion of organizational interests can influence correctional decisions, independent of any empirical data. It is quite conceivable that the personnel who helped to design the master plan based on correctional standards believed in the necessity of directing the organization according to occupational ideals. Many CYA personnel may also have believed that older youth would be more dangerous to the community if released after eight months instead of eleven. It was in the organization's interest, too, to continue to expand in order to realize the ideals of what constituted an optimum institutional treatment program.

Even if the promotion of occupational ideology and CYA organizational interests were not supported by empirical data, the acceptance of their arguments by the legislative budget committees and the executive branch provided social and fiscal legitimation for a policy of "strengthening and intensification of institutionalization." In 1963–64, the year of the critical subsidy study, a weaker institutional policy yielded an operating budget of about $20 million. By fiscal 1969–70, the stronger institutional policy yielded a support budget of $33.9 million (SCYA, 1972e, p. 27). The acceptance of the post-subsidy institutionalization policy by the executive branch and the legislature proved to be quite costly—about 69 percent more expensive. The per capita rise also reflects this increase in aggregate operating costs. An organization interested only in adaptive survival could have maintained a correctional/budgetary status quo by receiving an increase based on inflation alone—about 21.4 percent, according to the rise in the Consumer Price Index from 1963–64 through 1969–70 (State of California Joint Study, 1970, Appendix L-1).

The difference between a CYA fiscal increase of 69 percent

and one of 21 percent (between 1963-64 and 1969-70) could be perceived as the extra cost to the state of having accepted the arguments that legitimated a policy of strength and intensification. In fiscal 1969-70 the one-year difference between a CYA policy of strength or adaptive survival amounted to about $9.6 million ($13.9 minus $4.3 million). This noninflationary increase excludes the additional $13.3 million subsidy paid to the counties in the same fiscal year.

In practice, the state correctional organization received an extra $9.6 million in 1969-70 without penalizing the counties. The counties, in turn, received $13.3 million from the state for an intensification of local corrections, without penalizing the CYA. Each participating correctional system was able to intensify its control/treatment efforts fairly autonomously, since intersystem cooperation was required at only one critical decision point— county commitment to the state's authority. All other correctional decision points indigenous to each system were open to discretionary choices. These choices appear to have been influenced by occupational preferences and organizational interests. In addition, external constraints may have occurred where specific decision points were shared with other systems, as in the cases of local detention and police referrals to court.

The discretionary choices, at the state and county levels, produced a total statewide increase in the dominance of social control. While the additional social control also increased the total fiscal bill for the state, it is quite evident that correctional interests per se did not suffer. The CYA expanded its organizational resources and operating budget during the post-subsidy period. The county correctional systems experienced a comparable expansion, even though one-half of its new operating funds may have been expended for increased rates of detention. The fiscal answer to the traditional policy question, *cui bono*, seems clear: the primary beneficiaries of the post-subsidy period are the state and county correctional systems rather than the citizens of California.

9   Probation Subsidy: Issues
for Correctional Policy

The designers of probation subsidy, like the designers of the Community Treatment Project, were more interested in promoting a specific program than in inaugurating broad policy changes. The initiators of CTP appear to have been primarily interested in demonstrating the effectiveness of a new diagnostic typology and a differential treatment strategy; the designers of subsidy appear to have been primarily interested in obtaining state funds to strengthen and expand county probation services. In carrying out their program strategies, each relied on obtaining the cooperation of key decision makers to divert offenders from traditional institutional programs. National correctional leaders have perceived each of these program strategies as viable examples of community treatment, probably because they involve this diversionary characteristic. Outside observers also believe that each strategy has demonstrated effectiveness, including savings in social and economic costs. But detailed analyses of each strategy indicate that this outside approbation is premature.

Our assessment was made on the basis of what actually occurred, rather than on the basis of self-proclaimed success. The outcomes found in our analyses may not have been intended, but this does not erase the empirical reality of altered modes of social control and cost run-ups. If we address these findings as policy issues, we may be able to devise less costly strategies in the future.

Temporary Detention and Probation Subsidy

Part 1 suggested that reasonable evidence existed for believing that special CYA parole projects, like CTP, had not only inaugurated the extensive use of detention for treatment reasons, but had taught and legitimated this practice to the entire CYA parole program. It was also pointed out that this expansion of detention for treatment purposes did not apparently occur until the middle of 1968, approximately two years after the initiation of subsidy operations. During those two years initial commitments to the CYA had been reduced; in 1966-67 there were 460 fewer commitments than expected, while in fiscal 1967-68 there were 1,194 fewer commitments than expected (see chapter 8). These reductions occurred while the CYA was opening up two new, large institutional facilities, O. H. Close and Karl Holton. The available bed space in early fiscal 1968 must have been quite substantial, since the CYA did not begin the phasing out of other sizable institutional units until *after* fiscal 1969-70 (see data tables and discussion in chapter 8).

This availability of bed space removed one of the primary constraints from using temporary detention as a method of treatment on a larger scale. The CYA Task Force on Detention, in 1966, had identified some of the following factors as limiting the effective use of "therapeutic detention": availability of bed space; time and distance; and release procedures and timing (see chapter 3). Not only were beds probably available in 1968, but they were also potentially available in the north, around Sacramento, and in the south, around the Los Angeles area.

As noted in part 1, the policy of permitting regular parole agents to use detention for treatment purposes had been officially inaugurated by August 1968. The link between "special projects," like CTP, and regular parole was explicitly noted in the memorandum sent by the former Operations Chief of CTP to all CYA parole units. Without any change in the release procedures, but by the provision of beds, use of CYA institutions for "parole detention" rose sharply in 1968 and 1969. In September 1969, Section 29 was officially incorporated into the CYA *Board Policy*

Manual, thus making it easier both to "sign in" and "sign out" youth.

Another official reason for inaugurating detention—placement in detention prior to receiving a formal suspension/revocation hearing at a reception clinic—occurred at about this date, but this development appears unrelated to CTP. It is reasonable to conjecture that the requirement of being placed in detention at a clinic may have also been influenced by available bed space.

This flexible use of parole detention indicates that *a policy of lengthened institutional stay had been combined with a parole policy that involved a higher rate of short-term detention.* In 1965 there were 580 detention admissions out of a total parole caseload (as of the census day, 30 June 1965) of 13,544—or a rate of 4.3 per 100 youth on parole; by 1968 there were 1,627 detentions out of 14,383—or a rate of 11.3 per 100 parole youth; and by 1971 there were 2,902 detentions out of 13,330—or a rate of 21.8 per 100 parole youth (SCYA, 1971*a*, p. 42; SCYA, 1972*d*, pp. 9–10).

It is unknown how many youth may experience each type of detention while on parole, how many times they may experience each type, or how long the average detention stay may be for each type. However, the chances of being placed in detention while technically on parole or suspended parole status have certainly increased since 1965. Besides the rule changes of 1968 and 1969, the increase in the availability of bed space, and the geographical spread of these new resources, another factor may have increased the relative chances of being placed in detention, that is, the lengthening of the average time that wards remained officially on parole.

An increase in parole time occurred both for "nonviolators" and "violators." The mean time on parole for nonviolators was 24.9 months in 1965, 25.9 months in 1968, and 28.4 months in 1971. For violators, the parole time to revocation or dishonorable discharge increased from 12.8 months in 1965 to 18.7 months in 1971 (SCYA, 1971*a*, p. 35). On the basis of the CTP data, it seems reasonable to expect that the longer the period of "intensive supervision," the greater the average number of detentions per ward. However, detention per ward is not likely to be as high as occurred in the CTP for three reasons: (1) the ratio of wards to agents is probably closer to 45–50 to 1 than to 8–12 to 1, thus limiting the agent's available time per ward to use detention for treatment purposes; (2) while institutional resources are available in the north and south, they are not equally accessible to all parole centers; and (3) county detention facilities may not be as readily available as they were in Stockton and San Francisco.

The availability of CYA institutional resources is, of course, related to the apparent success of subsidy in reducing first commitments. This availability may also have aided in duplicating another set of CTP characteristics. For the first time since 1960, parole violations, as measured at fifteen months' exposure time, displayed a drop in the violation rate. Between 1960 and 1969 the violation rate had remained rather stable—fluctuating between 44.6 percent and 46.8 percent (SCYA, 1971a, p. 38). Since the rate dropped for both males and females and for both juvenile court and criminal court commitments, it is likely that these variables are not the primary causes for the overall changes in violation rate. In view of the findings of past acceptable research studies, as well as the pertinent findings that emerged from a reanalysis of CTP data, it appears quite reasonable to assume that *adult decision-making behavior* has been shifted. The 1971 CYA *Annual Report* stated that short-term detention is being increasingly used "in lieu of revocation" (SCYA, 1971a, p. 42). In addition, parole agents and CYA board members are probably exercising their discretion and behaving in a manner similar to the CTP experience; they are probably recommending fewer "revokes." And predictably, the organization may soon claim "success"—as if it were responsible for changing *youth behavior*. The claim will probably be based on strengthened institutional programs and an improved parole service—both made possible by reduced commitments (SCYA, 1971a, foreword).

There is, of course, nothing intrinsically wrong with substituting short-term detention for parole revocation. Many revocations are associated with renewed longer-term institutional stays that are unable to demonstrate "success" and are certainly more costly. But some revocation proceedings involve dishonorable discharge to county authorities, where the length of stay may be a good deal shorter. In the absence of clear and convincing evidence, it may be inappropriate to assume automatically that the "excess" of institutional days associated with increased detention is clearly outweighed by the "savings" attributable to lower parole violation rates. In addition, the increase in the *initial* institutional stay must also be taken into account in calculating a comprehensive balance sheet of institutionalization. The CTP data also indicate that many cases of temporary detention initiated by parole agents may be dictated by unclear and arbitrary criteria, without adequate independent review. Therefore, social and economic costs, as well as potential social and economic benefits, must be assessed in order to reach a reasonable conclusion concerning the new CYA institutional-parole policy. At present the requisite data are not publicly available.

While outsiders await the necessary data to assess the new parole policy, it might be useful to interested observers for the reports to include data concerning *youth behavior* for all paroled youth—unmarred by the discretionary decisions of parole agents and CYA board members or representatives—for various time periods, by age and sex. If this is done, we can distinguish between the issues of effectiveness, public risk, economic costs, and altered modes of social control. As noted in part 1, it is quite possible that while programs may be equally ineffective, comparisons on other grounds may yield empirical evidence that benefits are greater than those of past policies that relied on other types of control/treatment "packages."

Discretion and State Corrections

The subsidy years, 1966–71, were marked by a number of significant correctional choices: (1) institutional stay was lengthened from 8 months to 11.2 months in the CYA, and from 30 to at least 36 months in the CDC; (2) extra bed capacity, in the CYA, was permitted to outweigh the number of beds phased out; (3) the hiring of new CYA staff continued to increase, while the ratio of staff to wards was decreased; (4) the time on parole was lengthened in the CYA, from 24.9 months to 28.4 months; and (5) the rate of parole detention in the CYA was markedly increased. None of the decisions were required by law. In this sense these choices are examples of discretionary decision making in corrections. The Welfare and Institutions Code does not specify the rate of police referrals to a juvenile court, nor does it regulate increases or decreases in length of stay, bed capacity, staff/ward ratios, length of parole, and use of parole detention.

Since all of these choices can affect either the fiscal or social costs of institutionalization, they constitute major policy decisions. The fact that they were apparently instituted so easily, without opposition (except for objections to the premature phasing in of beds or institutional units by the legislative analyst's office), indicates that discretion at the state level of corrections is also fairly broad. This discretionary power can be assessed from two perspectives: first, at the level of the specific choices that were made, whether they were reasonable; and second, whether the mechanisms for developing and monitoring policy decisions are appropriate.

Regarding specific discretionary choices, it is evident that none of the costly decisions can be justified on the basis of available empirical evidence. An earlier chapter has analyzed the CYA budgetary claim that there was a need for the "strengthening and intensification of institutionalization." There is no need to repeat the arguments or the array of evidence that fail to support the specific decisions that implemented this general correctional philosophy. Even if administrators and legislators are unwilling to address the social costs of these discretionary decisions, it would seem reasonable that the fiscal consequences might be worth questioning. The analysis leaves little doubt that these choices have provided a potent contribution to the erosion of the expected correctional savings that were intended to offset the payments to the counties. In addition, these choices increased the actual costs of operating the institutions. Not only has the fiscal cost run-up been prodigious, but the trend will probably continue, unless changes are made regarding the specific decisions affecting operating costs. It seems odd that these facts have not been publicly recognized. If there is explicit recognition of the fiscal problem, remedies can be proposed and discussed.

One remedy, declaring a moratorium on subsidy payments, would probably be politically unfeasible and might yield undesired consequences. The counties would probably be dissatisfied with this solution, even if several years of "bail out" time were offered. They might even retaliate by increasing their commitments to the state in excess of the base-rate years. If this occurred, the state could reduce per capita fiscal costs. This reduction would have been purchased at the expense of many unnecessary commitments and cooperative state-county relations. It is unlikely that many proponents could be found to back this type of remedy.

A second remedy could involve a freeze on state construction and operating costs. This remedy would slow down the cost run-up. This remedy, of course, would not antagonize the counties, since subsidy payments would continue for reduced commitments. However, it would not provide any reduction in current level of costs; instead, it might lower the *rate* of the increase in costs.

A third remedy could attempt a policy of rolling back operating costs of the CYA to 1965 per capita levels. If state officials are interested in more than just halting immediate cost run-ups due to *state* action, then obvious choices for generating lower operating costs are precisely those discretionary decisions that helped push the costs up initially. This fiscal pruning would not have to be done blindly; instead, the state might have the minimum goal of reducing institutional stays, staff/ward ratios, bed capacity, and length of parole to 1965 levels. Executing this roll-back policy could, of course, involve severe organizational consequences. In order not to impose undue personal and organizational costs, consideration might have to be given to reaching these discrete roll-back goals over several years rather than in one fiscal year. This policy of "roll-back moderation" would also involve costs to inmates and to the state.

A successful CYA roll-back policy could halt the state run-up in costs, but it would not, in and of itself, restore the offset formula that had been eroded. Subsidy is related to the CDC as well as to the CYA. Therefore, it is also necessary to address the correctional choices that have been made in the adult sector. State officials might have more difficulty in rolling back the adult organizations because of possible opposition from citizen groups. After all, hadn't they recently been told that the newest state inmates were more dangerous than in past years? It is not as easy to roll back *fears* as it is to roll back fiscal *costs*—and rolling back costs may not be so easy either.

If a real roll-back policy evokes interest-centered opposition that cannot be overcome, then a fourth remedy might merely attempt to stabilize the annual costs of the subsidy program. It is quite conceivable that a ceiling for subsidy payments could be set, while simultaneously attempting to restrict further cost increases at a state correctional level. The myth of offset earnings could still be maintained, but legislative and executive attention would be directly focused on actual, rather than expected, costs. This

remedy may appear politically attractive, since there are indications that some counties may have reached their own self-
designated ceilings on commitment reductions (e.g., Los Angeles
county). From a county perspective, obtaining yearly subsidy
dollars from the state at 1973–74 levels, with appropriate adjust-
ments for price increases, would provide a welcome stability in
fiscal planning. This remedy could be worked out informally,
without requiring an embarrassing public announcement that
"earnings" were being limited.

The remedy of merely holding down *future* CYA and subsidy
cost rises appears pragmatic, politically feasible, and highly
probable.

In contrast, a fifth remedy, based on unorthodox but rigorous
rationality, could also be considered for discussion. Perhaps after
thinking the unthinkable and performing the impossible—rolling
back correctional policies, at a state level, to 1965 conditions—
attention might be addressed to generating actual offset savings
by engaging in a "strategy of search." A minimum strategy of
search, it will be recalled, should be guided by three interrelated
assumptions (see chapter 5): (1) current efforts are *ineffective*,
until proved otherwise by competent, well-designed research that
can withstand the scrutiny of the social science community;
(2) new proposals for experimentation (with due regard for
human dignity and ethics) must *actually* cost less on a per capita
basis than a base-year of institutional and parole per capita costs;
(3) institutional and parole programs must be *frozen* at predetermined base-year per capita levels (making due allowance for
inflation and mandatory expenses).

These proposals are similar to those that emerged from an
analysis of CTP cost run-ups (as of 1965). If state officials had
been regulated by these three interlocking proposals, the subsidy
years might not have been marked by a precipitous rise in
fiscal costs. These fiscal constraints can possibly prevent the
inauguration of new unsound correctional policies.

It is evident that the designers of subsidy assumed effectiveness
at the county level, controlled payments for the new programs at
1965 cost levels, but *paid no attention to the third assumption—
the need for control of state institutional costs*. The designers of
subsidy were aware of discretion at the county level, but
apparently overlooked the fact that the CYA and CDC could be

as discretionary as county judges and probation officers. Controlling only *one* discretionary decision point does not appear to be a sound basis for designing an economically reasonable correctional policy. Unless the discretionary actions of state correctional organizations are taken into account, the offset strategy is likely to continue to boomerang.

Utilizing Correctional Research

The CYA probably supports more correctional research than any other state in the country and distributes many research reports (SCYA, 1972*f*). This policy should be continued. However, many of the CYA's recent policies do not appear to be informed by acceptable studies emanating from criminological and correctional research. Earlier chapters have disclosed that: (1) the CYA initiated a master building plan that assumed a desired length of stay—but there is no acceptable evidence that supports that any length of stay is associated with successful outcomes; (2) the CYA lengthened institutional stay after subsidy—but did not utilize its own research findings concerning the new population mix or earlier studies regarding length of stay; (3) the CYA set a probation standard of fifty wards to an officer—but every acceptable study of reduced caseloads has failed to demonstrate any impact on outcome; and (4) the CYA extended the length of parole—but there are no acceptable studies that demonstrate that this variable has any demonstrable relationship to outcome.

The evidence indicates that policy is being formed and executed without utilizing existing research that meets the standards of the social science community, and this has proven costly. In addition, given the outcomes of past research, which failed to demonstrate correctional effectiveness, the current policies are quite likely to demonstrate the null hypothesis once again. The 1973–74 evaluation of subsidy versus regular probation is a current example, since neither program proved to be superior (SCYA, 1974, p. 39).

It seems highly probable that if a sample of California's esteemed criminologists and sociologists had been queried between 1960 and 1970, they would have advised against adding to institutional capacity, lengthening institutional stay, extending parole time, or believing that reducing probation caseloads or supervisory span of control had any demonstrable impact. The social scientists would probably have relied on their knowledge of studies that had been conducted with California populations or in California correctional settings, as well as other studies.

Many articles, books, and monographs conclude by suggesting more research. While it is difficult to quarrel with this policy, provided we are not continually studying variations of ineffective correctional technologies, it is evident that the critical decision makers appear unaware or do not utilize existing research. How to get critical organizational decision makers to use what has been studied so that decisions are better informed is an important policy issue. One strategy might be to make certain that there is an *outside*, independent review body that relies on social science evidence to make program and policy assessments. In self-defense, the program organization might begin to utilize available knowledge in an effort to stave off expected criticisms. In turn, organizational rebuttals could improve the level of policy assessments. At present, neither the structure nor the reward system appears to encourage utilization of prior knowledge. If this state of affairs continues, we may often find past failures functioning simply with new program names—and at an increased price.

Discretion and County Corrections

The designers of subsidy were not primarily interested in reducing institutionalization. Reduced commitments were a "fortuitous spin-off" of the primary achievement—obtaining state aid for county corrections. However, when subsidy is viewed as a community treatment strategy, it is assumed that institutionalization will, in fact, be reduced. The evidence indicates that discretion was also exercised at the county level regarding the multiple uses of detention.

Detention, unlike state commitments, involves a different set of decision makers. It involves police officers and probation officers, as well as judges. Some cases of detention are also due to courtesy requests from parole officers and other jurisdictions, but these are obviously a minute portion of the admissions in a year.

Subsidy legislation was not designed to regulate detention admissions. Counties were not penalized for using detention. In theory, they could even be rewarded for incorporating detention as part of a reimbursable subsidy program (but there is no firm evidence regarding this potential use). The evidence indicates that detention tended to accompany police referrals and outpaced probation decisions to file petitions. Post hoc reasons for this were offered, but the important issue for correctional policy is whether this mode of discretionary social control should continue to increase. If the issue is not addressed, the savings realized regarding institutionalization at a state level can be offset by an excessive rise in detention, and a portion of subsidy funds can be indirectly diverted to pay for increased use of detention.

Detention for juveniles is similar, in many respects, to city and county jails for adults. Both are much less noted, studied, or written about in the correctional literature than state institutions. The community treatment literature, either implicitly or explicitly, refers to diversion from state facilities. Yet it is apparent that more California youth experienced detention than state institutionalization (see chapter 7). Not only are more persons detained locally than incarcerated in state institutions, but in California more youth are detained than even appear in court on a formal petition. A deinstitutionalization strategy that misses the majority of a target population appears to be an unreasonable correctional policy.

The general empirical evidence concerning detention is quite sparse. However, we know of no study that clearly demonstrates that detention accomplishes any of the goals that are stated in the Welfare and Institutions Code of California. The evidence of our analyses indicates that: (1) the rate of detention can rise without an increase in the arrest rate; (2) the majority of detentions do not involve formal court petitions; (3) the majority of detentions are for "delinquent tendencies"; and (4) the majority of detentions are for either "delinquents without crimes" (i.e., delinquent tendencies or administrative/other reasons) or "crimes without victims" (e.g., drug offenses). These appear to be unreasonable consequences of county detention policies.

However, venturesome subsidy policy advocates could propose an interim remedy; namely, that the payments to the county include a CYA "standard" that the detention rate of each county be frozen at a predetermined level. Besides halting the increase in institutionalization and the fiscal diversion of subsidy funds, this new standard might even aid in the further "professionalization" of probation practice. Neither the legislation nor the CYA's discretionary power would prevent the imposition of this standard, any more than they appear to influence the choice of the existing standards. At present, the CYA standards theoretically encourage detention when youngsters are on probation. Perhaps these standards could be used to *discourage* all types of detention and could begin to inaugurate a significant reduction in rates of institutionalization and institutional youth days.

Standards, like discretionary decision making, can be used for a variety of purposes. During the subsidy years, probation standards have been used to institute organizational reforms. They can also be used to institute substantive reforms, if administrators are willing to focus on decisional points of discretion that affect overall rates of institutionalization—rather than on the single discretionary point that involves a reduction in state commitments.

Professionalization and Social Control

Both the CTP and probation subsidy strategies were implemented by trained correctional workers, and both programs were associated with increases in the use of institutionalization as a type of social control. This outcome casts doubt on one of the basic assumptions of American correctional ideology—namely, that the greater the degree of training and professionalization that organizational personnel possess, the greater the degree of correctional treatment that will occur. The findings of this study suggest an alternate hypothesis—namely, that the *greater degree of training and professionalization that organizational personnel possess, the greater the degree of correctional social control that will occur.*

The practice of therapeutic detention in the CTP and its widespread adoption within the CYA parole organization indicate that the hypothesis is worth pursuing. The increase in the length of institutional stay within the CYA, when extra bed capacity made it possible, also indicates it is worth pursuing. The increasing rates of detention at a county level, even though probation departments were being specifically subsidized to improve and strengthen local treatment services, should also be taken into account. While each example may have been affected by other variables, like available resources, it is of some interest *how* resources were used.

Perhaps California is unique in this regard, but we doubt that this is the case. Indirect evidence from another affluent state (New York), conducted with a post-1955 sample, indicates that one of the most esteemed, professionally operated correctional programs was also associated with greater reliance on institution-alization. This study, which I myself conducted, found that highly selected boys that were sent to a private residential treatment center and completed "treatment," stayed an average of two and a half years; those that did not complete treatment and were sent back to the courts as organizational "failures" stayed an average of sixteen months. At the same time, the less professionalized state institution only kept nonselected boys for an average of nine months. The post-release results were similar when all sources of "failure" were taken into account.

There are other data regarding professionalization and in-creased social control. Wilson (1968), for example, found that police arrest and referral rates were much higher in profession-alized departments than in backward, untrained organizations. He also found that the policy orientation of the trained chiefs of the departments influenced the rates of social-control processing. Since police chiefs could, and did, influence police officer behavior, there were differences between professionalized depart-ments. But professionalized departments, regardless of orienta-tion, produced sharply different arrest and referral rates. In another study, which focused on juvenile court judges, Wheeler (1968) found that judges who were closest in ideology to professional psychiatric thinking were more likely to sentence youngsters for "placement" in an institutional facility than judges who *verbalized* nonprofessional, punitive attitudes. Both of these studies indicate that professionalization may be asso-ciated with unintended consequences for all official organizations involved in the regulation and control of youth.

Among possible reasons for this unintended association between American professionalism and social control are the following. (1) Professional training emphasizes affective neu-trality rather than personal involvement, and this type of value orientation may be more compatible with enacting the role of an agent of a formal social control organization. (2) Professionals learn to keep formal records, and the number of previous recorded contacts may be a potent criterion in exercising discretionary social-control measures. (3) Professionals are taught that there is "an element of therapy" in whatever *they* might do, and this may justify using social-control measures. (4) Professionals are taught that they are capable of assessing "needs," and this diagnostic assessment may be compatible with "placement in a structured environment." (5) Professionals are taught that a "therapeutic intent" excludes any punitive attitudes, and this may justify the delivery of potent sanctions.

Whether the hypothesis will be sustained in studies designed to test it is not known. However, it appears evident that professionalization per se does not provide a guarantee that social control will be reduced. A broad policy perspective, therefore, cannot rely on professionalization per se to introduce change. A reasonable correctional policy can ill afford the historical failure of American corrections, regardless of increases in trained manpower, to distinguish between social control and treatment. We can further hypothesize that when American corrections learns to make this distinction, professionalism will modify its association with increased detention and other forms of social control. The policy implications of our hypotheses are too important not to be tested in the near future.

Summary and Conclusions

Probation subsidy, like other policies, can be perceived as pursuing explicit and implicit goals. The explicit goals can be found in the statement of legislative goals that accompany statutory inclusion in the Welfare and Institutions Code. The implicit goals are derived from examining the rationale for its enactment and the reasonable expectations that can be placed on probation subsidy as an exemplar of a general community treatment strategy. This study has focused on the twin implicit goals of probation subsidy: the saving of state funds to pay for county subsidies, and the reduction in total, statewide institutionalization. It is clear that implicit goals were not achieved, and a good part of the analysis was devoted to determining how and why the policy failed to realize these basic expectations of a community treatment strategy. A discussion of policy issues was conducted on the basis of the findings related to these implicit goals.

In contradistinction to this line of analysis, a recent *Progress Report to the Legislature: 1966–1973*, prepared in January, 1974, presented data and interpretations concerning the explicit goals

contained in the authorizing legislation. These goals were identified as follows:

1) To increase the protection afforded the citizens of this state;
2) To permit a more even administration of justice;
3) To rehabilitate offenders; and
4) To reduce the necessity for commitment of persons to state
correctional institutions. [SCYA, 1974, pp. i–ii]

Regarding the first goal, the report presents the following
conclusion:

The Probation Subsidy program has neither increased nor
decreased reported crime in California. Rather, reported crime
rates in California have continued to rise, paralleling increases in
national rates.
   The most probable explanation for the failure of Probation
Subsidy to reduce reported crime in California lies in the fact that
reported crime is an extremely gross measure. While it is
impossible to determine exact numbers, it is apparent that only a
small percentage of the total crimes reported in California are
actually committed by persons who are on probation caseloads.
Furthermore, since Subsidy caseloads (adult and juvenile) in 1972
constituted less than 10 percent of the total active probation
caseload for that year, their potential for affecting the overall
crime rate was negligible. In other words, even if criminal
activities among Probation Subsidy caseloads were reduced to
zero, we still would probably not expect crime rates to be
decreased significantly. [Ibid., p. 35]

These inferences seem eminently reasonable; it seems unlikely
that any specific program, or even all state correctional programs
combined, are capable of producing an appreciable impact on the
rates of criminal complaints to police departments in a state. Not
having taken the explicit goal seriously, we are not surprised at
the empirical results.

More positive results are claimed for accomplishment of the
second explicit goal, "a more even administration of justice."
Relying solely on rates of commitments to state institutions, the
Report to the Legislature concludes "that there was a greater
amount of consistency among the participating counties with
respect to their use of state institutions during the 1972–73 fiscal
year than there was during the base period of the Subsidy
legislation" (SCYA, 1974, p. 32).

This analysis, as well as other data contained in the 1974
Report, excludes *any* mention of juvenile detention rates. Since

this is the primary form of institutionalization for juveniles, it is difficult to understand why detention data were excluded. This study's examination of all major forms of institutionalization indicates that incarceration of juveniles has risen faster than official arrests during the post-subsidy period; more juveniles are locked up than adjudicated; and more juveniles are detained than placed on probation. Since many more juveniles are involved with the administration of justice at this critical juncture, it seems quite unreasonable to claim that the goal of more even-handed justice "has been achieved since the program's initiation" (ibid., p. 32). The data reported in chapter 7 indicate that on a total, statewide basis the juvenile administration of justice dispensed more unnecessary incarceration in 1970 than it did in either 1965 or 1960. From a policy perspective, the issue is how to reduce the unfairness—not to ignore its existence.

The third explicit goal, the rehabilitation of offenders, has been noted in the discussion of earlier chapters. Regarding juveniles, there is an absence of any significant differences between the arrest rates of subsidy and regular probation caseloads. While the findings are reported as tentative, there is little reason to be surprised by an additional confirmation of the null hypothesis, controlling for comparable offender characteristics. Our analysis disclosed that probation subsidy did not require a correctional technology that was appreciably different than had been used in projects like CTP. As a reasonable strategy, probation subsidy did *not* require a demonstration of greater effectiveness; rather, it had to demonstrate accomplishment of the implicit goals: reducing the fiscal and social costs of current correctional programs at a statewide level.

Probation subsidy did, of course, accomplish the fourth explicit goal, reduction of first commitments to state institutions. However, the decision makers accomplished this desirable goal by a strengthening and intensification of institutionalization at state and local levels. In addition, it produced these undesirable social impacts by raising the fiscal costs for California corrections by an appreciable amount on an annual basis after the initial year. Unfortunately, the 1974 *Report to the Legislature* does not deal with these facts, or the policy issues posed by a reasonable interpretation of the data.

10   Summary and Conclusions

Until the initiation of the community treatment strategy, the dominant concern of correctional evaluation was to determine whether new programs were more effective than traditional ones. The classic Cambridge-Somerville study is probably the best example of this concern prior to the 1950s (Powers and Witmer, 1951). The 1958 study of Highfields exhibits passing attention to the potential fiscal and social benefits of a four-month, small residence program. However, it is clear that the major concern of the evaluator, Weeks, was to assess the relative effectiveness of the correctional strategy for first-time institutionalized boys (Weeks, 1958). The CTP strategy, initiated in 1960, continued this emphasis, but it also provided more detailed evidence that fiscal costs could be a legitimate evaluational criterion. The President's Commission on Law Enforcement and the Administration of Justice injected another criterion, by suggesting the possibility that new programs could also replace the socially undesirable consequences of institutionalization (1967*b*).

From a historical perspective, the strategy of community treatment is associated with a modification of the criteria whereby correctional policy can be assessed. Besides a concern for effectiveness, a new strategy can also be examined for related social and fiscal benefits. This newer approach to policy assessment was capitalized on by the designers of probation subsidy—and raised the possibility that alternative strategies could even be comparable in relative effectiveness, but might vary by social and fiscal costs and benefits. The potential of this newer mode of policy analysis is amply demonstrated by this study's examination of prototypes of the new correction strategy—CTP and probation subsidy.

This newer type of policy analysis extends the older evaluation tradition by utilizing impact criteria that do not rely solely on indications of technical effectiveness. Nor do newer impact criteria focus solely on measures of individual change. Attention is also directed toward assessing organizational, systemic consequences of program execution, whether intended or unintended by designers of new correctional strategies and treatment techniques. Assessing these broader indications of impact requires a valuation of the costs, as well as the benefits, of the consequences that can be empirically documented. This means that analysts are forced to specify and engage in valuations of a variety of societal standards pertaining to fiscal expenditures, fair procedures, just dispositions, reasonable sanctions, and other cherished values. While the empirical data and analyses are separate and distinct from these broad standards, it is evident that the facts can take on meaning regarding an assessment of costs and benefits only if there is clarity and agreement concerning these social standards.

This study has examined the impact of actual practices and policies of esteemed community treatment programs and has found them to be too costly—in social as well as in economic valuations. It is possible to read and interpret the findings concerning the two case studies with a broad or strict construction of their impact for correctional policy. Viewing the findings in a strict sense involves treating each case study on its own merits and generalizing only to the extent that other cases (i.e., programmatic expressions of a similar community treatment policy) are comparable in most major characteristics. A less narrow construction could treat CTP as an example of parole practices and policies adapted to an in-lieu-of-institutionalization strategy; and in a similar vein, could treat probation subsidy as an example of providing subsidies to counties as a mechanism for inducing shifts in judicial practices and policies. A broad construction could view both cases as efforts to influence official organizations to alter their modes of offering social control and treatment, and use these cases to probe the implications for America's juvenile social control/treatment system. This final chapter will attempt to synthesize the findings from these varied perspectives in order to derive maximum benefit from the California experience.

The ideal design of CTP proposed to demonstrate that intensive supervision and differential treatment of adjudicated juveniles could be substituted for a traditional institutional-parole program. Youth could be released early to parole and thereby miss the institutional phase of the program. CTP, as a special parole program, functioning within the policies, guidelines, and traditions of the CYA, attempted to demonstrate that it could be more effective than the traditional strategy. The evidence, upon reexamination, fails to sustain the claim that CTP was the more effective program. Even a narrow construction of the findings would have to conclude that CTP cannot provide an improved model of an effective control/treatment strategy. When pooled with the reexaminations of other case studies, it is also evident that an effective juvenile control/treatment strategy has yet to be scientifically demonstrated. Any emulation of the CTP strategy would have to be governed by criteria other than the traditional one of effectiveness.

Assuming that the CTP strategy was no more effective (or no riskier) than the traditional CYA approach, it could be favored if the social and/or economic costs were demonstrably less. If the ideal design of eight months of in lieu control/treatment had been actually adhered to, then the CTP would have been less fiscally expensive than the traditional program package. In practice, of course, it was not adhered to, and the CTP was unable to demonstrate any economic savings; in fact, it demonstrated the opposite, by incurring undesirable cost overruns at a time when institutional costs were relatively stable (and not confounded by the cost run-ups associated with the second community treatment program, probation subsidy). Any emulation of CTP, using fiscal criteria, could only be warranted if the period of intensive supervision were administratively cut back from two and a half or three years to about eight months (assuming that caseloads of ten wards per agent and other organizational factors remained constant).

It seems quite probable that the economic costs of CTP-type programs could be sufficiently reduced to compete favorably with the old institution strategy while having no demonstrable impact on its relative inefffectiveness or social risk. It also seems probable that a less expensive CTP could also reduce the unnecessary social costs associated with parole detention. Given that unnecessary deprivation of liberty had no demonstrable impact on effectiveness, risk to the community, or side benefits, there appears to be little reason to use this potent sanction in a revised program. CTP demonstrated that short-term lockups could be used for reasons that had little direct relation to criminal offenses. Analysis of actual practices disclosed that parole detention could be associated with broadened definitions of deviance, discretionary criteria in defining deviance, unregulated procedures, and other undesirable and unreasonable characteristics. Inadvertently, CTP also demonstrated that short-term lockups could be used as a substitute disposition in lieu of formal revocations or unfavorable discharges from parole.

The use of short-term detention as an in lieu disposition, based on a sustained complaint of renewed criminal-type behavior, is a potentially useful strategy—but its use would have to be regulated by proper tribunals, written guidelines, fair procedures, and responsible monitoring. This type of use of parole detention is distinguishable from other types that were used in CTP: therapeutic, administrative, and preventive detentions. These latter types of parole detentions rely on presumed violation of treatment or organizational expectations, and hypothetical predictions about future behavior. By adding these non-offense-related criteria to its program package, and by using them, CTP delivered more control than treatment to its youth and decreased part of the social benefits accruing from the original suspension of institutionalization. Had CTP been limited to detention in lieu of revocation, for a criminal offense, then it is unlikely that the rates of detention would have been so much higher than the regular program.

Viewing CTP as a parole program, it is possible to gain insights into the functioning of the sanctioning power of an existing community-based program. This study provides ample evidence that parole agents possess enormous discretion to define, enforce, judge, and justify technical violations of parole. Violational rates can increase or decrease according to the exercise of discretion in defining renewed signs of deviance. In addition, rates of recidivism can also be influenced by the discretionary revocation decisions of parole organizations. Using these organizationally produced rates of recidivism as indicators of correctional effectiveness can be extremely misleading. The CTP data offer a vivid case illustration of the potential importance of regulating and monitoring existing parole policies, practices, and statistics.

As a sub-unit within the CYA parole organization, CTP also illustrates how correctional organizations can learn to modify social control practices and policies. This type of organizational impact is usually excluded from traditional evaluations, but it is probable that it may prove to be more significant than demonstrating new diagnostic and treatment techniques. The evidence seems persuasive that CTP, together with other special programs, helped to teach the CYA parole organization how to incorporate systematically into its policies and operations the discretionary uses of therapeutic detention and detention in lieu of revocation. The dramatic increases in the rates of parole detention between 1965 and 1970 are related to the availability of beds in existing reception centers, the opening of new facilities, lengthier parole terms, administrative rule changes, and other organizational changes (related to probation subsidy). However, the rationale, procedures, and practices had been demonstrated earlier by special parole projects like CTP.

Unlike CTP, probation subsidy was not designed to prove the greater effectiveness of a community treatment strategy. The designers of this funding strategy argued that county programming was superior to, or equal to, the traditional stragegy of state institutionalization and parole for both youth and adults. The goals of probation subsidy involved a decrease in the rates of first commitments to state facilities and the growth of special supervision units located in county probation departments. If these goals could be accomplished by using new revenues as an incentive, then it could be assumed that the state would save money and that institutionalization would be reduced. In a sense, operationalization of the program could be used as an indicator of its success, since the greater the amount of subsidy expenditures the greater the likelihood that social and fiscal benefits were also occurring.

Unfortunately, the designers of subsidy focused primarily on one critical discretionary decision point of the juvenile social control/treatment system—the formal commitment recommendation and decision of the probation officer and judge. They did attempt to discourage the use of county camps, ranches, and schools as substitutes for youth commitments by withdrawing subsidy payments for cases so treated. However, state decisions to lengthen institutional stay, strengthen and intensify institutionalization, lengthen parole, and increase the use of parole detention were unaffected by subsidy payments to the county. In addition, county decisions to increase referrals to juvenile intake, to increase rates of court petitions, and to increase the use of detention were also unaffected by subsidy payments to local probation departments. These unregulated, discretionary decisions occurred during the post-subsidy period. Though less visible, such choices dramatically transformed the social and fiscal balance sheets that were used to assess the impact of this novel correctional experiment.

The social balance sheet for California clearly indicates that many more youth were locked up at a local level in 1970 than in 1965 or in 1960. This occurred while fewer youth were being locked up at a state level, and committed youth were having their length of institutional and parole stay increased. In sheer numbers, even discounting drug detentions, the amount of local youth lockups more than compensated for the fewer state lockups of juveniles. Using institutional days as an indicator of social control, the amount of social control was nearly the same; adding up the days from all sources tips the institutional day balance sheet toward a reading of greater social control in 1970 than in 1965. Since the gains in social control outstripped the increase in criminal arrests, it is difficult to discern the offsetting social benefits that such a shift in correctional decision making produced for either adults or youth.

The altered patterns of decision making that occurred at a state level also upset the fiscal computations of the ideal subsidy policy. The steep rise in per capita institutional costs, for both adult and youth inmates, wiped out any offset savings after the first year of the subsidy strategy. The actual operational budget increased far in excess of inflation of the dollar, and subsidy payments were drawn from general state revenues rather than offset savings. At a county level increased detention costs reduced the benefits accruing from the subsidy. This state cost run-up has been substantial, and appears to be increasing each year. The only discernible benefit is that the CYA slowed the implementation of its outdated and untenable building program.

Any state considering the initiation of a subsidy strategy would have to take into account these potent unintended consequences. An altered subsidy strategy might have to incorporate a freeze on per capita institutional costs and new construction, as well as a freeze on local and state detention rates and average length of stay. As for California, it may be extremely difficult to roll back simultaneously fiscal costs and lockup rates to a 1965 level for both youth and adults. It seems more probable that the state legislature and/or governor might soon recommend a ceiling on total subsidy payments, thereby holding down the steady rise in correctional costs.

The major findings of this study indicate that major goals of the community treatment strategy were not realized in practice. Community treatment was proposed as an effective alternative to traditional institutionalization and proved to be no more effective. Community treatment was proposed as a noncoercive substitute for state-delivered sanctions, and proved to be associated with increases in state and local social control. And community treatment was supposed to be less expensive, but proved to be associated with cost overruns. These disappointing results occurred with esteemed prototypes in one of America's state leaders in corrections. The findings compel one to question whether the prototypes can be recommended without undergoing critical modifications. Specific modifications have been suggested in this summary as well as in the summary chapters (5 and 9) of parts 1 and 2.

The suggested modifications may help to bridge the gap between intentions and reality, but they do not fully address the functioning of a total statewide system. The findings of this study indicate that a total system does not actually function in accord with the ideal conceptions set forth by modern correctional thinking. More institutionalization occurs at the local level than at the state level, and rates of local institutionalization can increase without any comparable increase in rates of harmful offenses. These facts must be incorporated into a broader conception of the public response to youth. In order to fashion a strategy that is less limited, and that can address the unnecessary social and fiscal costs associated with all forms of institutionalization, a revision of our image of community-based corrections is required. The findings of this study, combined with other empirical evidence, can be used to formulate a more accurate portrayal of the American approach to suspected youthful deviants.

According to the dominant appraisal of American corrections, we have progressed as a nation from a spirit of revenge and restraint toward realizing the goals of reformation and reintegration of youthful deviants. This view is not only held by professional correctional officials; it is also set forth by respected members of the academic community (Empey, 1967). But the disparity between these lofty intentions and actual practice is much greater than we have wished to believe. This disparity exists on a national level, as well as in California. In 1967 the National Council on Crime and Delinquency reported the results of the first nationwide study of corrections. This study was prepared for the President's Commission on Law Enforcement and the Administration of Justice. Some of the study's most significant findings have yet to be fully absorbed into an empirically based conception of what public policy actually offers American youth on a national scale:

> In 1965 the total number admitted to detention facilities was more than 409,000, or approximately two-thirds of all juveniles apprehended .... These youngsters were held in detention homes and jails for an estimated national average stay of 12 days at a total cost of more than $53,000,000—an average cost of $130 per child ....
> The statistics show 409,218 children detained but only 242,275 children placed on probation or committed to an institution. [President's Commission, 1967a, pp. 121 and 129]

The figures clearly indicate that on a national level the dominant public response to arrested juveniles is likely to be a local twelve-day lockup. Since about one-half of those formally arrested (about 300,000 of the 600,000) are not even officially handled by the court, but are screened out, the national data also indicate that more youth receive community-based institutionalization than are even formally adjudicated as delinquent (U.S. Department of HEW, 1970, p. 12). In addition, only about 189,000 youth received probation in 1965, but over twice as many were detained. It seems extremely unlikely that these 189,000 youth received twelve full days of treatment services during the year, since not even CTP youth received this level of service. The data indicate that more arrested youth are locked up than receive juvenile justice or probationary treatment. These empirical facts lead to the inference that restraint is still the dominant public policy response toward youth—not rehabilitative and reintegrative services.

The empirical facts also suggest that juvenile justice and treatment services are actually secondary units of a larger social control system. It seems more accurate to conceive of law enforcement, the juvenile court, and corrections as units within a broad social control/treatment system. Within this system, once youth are formally arrested, they are more likely to receive sanctions than either justice or probationary treatment. Obviously, this outcome does not represent the ideal policy of the system but, rather, refers to the manner in which it actually operates. On a national level, as well as in California, there is a discrepancy between what are professed as ideals and what actually emerges from empirical measurements of the system's functioning.

The national 1965 survey data indicate that local, community-based sanctioning resources are available throughout the country, particularly in and near urban centers. Less populous areas often use local jails; in 1965, of the 409,000 detentions, approximately 88,000 occurred in local jails. The costs of constructing a detention facility can be expensive; in 1965, the cost was estimated to be at least $10,000 per bed. The costs of operating juvenile lockups were computed at over $11.00 per capita per day in 1965. Given these construction and operating costs, it may not be surprising to learn that an affluent state like California is considered one of the country's leaders in juvenile detention (Lemert, 1970). Since California is also considered a national leader in corrections, the state's superior statistics can help to describe more precisely the unstated operational policy that guides the delivery of more social control than formal adjudication or probation services.

In 1960 and 1965 the data of this study clearly reveal that more

California youth were detained than appeared on a formal petition before a juvenile court judge. This social control dominance continued in 1970, despite a statewide emphasis on community treatment. The data for 1970 also reveal that California local lockups are primarily related to charges where there is an absence of a victim. The preponderant reasons for detention are delinquent "tendencies," administrative reasons, and drugs (primarily marijuana). It is clear that the boundaries of this state's juvenile social control/treatment system are quite broad. There is evidence that a state like New York, with comparable levels of resources, also provides similar boundaries in operating their local social control/treatment systems (Lerman, 1971).

Recent data suggest that a greater emphasis on due process within the juvenile court has not yet had an appreciable impact on detention usage. The 1970 California data reveal that statutory changes and Supreme Court decisions have not decreased the relative dominance of social control. A recently completed national survey, conducted by Sarri and other University of Michigan researchers, provided the following empirical estimates: in 1973 at least 100,000 children will have spent at least one day in an adult jail, while nearly 500,000 other youth were confined in local detention facilities (U.S. Department of HEW, 1973, p. 2). Between 1965 and 1973 the number of youth detained has grown from roughly 400,000 to 600,000—a gain of 50 percent. This gain is greater than the growth in the age-specific growth population that faces the risk of detention (ibid., 1974, p. 7).

A recent study offers some insights regarding how difficult it can be to try and reverse the steady rise in detention rates. In 1967, the Chief Judge of Cuyahoga County (based in Cleveland, Ohio), launched a determined effort to reduce detention. He comments about his efforts as follows:

Social workers, probation officers, and police officers, who had previously for all practical purposes made the decision as to the necessity of detaining the child, reacted strenuously to our screening process.
Naturally, these criticisms, those from within the court and more especially those from outside agencies, militated against acceptance of our new policy . . . .
The social agencies which staunchly proclaimed their

non-punitive philosophy wanted us to detain children as part of their "treatment" process . . . .

Helpful in discouraging one of the social agencies from the overuse of detention was our new requirement that an official complaint must be filed concerning each child placed in the detention home . . . .

It had been a common practice for a probation officer to place a child in detention who was uncooperative, who failed to keep appointments, who truanted from school, or when upon a complaint of the parents was considered out of control at home . . . . The 380 children admitted by probation officers in 1967 was reduced to 125 in 1971, a reduction of 60 percent . . . .

As we began our initial effort to reduce population, we found that many children were being detained, awaiting acceptance by various state, county, and private facilities who, often arbitrarily and for their own convenience, imposed quotas and admission requirements on the court. [Whitlatch, 1973]

This unusually frank report indicates that detention can be used as a multipurpose resource for a variety of preventive, treatment, and administrative reasons in Cleveland, Ohio, as well as in California. For three years (1967–69), Judge Whitlatch was unable to demonstrate empirically that the Chief Judge could administratively regulate the use of detention by police, probation officers, treatment agencies, and correctional organizations. Finally, in 1970 and 1971, his detention reduction policy began to show signs of success—particularly with police and his own probation staff. However, a separate reading of the 1971 Annual Report of the Cuyahoga County Court reveals that more local youth still received formal detention than received formal probation—3,439 to 2,387 (County of Cuyahoga, 1971, pp. 26 and 27).

The unstated policy of America's public response to juveniles, as indicated by actual empirical data of current practices, appears to contradict the sanguine ideal image of an evolutionary correctional policy. There is a lack of empirical evidence that correctional policy has progressed from restraint to rehabilitation. In practice we may attempt to do both, but restraint appears to be the more dominant expression of our operational, unstated policy. In addition, the current unstated policy displays a historical continuity with past policies and practices. Recent historical research suggests that the advent of the modern correctional era has probably led to a growth in the degree of local social control over youth.

Beginning in 1824 with the inauguration of the first House of Refuge, American urban centers began the development of a separate juvenile correctional system. By the time of the invention of the first juvenile court in Chicago, at the turn of the century, a substantial juvenile correctional system had been created in the more populous, industrialized states. This pre-modern, publicly supported system relied on broad and vague statutes of juvenile misconduct, as well as the adult penal code, to set the boundaries for an evolving definition of juvenile delinquency. The nineteenth-century Houses of Refuge, Reformatories, Industrial and Training Schools, and Homes for Boys and Girls, were confining, strict, and punitive places to be sent to—even though a child-saving, rehabilitative intent was proclaimed as the dominant philosophy. While some private individuals and agencies, as well as municipalities, began to experiment with "placing out" in foster homes (preferably in rural settings), it is clear that the dominant nineteenth-century public correctional service was institutionalization (Rothman, 1971; Bremner, 1971; Mennel, 1973).

Prior to the creation of the juvenile court, most American urban centers also relied on existing local jails to house youth awaiting adjudication and sentencing. Founders of the juvenile court were interested in setting up a separate tribunal to hear cases involving youth, and a special facility for housing youngsters while they awaited trial in a noncriminal court. If adults and juveniles were separated at all stages of judicial and correctional processing, then the full promise of modern correctional ideas would have an opportunity to be realized. For accompanying the idea of strict age (and sex) separation was the creation of community-based probation dispositions for worthy youths. The creation of separate juvenile detention facilities seemed to be a reasonable and logical corollary of the new community-oriented approach to youth. In practice, this meant that attached to the social invention of public probation, and the invention of a juvenile court with a broad jurisdictional mandate that codified many existing juvenile statutes, there was one additional invention—a local detention facility for children of court age only.

In Chicago, the birthplace of the first modern court, reformers secured a large house, staffed by women volunteers, to operate a holding facility for children awaiting adjudication and disposition. By 1915, this commmunity "group home" was replaced by a bigger, sounder, and more secure residence—the Audy Home. This new, publicly funded place of detention had bars on the windows, secure locks and doors, guards, and a more orderly correctional routine; it was also surrounded by a wall. Chicago had constructed the country's first juvenile facsimile of a local jail, along with its community-oriented court and probation department (Sanders, 1970, pp. 449–53).

In the ensuing years, many professionals, reformers, and academics devoted major attention to the new probation departments that were attached to the court. Meanwhile, many more youth were exposed to local lockups than under the older, less progressive system—since judges had been increasingly reluctant to place youth in adult jails (Platt, 1969). The use of local lockups appears to have been facilitated by the infusion of new public resources to help realize the broad mandate of the court. On behalf of this mandate, the larger urban centers also added new occupations and organizational resources. Specialized juvenile officers and bureaus, as well as probation offices and departments came into being to aid the work of the court. The building of detention facilities was a critical multipurpose resource for the new juvenile police officers, juvenile judges, and juvenile probation officers—the new officials of the modern juvenile social control/treatment system (Bremner et al., 1971, vol. 2).

As new detention facilities or beds were made available, the new officials made rapid use of their community-based resources. In the 1965 survey the dominance of this local correctional resource was revealed for the first time on a national level. But it is quite probable that this dominance emerged between 1915 and the onset of World War II. It is also likely that the rates of local institutionalization of youth have been rising ever since the first Youth Homes, Halls, Reception Centers, and Shelters were built as places of segregated juvenile detention. The rise in detention rates during the decade of the 1960s and early 1970s appears consistent with the unstated policy and public investments of earlier years. The California data illustrate how the policy operated during the past decade.

The emergence and expansion of local forms of sanctions was also accompanied by the emergence and expansion of new occupations and organizations devoted to the regulation and control of suspected youthful deviants. Since 1900 we have

increasingly relied on paid personnel, preferably with professionalized training, to specify and operationalize a community's
policy toward its youth. In carrying out this policy the new
officials were expected to make individual judgments about each
case, employing such nonlegal criteria as emotional development,
family composition and relationships, adjustment at school, and
relationships with adults. The practical impact of using nonlegal
as well as legal criteria for deciding whether youth "needed" the
rehabilitative services of the modern system, meant that the
meaning of "delinquency" included more than just the commission of penal offenses. While the pre-modern era also
included noncriminal, juvenile status offenses, it did not have the
explicit statutory permission and resources to transform a case of
"tendencies" and "need for supervision" into a bona fide arrest
or juvenile court complaint. Part of the rationale for obtaining a
new juvenile law and juvenile court was to gain this permission.
The modern era did not invent delinquency; but the new officials
added a breadth to its meaning that expanded the criteria for
being placed under the parental care of the juvenile control/treat-
ment system (Platt, 1969; Mennel, 1973).

This expansion of the potential meaning of delinquency
provided professionals with broad discretionary power to interpret what constituted a deviant act, a deviant character, or a
deviant situation. Recent studies of the exercise of discretion in
practice indicate that professionals can make an independent
contribution to increasing the rates of deviance and/or increasing
the rates of social control. Wilson has documented how the
growth of specialized juvenile units and police professionalization
is associated with far higher rates of juvenile delinquency
(Wilson, 1968). For example, Oakland, California, which has a
professionalized police department, was found to have a juvenile
arrest rate that was ten times as high as that of Albany, New
York, which has a nonprofessionalized department. The statutes
of California and New York are equally broad in their potential
mandate and leeway for the exercise of discretion—but the
Oakland police were far more likely to arrest youth for "delinquent tendencies" than were Albany police. In a very real sense,
the Oakland police were independently expanding definitions of
deviance, since both departments were likely to make "pinches"
for serious penal offenses.

Besides making an independent contribution to rates of deviance, professionals exercising discretion can also make an independent contribution to rates of social control. In this study, data associated with the pre- and post-probation subsidy periods illustrate how county rates of referral to probation and detention admissions can rise independently of any comparable increase in rates of criminal offenses. The CTP data disclose that parole officers can make an independent contribution to rates of deviance and detention, since the rates of criminal infractions were comparable for experimental and control youth. The historical and empirical evidence indicates that an expansion of occupations and organizations that are granted discretion to exercise powers of complaint and sanction can be associated with increases in the rates of official deviance and community-based sanctions. It appears, too, that therapeutic intentions and standards can be readily incorporated into the ongoing juvenile control/treatment system—thereby creating an additional source of deviance definition and an additional rationale for creating sanctions.

The inference that social control/treatment officials can make an independent contribution to the creation of deviance and societal responses is drawn from this and other empirical studies. However, the inference is consonant with recent intellectual perspectives of the labeling theorists (Lemert, 1967; Becker, 1963; Schur, 1973). According to this sociological perspective, deviance is not an attribute or trait of a person. Rather, it is a social invention, or definition, that arises out of the interaction between social actors and persons or organizations possessed with legitimate power. Deviance, therefore, is a negative characterization of the actor by persons and organizations with sufficient power to create, interpret, and enforce social, moral, or legal standards. This labeling process is characterized by a potential variability in concensus regarding the standards for many types of behaviors and situational conditions. This process is also characterized by a potential variability in access and use of sanctioning resources to impose and enforce the standards. Until recently, those concerned with such variability have exhibited a major interest in understanding how the definitions and responses of the labelers are reacted to by suspected deviants. Regarding juveniles, there has been an interest in determining how stable deviant roles and careers are facilitated by the stigmatic actions of the labeling system (Wheeler, Cottrell, and Romasco, 1966). While it is possible that future research will support some or all of the hypotheses about the impact of the labeling process on the self-conceptions of youth, it is important to note that the labeling process is socially sponsored and organized; therefore it can have objective consequences that are independent of the subjective images of either the labelers or the labeled.

In this study, evidence has been provided that the activities of correctional personnel and organizations are part of a larger deviance-defining and sanctioning system. For purposes of convenience and ready communication, this complex system has been termed the social control/treatment system. As members of this system, correctional personnel can have a direct and indirect impact on rates of deviance processing and sanctioning. Adding a broader mandate to correct youth can result in a widening of the deviance-defining boundaries and the creation of new forms of deviance and higher rates of sanctions—as occurred in CTP. Changes in the allocation and distribution of the system's financial and organizational resources can result in alterations in the deviance-defining rates, the sanctioning rates, or the duration of the sanctions—as occurred in the post-subsidy period. In drawing these kinds of inferences from the empirical data, it is not necessary to assess the subjective intent of the definers and enforcers of community, organizational, and treatment standards. Nor is it necessary to assess the self-conception of those that are labeled and processed by the system.

The idea that an expanding system of social control and treatment can actually produce added amounts of deviance and sanctions poses a paradoxical problem for social policy. For instead of just one delinquency problem, we are liable to be faced with two: one presented by youth and one created by adults. In practice, this means that when we read that the delinquency rate in Oakland, California, is ten times the rate of Albany, New York, we doubt that the entire difference is due to youth behavior (Wilson, 1968). Or when we read that California rates of referral to juvenile courts have risen by nearly 50 percent in the post-subsidy period, we doubt that the entire increase is due to youth behavior. These areas of doubt represent independent contributions to the delinquency problem.

The evidence indicates that we can compound the original problem by permitting systems of control/treatment to expand and to operate under discretionary standards. Many of these standards appear unreasonable when subjected to close scrutiny. The system, if left to operate according to the unstated policy, tends to result in a dominance of social control. The evidence also indicates that merely adding more fiscal and organizational resources to the existing system can further the relative dominance of social control over treatment.

The community treatment strategy, as currently formulated, attempts to control one discretionary part of the social control/treatment system—while adding additional resources to other parts of the system. The evidence provided above indicates that this limited approach can yield unintended and undesirable consequences. In order to have an impact on definitional boundaries, total institutionalization rates, the balance between sanctions and treatment, and the duration of sanctions, it appears necessary to address all of the critical, discretionary decision points. A policy of rolling back or freezing the boundaries and all types of institutional usage would probably involve the creation of a monitoring, regulating, reporting system that would be directed at police, judges, probation officers, and parole officers. Even if a cooperative consensus about narrower deviance and detention standards were agreed to verbally, actual compliance would have to be monitored at all decision points.

A strategy of decreasing the definitional boundaries and coercive dominance of the total system could be coupled with a policy of searching for less extreme forms of social control and less costly forms of treatment. However, a strategy of reducing the boundaries of deviance definition and institutional forms of sanctions need not be rationalized by claiming a rehabilitative technology where none has been scientifically demonstrated. The reduction of excessive social and fiscal costs associated with unreasonable uses of institutionalization possesses a social value that is superior to pursuing relatively ineffective modes of treatment. From an empirical perspective a better case can be made for reducing the total system's unnecessary social and fiscal costs than pursuing treatment strategies that contribute to increasing these costs. In practice this means that our juvenile system could become less costly if we concentrated less on expanding treatment and more on reducing the rationales and practices associated with sanctions. The delivery of treatment, limited as its impact may be, might begin to expand as the social and fiscal dominance of institutionalization at state and local levels actually diminished. The evidence suggests that we have to be clear about the priorities, or else we can unwittingly continue to incur unnecessary costs, and leave the system essentially unchanged.

At this time, it is uncertain whether a sufficient degree of agreement and political authority could be mustered on behalf of trimming down the boundaries or sanctioning capabilities of the total juvenile control/treatment system. New directions in public policy often require the support of political elites, interest group leaders, and leaders of the local and state subsystems of enforcement, adjudication, and correction. While appeals to reason and empirical evidence can play a part in formulating public policy, it would be naïve to think that traditional assumptions, values, rationales, occupational interest, and political and fiscal interests do not influence policy choices to an important degree. The blunt fact may be that fundamental reforms of the total operation of the juvenile control/treatment system may not be deemed to be politically acceptable or feasible—even when costs are documented to outweigh benefits.

In the event that local communities are unwilling or unable to engage in a fundamental reexamination of the operation of the control/treatment systems, there are other strategies that could be considered. One, of course, is a modified community treatment strategy that attempts to reduce the specific social and fiscal costs that have been identified for special programs like CTP and probation subsidy. A second strategy involves a policy of diverting significant numbers of youth away from the existing system into alternative institutional arrangements, and thereby mitigating the consequences of penetrating beyond the arrest or court referral stages of deviant definition and processing. A third strategy, related to the diversion strategy, attempts to create new, competing definitions of deviance and less coercive societal responses to deal with family and youth problems (Lemert, 1972). A fourth strategy favors the ignoring of many forms of youthful deviance by the control/treatment system, with the expectation that the benefits of nonlabeling will outweigh the costs of stigmatization and inappropriate responses (Schur, 1973).

Each of these limited strategies leaves the existing system intact, while hoping that the numbers of youth subjected to discretionary definitions and sanctions will be reduced. In addition, each limited strategy requires some degree of cooperation by existing sub-units of the juvenile social control/treatment system. This cooperation can be obtained by agreement, incentives, or by the use of superior political authority. But it appears that some degree of cooperation with exising units within the system is a significant precondition for obtaining altered patterns of deviance processing in a local community or on a state level.

It is instructive to note that strategies of limited reform, as well as more fundamental policy changes, often require direct political authority or cooperation of significant interest groups and elites to initiate and stabilize change (Marris and Rein, 1967). The political dimension of the delinquency problem is rarely highlighted, but the dominance of social control and the broad discretionary use of authority could not have been permitted for the last century and a half without the acquiescence or approbation of community elites and representatives. The construction and operational maintenance of varied forms of institutional control required budgetary and political approval. The recent rise in national detention statistics, in a period of experimentation with community treatment and legal rights, indicates that the modern, community-based system of juvenile control continues to command widespread political support.

An unstated policy that has received expanding fiscal and organizational resources and continued political support for such a long period may seem impervious to dramatic change in the near future. But the spread of juvenile control/treatment systems into suburbia and more affluent residential areas may lead to a belated democratization of the delinquency problem, and to the entry of new groups and individuals concerned about control and treatment issues. Further, as more middle-class youth are drawn into the discretionary boundaries of the expanding system, they are likely to be defended by lawyers. Legal representation for juveniles, in turn, has only recently been legitimated by statutes and a precedent-setting Supreme Court decision. Private lawyers have been joined by lawyers assigned by legal aid, public defenders, child advocate, and civil rights groups—and have begun to attack vulnerable parts of the system on behalf of individual clients and class action categories. This newly added interest group is having difficulty in carving out a traditional legal role, but the rise in juvenile advocacy is a reality that few would have predicted in the mid-1960s (Stapleton and Teitelbaum, 1972).

The addition of advocate lawyers to the juvenile social control system is producing an impact on the organizational roles and locus of decision making within one unit of the system, the court. An increasing number of states are now assigning official state prosecutors, rather than probation officers, to formulate a case against juveniles. Besides adding another segment of the legal profession into the system, the addition of the prosecutor has injected into the work of the court the notion of plea bargaining. Plea bargaining has already begun to be described in the literature, and is likely to increase in the near future (Stapleton and Teitelbaum, 1972). Plea bargaining can lead to reduced charges, dismissal of cases based on poor evidence, and pre-adjudication bargaining regarding dispositions—outcomes that have little to do with treatment preferences or techniques. Prosecutors and defense lawyers are likely to gain influence in specifying the boundaries of legal deviance and the use of specific sanctions attached to dispositional recommendations. Regardless of whether participants or outsiders applaud or decry these new developments, the injection of defense lawyers, prosecutors, legal traditions, and plea bargaining are likely to have systemic consequences that result in altered decision-making patterns and choices.

The national dominance of social control has not yet been influenced by the recent introduction of lawyers into juvenile courts, perhaps because a good deal of detention occurs at the pre-adjudication stage of decision making. But lawyers and persons representing other new interests can also attempt to influence events by engaging in outside political activities. It is possible that the advocates of legal rights, minority rights, and the rights of children will begin to forge a variety of alliances to challenge the existing system on local and state levels, and push for changes that affect pre-court, as well as post-court, processing. If this occurs, then the advocates of reason, researchers using empirical evidence to assess the actual operation of the system, may have groups outside of academia that will use their studies in the broader policy-making arena. If changes occur, further research can examine whether the system is moving from an unstated national and local policy of restraint to a policy of informed reasonableness, fairness, and humane concern for youth.

Future signs of progress should not be too difficult to discern. Rates of total institutionalization and length of stay are two signs. We can also find out if the rates of formal complaint, formal adjudications, and noncoercive probation dispositions exceed the rates of institutionalization. Progress could also be noted by decreases in the arrests and coercive processing of cases of delinquent tendencies, juvenile status offenses, or children in need of supervision. In monitoring this latter indicator of progress, analysts may have to assess new alternative societal responses toward the new legal category, juveniles in need of supervision (or JINS, PINS, MINS, and CINS, depending on the jurisdiction). Since past evidence indicates that this category of youth is most likely to be detained, to remain in detention longer, and to be institutionalized in state institutions for a greater length of stay, it is possible that programs operated under new sponsorship and titles may recreate traditional, costly examples of restraining institutions (Lerman, 1971). It is useful to remember, too, that reforms initiated at the turn of the century also began by creating an alternative community-based response to the traditional system of social control.

During the first seventy-five years of this century, we have been creating a modern juvenile control/treatment system to regulate the conduct and character of America's youth. We have accomplished this while believing that we were primarily engaged in saving or rehabilitating youth. The image of a nonrestraining society was set forth, while we constructed new institutions that were classified as detention facilities, residential schools, diagnostic centers, and reception clinics. During this time we also created probation and other less coercive services, but the dominance of our reliance on institutionalization is clearly revealed by national and state data. In the last part of this century we may continue to maintain the discrepancy between reality and our intentions, or we can begin the troublesome task of determining where social control ends and treatment begins.

Appendixes

APPENDIX A

A Methodological Note on the CTP Analysis

As noted in the text, the findings reported in part 1 were based on a reanalysis of CTP research reports and related documents. The major portions of this secondary analysis were completed as of 15 December 1972. A critical part of this analysis involved choosing the best indicator of probable renewed delinquent behavior that was available in the CTP research reports. Suspension of parole was chosen, even though I was aware that suspension, like revocation of parole, could involve elements of discretionary decision making. However, suspensions could arise from the arrest decisions of non-CYA law enforcement officers—and not only from CYA parole officer decisions. The arrest decisions of police and sheriff representatives were deemed to be less biasing than those of interested CYA personnel, and a closer approximation of probable youth behaviors in the community. The publicly available data indicated quite clearly that the rates of arrest (associated with parole suspensions) *initiated by non-CYA law enforcement officers* were virtually identical for experimental and control samples for similar community exposure periods. Unfortunately this type of arrest was not broken down by specific offenses for each of the samples. In order to get at detailed offense data that was probably linked to police or sheriff arrests, the reports that provided the most specific suspension data were utilized. After examining all of the available documents, I chose *CTP Research Reports No. 6* and *No. 7.* As table 4 indicates, *CTP Research Report No. 7* proved to be the most useful in understanding the differences between probable youth behavior and adult behavior.

Besides containing the best indicator of specific youth behavior associated with a police or sheriff arrest, *CTP Report No. 7* had another major advantage. It provided detailed evidence that the total eligible experimental and control samples were comparable regarding sex, socioeconomic status, type of commitment offense, age, and IQ. Regarding race there was a tendency for the two samples to differ, but this was not statistically significant at the .05 level. There were, however, a number of significant differences in population characteristics between the experimental and control group diagnostic subtypes, even though the overall proportions appeared comparable. By restricting the analysis to the total samples, it was possible to avoid the errors involved in making subtype comparisons that could be confounded by population variables that could not be analytically controlled when using available research reports. The total *available* samples, however, are not identical with the total *eligible* samples. Attrition occurred because of a necessity to control periods of community exposure and because some youth were classified as moving out of the parole area. A comparison of available experimentals and controls, by diagnostic subtype, indicated that the two groups were comparable.

The issue of comparability of sample groups is a serious problem in all evaluation research. To assume that random sampling has occurred, and that experimental and control groups are comparable—merely on the basis of a stated intention—may prove to be erroneous. For example, in *CTP Research Report No. 9*, part 1, issued in October 1968, there is evidence that the comparability that had been accomplished in 1966 (between the *total* experimental and control groups) was no longer true for specific variables considered independently. While the two eligible samples were comparable on socioeconomic status, race, IQ, and type of commitment offense, they differed significantly on the variables of age and sex. It is well known that both of these variables are strongly associated with delinquency; therefore, differences between the two eligible samples that might be found could be due to sampling variability—and not because of any program differences.

In addition to casting doubts about sample comparability, *CTP Research Report No. 9* lacked specific information concerning suspension data. If it had contained the requisite suspension data, it would have been necessary to control for the influence of age and sex in order to conduct appropriate analyses. However, none of the reports detailed findings by a combined controlling for age and sex.

These considerations supported the choice of *CTP Research Report No. 7* as the best data source for the major findings depicted in table 4. The choice of this report had additional advantages. It seemed useful to pick a period in which length of institutional stay, type of youth commitments, and parole practices were relatively stable and unaffected by the impact of probation subsidy on the operations of the CYA. As part 2 of the present study documents, post-1967 developments in California had a profound impact on the CYA. Fortuitously, the dates chosen also coincided with the time period of the CYA report on detention. Finally, the best available data on CTP fiscal costs were also available for this period, and the control costs were not influenced by the atypical cost run-ups associated with the probation subsidy period (post-1967). After completing the analysis by 15 December 1972, I mailed several drafts of the manuscript to interested parties to solicit comments. In October 1973, I was offered a "new" and "updated" analysis by the CTP research organization, in response to the analysis contained in the draft manuscript. I was informed that twelve years of research findings were deemed to be "obsolete." Therefore, any assessments based on the 1961–69 reports were also considered "obsolete." The CTP post-manuscript analysis did not directly challenge the data reported in table 4, but rather presented new samples that were compared with "new" data on both suspensions and law enforcement arrests. Unfortunately, the comparability of the samples used in this post-manuscript analysis is not discussed or reported. However, there are very good reasons for questioning whether the "updated" experimental and control groups represent random samples that could have been drawn from a common male population (girls were excluded in the updated analysis).

The CTP post-manuscript analysis appears to present new findings that rely on two types of male populations. The first type contains 104 experimentals and 90 controls that had received a favorable or unfavorable discharge from the CYA by the end of 1969. The second type contains 310 experimentals and 225 controls that had been on parole a total of 117 months. Regarding the first type of population, the favorable/unfavorable groups, there exists evidence that experimentals and controls did not have an equal chance to reach this CYA-defined status. In 1969, *CTP Research Report No. 9*, part 3 (p. 25), evidence was reported that "differential" decision making, associated with revocation of parole, was significantly associated with the "greater likelihood of favorable discharge within the Experimental as compared with the Control Program, on four-years' follow-up." Given this kind of knowledge, it now appears quite unreasonable—without supporting evidence—to assume that nonrandom, purposeful decision making resulted in comparable samples of experimental and control youth.

Earlier evidence exists that indicates that the organizationally screened samples result in significant differences between experimental and control favorable discharge samples (SCYA, 1972c). In March 1972, the CTP reported on a 24-months cohort and a 48-months cohort of post-discharge male youth. The 24-months cohort yielded differences on four of ten population characteristics at a probability level of .05 or .01. In both samples experimentals tended to differ significantly on two critical population variables: socioeconomic status and IQ. Experimentals were favored on both characteristics. It seems reasonable to believe that comparable differences are likely to exist in the type of population used in the post-manuscript analysis. It is also likely that this type of screened sampling yields groups that are unrepresentative of the original pool of eligible youth.

The second type of population that is presented in the CTP post-manuscript analysis contains 310 experimental and 225 control males. Since the original sampling design called for a 50–50 split in sample selection, it is evident that there is a marked disparity in the actual numbers between the two groups. As of 31 March 1968, in *CTP Research Report No. 9*, part 1 (p. 2), information is provided that the *eligible* population pool yielded 287 experimental and 296 control males, very close to a 50–50 split. Yet in the CTP post-manuscript analysis, presumably written more than four years later, the number of available experimental boys increased to 310—a gain of 23—while the control boys *decreased* to 225—a loss of 71. This loss may stem from eliminating the categories "parole out of area" (POA) and "Non-Interviewed Controls" (NIC) from the eligible samples.

The possibility that some eligible boys may be lost in a follow-up and not included in the final available sample is not unusual. However, it is unusual to find out that in 1968, according to *CTP Research Report No. 9*, part 1 (p. 36, n. 2) the eligible experimentals lost only 2 youth while the controls lost 84 wards as POA and 22 as NIC. A few years earlier, in *CTP Research Report No. 7*, the loss had been 2 experimentals and 63 controls as POA, with no NIC youth. In 1966, 22 percent (63 of

283) of the controls were dropped from the eligible sample, but in 1969 this increased to 28 percent (106 of 381).

Meanwhile, the experimental loss remained at less than 1 percent. This increased attrition of the control youth certainly evokes the doubt of whether the "updated" available samples adequately represent the original pool of 1961–69 eligible males.

In addition to the "numbers" problem, the second type of population used in the CTP post-manuscript analysis appears to have experimentals and controls that are noncomparable. A secondary analysis of the footnoted data and "new" classifications used in the post-manuscript analysis reveals the following distribution of available diagnosed personality subtypes: (a) experimental boys had 185 "neurotic" types (Na and Nx subtypes), 57 "power-oriented" types (Cfc and Mp subtypes), 33 "passive conformists" (Cfm subtype), and 35 all other types; (b) control boys contained 103 "neurotic types," 54 "power-oriented" types, 40 "passive conformists," and 28 all other types. If these two distributions are submitted to statistical analysis, the following finding emerges: there is one chance in a hundred that the experimental and control boys were randomly drawn from the same available population (chi-square = 11.8, df = 3, and $p < .01$).

It is possible that the differences between the above two distributions could be attributed to unreliable diagnoses rather than to unreliable samples. However, additional secondary analysis of the "updated" population for 1961–64 yielded distributions more nearly comparable according to personality assessments than those of 1964–69. Reliability usually increases with practice, and we might have expected a reverse set of findings. In addition, the final available samples in *CTP Research Report No. 7* did not exhibit marked discrepancies between experimentals and controls.

There are very cogent reasons for believing that the diagnostic differences between the available 310 experimentals and 225 controls are linked to two significant population variables—age and intelligence. The evidence and reasons are as follows:

1. In *CTP Research Report No. 9*, part 1, the latest publicly available document that presents population characteristics, evidence is provided that in March 1968 the total eligible experimentals and controls differed significantly on the variables

of age and sex (pp. 3–4). Specifically, the evidence indicates that the experimentals were overrepresented in the seventeen-year-old age category, in comparison to the controls (27 percent versus 17 percent).

2. In *CTP Research Report No. 9*, part 1, evidence is also presented that the CTP personality classifications are significantly associated with age and IQ. For the total population of eligible youth (girls included), the contingency coefficients are .20 for age, .225 for IQ, and .29 for age and IQ combined (p. 8).

3. In the updated analysis the two subtypes that are overrepresented in the available experimental sample are the "neurotics (Na and Nx types). The neurotics are from the higher interpersonal maturity levels and would be expected to have more older and brighter youth.

4. In *CTP Research Report No. 9*, part 1, evidence is presented that in March 1968 the "neurotics" comprising the eligible control group were underrepresented within the seventeen-year-old category and overrepresented in the fifteen-year-old category (p. 7). This finding suggests that the "neurotics" contained in the updated experimental sample are even older than what might have been expected by just considering overall trends of the eligible population.

On the basis of the evidence, it is quite reasonable to believe that the available 310 experimental males are older (and probably brighter) than the 225 controls. The probable difference regarding age is of critical importance, since correctional researchers have known for some time that the older parts of youth and adult correctional populations have tended to be better parole risks than their younger counterparts. Therefore, it seems quite likely that the second type of updated experimentals used in the post-manuscript analysis are biased toward "success"—before being exposed to any particular correctional program.

In questioning the reliability and validity of the two new populations offered in the post-manuscript analysis, I do not suggest that the biased samples were constructed intentionally. The evaluation literature contains other examples of samples that were unwittingly biased. In an earlier article (Lerman, 1968), I cited the Fricot Ranch Study, conducted by Jesness for the CYA, as an example of random sampling intentions that had not been executed in practice. After presenting evidence that the experimentals and controls differed significantly on critical population variables, Jesness conducted his analysis as if the sampling bias did not exist. However, the claims of success were probably explained on the basis of the uncontrolled population variables. The CTP post-manuscript analysis appears to have experienced a similar difficulty—namely, failing to maintain a random sample.

A second type of sampling bias that can be found in the literature, and that is comparable to the favorable/unfavorable discharge sampling bias noted earlier, is the Hawthorn-Cedar Knolls Study (Lerman, 1968). In this study, the population that was eventually chosen for evaluative follow-up consisted of boys that had not been deemed "failures" while in the institution, and had survived two years of after-care without being considered post-program "failures." This type of screened sample—one that survives internal and external program "failure"—is quite analogous to the favorable/unfavorable discharge population offered in the post-manuscript analysis. Youth that are continuously screened by the *CYA organization*—and not by random assignment—are presented as available samples to be compared and evaluated in the post-manuscript analysis.

On the basis of these considerations, it seems quite unreasonable to accept updated CTP post-manuscript samples in preference to the less biased samples reported in earlier published documents. The updated samples may be newer, but this does not necessarily mean that they are less prone to sampling bias. On the basis of the evidence, it appears that *CTP Research Report No. 7* provides experimental and control samples that are much more likely to have been randomly drawn from an eligible youth population than the types of samples used in the CTP post-manuscript analysis.

While the choice of the samples used in our secondary analysis appears quite reasonable, the CTP post-manuscript analysis raises doubts about the use of suspensions as an indicator of probable youth behavior. According to the CTP post-manuscript analysis, there now exists evidence that both control and experimental parole agents did not always convert arrest reports into suspension reports. There is also evidence that arrest information may not have been completely reported in a parolee's folder. Evidently, the CTP researchers had relied primarily on suspension reports—except for their follow-ups of favorable/unfavorable discharges. The CTP post-manuscript analysis contends that non-CYA official arrest data was probably under-reported for both control and experimental groups—and may be part of a CYA parole operation practice. The updated analysis also contends that underreporting was greater in the control parole organization, and that new evidence exists to demonstrate the greater effectiveness of the experimental program—particularly for the two "neurotic" subtypes. However, the new analysis does not control for population variables.

It is apparent that acceptance of these new conclusions inevitably includes an acceptance of the biased samples that forms the bases of the updated comparisons. It is quite conceivable that the updated findings are spurious, and could be attributable to age, IQ, or social class. Acceptance of these new conclusions also involves an acceptance of updated counting as more accurate than earlier counting of deviant behavior recordings. While the newer counts could turn out to be more accurate, any new assessment of effectiveness would have to be based on nonbiased samples that represent eligible youth. But the claim that twelve years of data reporting is now to be cast aside as "obsolete" raises serious questions about who should update the updated post-manuscript analysis.

The National Institute of Mental Health supported the CTP evaluation of the demonstration project from 1961 through 1973. After twelve years, it should be reasonably confident about what portions of the full and representative samples of experimentals and controls had come into contact with non-CYA law enforcers at eight months and sixteen months. The CTP post-manuscript analysis indicates that the CTP researchers have not yet been able to provide the NIMH with convincing evidence that is based on complete and unbiased information. If the NIMH wanted to have the evidence reassessed once again, it might be prudent to contract for a disinterested researcher to conduct an independent audit of the total samples, CYA records, and the California Department of Justice records of all of the eligible youth. This independent audit might be able to document how the data of the past twelve years should be reanalyzed and reported to the scientific and correctional communities.

Pending an independent reanalysis, a conservative judgment can certainly be made. It appears reasonable to conclude that the

CTP has again been unable to scientifically demonstrate that its strategy of differential treatment has had a significant impact on the behavior of *youth*. Using the least biased data currently available, I believe that part 1 of this book is based on the best information we now have concerning the relative impact of CTP on youth behavior and the responses of adults. This conclusion was reaffirmed on 12 November 1973, while I was editing the manuscript for publication. I have attempted to incorporate into the text responses to any valid criticisms and questions posed by CTP personnel or other reviewers of the draft of the manuscript. At some point, there must be a halt to substantive revisions in order to prepare a manuscript for publication. For this manuscript, the cut-off date for considering new and "updated" findings and samples occurred on 12 November 1973. Textual revisions that improved the style, organization, clarity, and reasonableness of the analysis continued until the manuscript went to the printer. I am willing to have my analysis, based on the information I have set forth, judged by the test of time and a jury of my peers.

APPENDIX B

TABLE B-1

Time on Parole Prior to Violation for Two Cohorts of CYA Boys Released to Parole by Sentencing Court (by percentage revoked or discharged on a cumulative basis)

Time on Parole Prior to Violation	1964–65 Cohort[a] (Total N = 14,188)		1968–69 Cohort[b] (Total N = 6,880)	
	Juv. Ct.	Criminal Ct.	Juv. Ct.	Criminal Ct.
3 mos. or less	15.0	10.1	12.5	10.4
6 mos.	29.4	18.4	31.5	17.5
12 mos.	46.5	31.1	45.9	28.1
15 mos.	52.2	36.1	49.4	30.9
24 mos.	61.6	44.9	NA	NA
36 mos.	67.6	50.1	NA	NA
49 mos. or more	70.1	51.9	NA	NA
Total number paroled	N = (10,286)	N = (3,902)	N = (4,525)	N = (2,355)

[a]*CYA Annual Report, 1970* (Sacramento: Department of the Youth Authority), table 26, p. 37. Only the first release to parole was counted for wards with more than one release in the two-year period shown.

[b]Ibid., table 28, p. 38. Wards were released to parole in the twelve-month period between 1 October 1968 and 30 September 1969.

TABLE B-2
Violence Risks of CYA Male Parolees, 1961, 1962, 1963, and 1970

	1961	1962	1963	1970
No. of males on census day[a]	7,508	8,235	8,631	11,481
Offenses against persons[b]	489	628	684	894
Violent offenses/100 male youth on parole on census day	6.5	7.6	7.9	7.8

Sources: (1) *Analysis of the Budget Bill for Fiscal Year July 1, 1964 to June 30, 1965*, Report of the Legislative Analyst to the Joint Legislative Budget Committee (California Legislature, 1964 session), p. 123. (2) *CYA Annual Report, 1970* (Sacramento: Department of Youth Authority), table 24, p. 36. (3) *A Comparison of Characteristics of Youth Authority Wards, June 30 each year, 1962-1971* (Sacramento: Department of Youth Authority), September 1971, table 3, p. 8.

[a]Data on parolees and offenses for 1961-63 are based only on males 16 years and over, as collected by CYA, but reported by legislative analyst. Data on 1970 are reported by CYA in *A Comparison of Characteristics....*, but includes all boys on parole on 30 June 1970. The median ages of these 11,841 boys is 19.9.

[b]Offenses against persons in 1961-63 included: homicide, robbery, rape, sex offenses, assaults, and purse snatching, and were already combined in report of legislative analyst. In 1970 all offenses against persons were combined from *Annual Report* and included: homicide, robbery, assault and battery, and sex offenses.

Bibliography

Adams, S. A., and Grant, M. Q. 1961. *See* State of California Youth Authority, 1961*a*.

American Friends Service Committee. 1971. *Struggle for Justice: A Report on Crime and Punishment in America.* New York: Hill and Wang.

Bailey, W. 1966. Correctional Outcome: An Evaluation of 100 Reports. *Journal of Criminal Law, Criminology, and Police Science* 57.

Becker, H. S. 1963. *Outsiders: Studies in the Sociology of Deviance.* New York: Free Press of Glencoe.

Beker, J., and Heyman, D. S. 1972. A Critical Appraisal of the California Differential Treatment Typology of Adolescent Offenders. *Criminology* 10:3-59.

Beverly, R. F. 1965. *See* State of California Youth Authority, 1965*a*.

Black. D. J., and Reiss, A. J. 1970. Police Control of Juveniles. *American Sociological Review* 35:63-70.

Bremner, R. H.; Barnard, J.; Hareven, T. K.; and Mennel, R. M. 1971. *Children and Youth in America: A Documentary History.* 2 vols. Cambridge: Harvard University Press.

California Probation, Parole, and Correctional Association. February 1972. *Correctional News.* Sacramento: CPPCA.

County of Cuyahoga. 1971. *Cuyahoga County Juvenile Court Annual Report, 1971.* Cleveland, Ohio: Cuyahoga County Juvenile Court.

County of Los Angeles. 1970. *County of Los Angeles Probation Depart-*

ment Notice No. 245 (27 January). Los Angeles: Los Angeles County Probation Department.

CTP Nos. 1-9. See State of California Youth Authority, 1962-68.

Davis, G. F. 1964. A Study of Adult Probation Violation Rates by Means of the Cohort Approach. *Journal of Criminal Law, Criminology, and Police Science* 55:1-16.

Davis, K. C. 1967. *Discretionary Justice.* Urbana: University of Illinois Press.

Empey, L. T. 1967. *See* U.S. Department of Health, Education, and Welfare, 1967.

Empey, L. T.; Newland, G. E.; and Lubeck, S. G. 1965. *The Silverlake Experiment: Progress Report No. 2.* Los Angeles: Youth Studies Center, University of Southern California.

Hood, R. H., and Sparks, R. 1970. *Key Issues in Criminology.* New York: McGraw-Hill, World University Library.

Lemert, E. M. 1967. *Human Deviance: Social Problems and Social Control.* Englewood Cliffs, N.J.: Prentice-Hall.

————. 1970. *Social Action and Legal Change.* Chicago: Aldine.

————. 1972. *See* National Institute of Mental Health, 1972.

Lerman, P. 1968. Evaluating Institutions for Delinquents. *Social Work* 13:55-64.

————, ed. 1970. *Delinquency and Social Policy.* New York: Praeger.

————. 1971. Child Convicts. *Trans-Action* 8:35-45.

Marris, P., and Rein, M. 1967. *Dilemmas of Social Reform: Poverty and Community Action in the United States.* New York: Atherton Press.

Mennel, R. M. 1973. *Thorns and Thistles: Juvenile Delinquents in the United States, 1823-1940.* Hanover, N.H.: The University Press of New England.

Meyer, H. J.; Borgatta, E. F.; and Jones, W. C. 1965. *Girls at Vocational High.* New York: Russell Sage Foundation.

National Commission on the Causes and Prevention of Violence, 1969. *Crimes of Violence.* Vol. 12. A Staff Report Prepared by Donald J. Mulvehill, Melvin M. Tumin, with Lynn A. Curtis. Washington, D.C.: U.S. Government Printing Office.

National Council on Crime and Delinquency. *Locking Them Up: A Study of Initial Juvenile Detention Decisions in Selected California Counties, 1970.* Davis, Ca.: Western Region of NCCD.

National Institute of Mental Health, Center for Studies of Crime and Delinquency. 1971*a. Community-Based Correctional Programs.* Washington, D.C.: U.S. Government Printing Office, Public Health Service Publication No. 2130.

————. 1971*b. Development and Legal Regulation of Coercive Behavior*

Modification Techniques with Offenders. Prepared by Ralph R. Schwitzgebel. Ibid., No. 2067.

———. 1971c. *Perspectives on Deterrence.* Prepared by Franklin E. Zimring. Ibid., No. 2056.

———. 1972. *Instead of Court: Diversion in Juvenile Justice.* Prepared by E. M. Lemert. Washington, D.C.: U.S. Government Printing Office, DHEW Publication No. (HSM) 72-9093.

Palmer, T. B. 1971. California's Community Treatment Program for Delinquent Adolescents. *Journal of Research in Crime and Delinquency* 8:74-92.

———. 1973. Matching Worker and Client in Corrections. *Social Work* 18:95-103.

Phillips, E. L.; Wolf, M. M.; Bailey, J. S.; and Fixsen, D. L. 1972. *The Achievement Place Model.* Lawrenceville, Kansas: Bureau of Child Research and Department of Human Development, University of Kansas.

Pilliavin, I., and Briar, S. 1964. Police Encounters with Juveniles. *American Journal of Sociology* 70:206-14.

Platt, A. 1969. *The Child Savers: The Invention of Delinquency.* Chicago: University of Chicago Press.

Powers, E., and Witmer, H. 1951. *An Experiment in the Prevention of Delinquency.* New York: Columbia University Press.

President's Commission on Law Enforcement and Administration of Justice, 1967a. *Task Force Report: Corrections.* Washington, D.C.: U.S. Government Printing Office.

———, 1967b. *Task Force Report: Juvenile Delinquency and Youth Crime.* Washington, D.C.: U.S. Government Printing Office.

———, 1967c. *Task Force Report: Crime and Its Impact—An Assessment.* Washington, D.C.: U.S. Government Printing Office.

Reckless, W., et al. 1956. Self Concept as an Insulator against Delinquency. *American Sociological Review* 21:744-46.

———, 1957. The "Good" Boy in a High Delinquency Area. *Journal of Criminal Law, Criminology, and Police Science* 48:18-26.

Robison, J., and Smith, G. 1971. The Effectiveness of Correctional Programs. *Crime and Delinquency* 17:67-80.

Rothman, D. J. 1971. *The Discovery of the Asylum: Social Order and Disorder in the New Republic.* Boston: Little, Brown and Co.

Saleeby, G. F. 1971. Five Years of Probation Subsidy. *California Youth Authority Quarterly* 5:3-13.

Sanders, W. B., ed., 1970. *Juvenile Offenders for a Thousand Years.* Chapel Hill, N.C.: University of North Carolina Press.

Scarpitti, F. R., et al. 1960. The "Good" Boy in a High Delinquency Area: Four Years Later. *American Sociological Review* 25:555-58.

Schur, E. M. 1973. *Radical Non-intervention: Rethinking the Delinquency Problem.* Englewood Cliffs, N.J.: Prentice-Hall.

Schwitzgebel, R. R. 1971. *See* National Institute of Mental Health, 1971*b*.

SCYA. *See* State of California Youth Authority.

Seckel, J. P. 1967. *See* State of California Youth Authority, 1967*b*.

Sellin, T. 1962. The Significance of Records of Crime. In *The Sociology of Crime and Delinquency,* ed. M. Wolfgang, L. Savitz, and N. Johnston. New York: John Wiley and Sons.

Sellin, T., and Wolfgang, M. E. 1964. *The Measurement of Delinquency.* New York: John Wiley and Sons.

Smith, R. L. 1965. Probation Supervision: A Plan of Action. *California Youth Quarterly* 18:1–4.

————. 1972. *See* U.S. Department of Health, Education, and Welfare, 1972*b*.

Stapleton, W. V., and Teitelbaum, L. E. 1972. *In Defense of Youth.* New York: Russell Sage Foundation.

State of California Board of Corrections. 1964. *1964 Probation Study: Final Report.* Prepared by R. L. Smith. Sacramento: Board of Corrections.

State of California Budget for the Fiscal Year July 1, 1964, to June 30, 1965. Submitted by Edmund G. Brown, Governor, to the California Legislature, 1964 Budget Session. Sacramento.

State of California Department of Justice, Division of Criminal Law and Enforcement. 1960–64. *Delinquency and Probation in California, 1960, 1961, 1962, 1963, 1964.* Sacramento: Bureau of Criminal Statistics.

————. 1966. *Juvenile Detention Statistical Reporting: A Reference Manual for County Juvenile Halls and Camps, Ranches, and Homes.* Ibid.

————. 1966–69. *Crime and Delinquency in California, 1966, 1967, 1968, 1969.* Ibid.

————. 1970*a*. *Juvenile Probation and Detention: Reference Tables, BCS, 1970.* Ibid.

————. 1970*b*. *Crime and Arrests in California: Reference Tables, 1970.* Ibid.

————. 1971*a*. *Characteristics of Adults and Juveniles in Regular and Subsidy Caseloads on December 31, 1970.* Ibid.

————. 1971*b*. *Criminal Justice Agency Resources in California: Reference Tables.* Ibid.

State of California Joint Legislative Budget Committee. 1966–70. *Analysis of the Budget Bill of the State of California for the Fiscal Year July 1, 1966, to June 30, 1967; July 1, 1967, to June 30, 1968; July 1, 1968, to June 30, 1969; July 1, 1969, to June 30, 1970: A Report of the Legislative Analyst.* Sacramento: California Legislature.

State of California Joint Report by the Special Crime Study Commissions on Juvenile Justice and Adult Corrections and Release Procedures. 1949. *Probation Services in California.* Sacramento: Special Crime Study Commissions.

State of California Joint Study by Department of Finance, Department of the Youth Authority, and County Probation Representatives. 1970. *Report on State Aid for Probation Services (Probation Subsidy).* Sacramento: Department of Finance.

State of California Special Study Commission on Correctional Facilities and Services. 1957. *Probation in California.* Sacramento: State Board of Corrections.

State of California Support and Local Assistance Budget for the Fiscal Year July 1, 1965, to June 30, 1966; July 1, 1966, to June 30, 1967; July 1, 1967, to June 30, 1968; July 1, 1968, to June 30, 1969; July 1, 1969, to June 30, 1970. Submitted by the Governor to the California Legislature, 1965, 1966, 1967, 1968, 1969. Sacramento.

State of California Youth Authority (SCYA). 1954. *Standards for the Performance of Probation Duties.* Sacramento: Department of Youth Authority.

———. 1959. *A Method of Determination of Base Expectancies for Use in the Assessment of Correctional Treatment.* Prepared by R. F. Beverly. Sacramento: Division of Research.

———. 1961a. *A Demonstration Project: An Evaluation of Community-Located Treatment for Delinquents.* Prepared by Stuart Adams and Marguerite Q. Grant. Ibid.

———. 1961b. *Standards for the Performance of Probation Duties.* Sacramento: Department of Youth Authority.

———. 1962-68. *Community Treatment Project Research Reports, Nos. 1-9* (cited as *CTP No. 1,* etc.). *No. 1* (August 1962), prepared by M. Q. Grant, and M. Warren; *No. 2* (June 1963); *No. 3* (August 1963), prepared by M. Q. Grant, M. Warren, and J. K. Turner; *No. 4* (February 1964), prepared by J. E. Riggs, W. Underwood, and M. Q. Warren; *No. 5* (February 1964), prepared by M. Q. Warren, T. B. Palmer, and J. K. Turner; *No. 6* (October 1965), prepared by M. Q. Warren and T. B. Palmer; *No. 7* (August 1966), prepared by M. Q. Warren et al.; *No. 8,* 2 parts (September 1967), prepared by M. Q. Warren et al.; *No. 9,* 3 parts (September 1968), prepared by T. B. Palmer et al. Sacramento: Division of Research.

———. 1965a. *An Analysis of Parole Performance by Institution of Release (1959-1962).* Prepared by R. F. Beverly. Sacramento: Division of Research, Report No. 40.

———. 1965b. *Standards for the Performance of Probation Duties.* Sacramento: Department of Youth Authority.

———. 1966a. *Temporary Detention: A Task Force Evaluation.* Prepared by CYA Committee of A. Scott, J. Allbright, G. Hopkins, O. Imal, and M. Warren. Sacramento: Files of California Treatment Project.

————. 1966b. *Interpersonal Maturity Level Classification: Juvenile Diagnosis and Treatment of Low, Middle, and High Maturity Delinquents.* Prepared by M. Q. Warren and staff. Sacramento: Division of Research.

————. 1967a. *Forestry Camp Study: Comparison of Recidivism Rates of Camp-Eligible Boys Randomly Assigned to Camp and Institutional Programs.* Prepared by M. J. Molof. Ibid., Report No. 53.

————. 1967b. *The Fremont Experiment.* Prepared by J. P. Seckel. Sacramento: Division of Research.

————. 1968. *Group Home Project.* Ibid.

————. 1969a. *(California's) Probation Subsidy: A Report to the Legislature, 1966–68.* Sacramento: Division of Delinquency Prevention and Division of Research.

————. 1969b. *Rules, Regulations, and Standards of Performance for Special Supervision Programs.* Rev. ed. Sacramento: Department of Youth Authority.

————. 1970a. *Annual Report, 1970.* Sacramento: Division of Research.

————. 1970b. *California Laws Relating to Youthful Offenders.* Sacramento: Department of Youth Authority.

————. 1970c. *Community Treatment Project Post-Discharge Analysis: A Brief Review.* Sacramento: Division of Research.

————. 1970d. *The Los Angeles Community Delinquency Control Project.* Prepared by Esther Pond. Ibid.

————. 1970–72. *Probation Subsidy Evaluation, Progress Reports, Nos. 1–4.* Prepared by D. Johns. *No. 1* (1970); *No. 2* (1971); *No. 3* (1971); *No. 4* (1972). Sacramento: Division of Research.

————. 1971a. *Annual Report, 1971.* Sacramento: Department of Youth Authority.

————. 1971b. *Characteristics of California Youth Authority Wards, December 31, 1971.* Sacramento: Division of Research.

————. 1971c. *Institutional Experience Summary: 1969 Parole Releases.* Ibid.

————. 1971d. *California Youth Authority Board Policy Manual.* Sacramento: California Youth Authority Board.

————. 1972a. *Annual Report, 1972.* Sacramento: Department of Youth Authority.

————. 1972b. *Characteristics of Youth Authority Wards, June 30, 1972.* Sacramento: Division of Research.

————. 1972c. *Community Treatment Project Post-Discharge Analysis: An Updating of the 1969 Analysis for Sacramento and Stockton Males.* Ibid.

————. 1972d. *A Comparison of Characteristics of Youth Authority*

Wards: June 30, Each Year of 1963-1972. Ibid.

———. 1972e. *Some Statistical Facts on the California Youth Authority.* Sacramento: Department of Youth Authority.

———. 1972f. *The Status of Current Research in the California Youth Authority.* Sacramento: Division of Research.

———. 1973a. *The Community Treatment Project in Perspective: 1961-1973.* Prepared by T. B. Palmer. Ibid.

———. 1973b. *Some Statistical Facts on the California Youth Authority.* Sacramento: Department of Youth Authority.

———. 1974. *California's Probation Subsidy Program: A Progress Report to the Legislature, 1966-1973.* Sacramento: Division of Delinquency Prevention and Division of Research.

U.S. Department of Health, Education, and Welfare. 1967. *Alternatives to Incarceration.* Prepared by LaMar T. Empey. Washington, D.C.: U.S. Government Printing Office, Office of Juvenile Delinquency and Youth Development Publication No. 9001.

———. 1972a. *Juvenile Court Statistics, 1970.* Washington, D.C.: U.S. Government Printing Office, DHEW Publication No. (SRS) 72-03452.

———. 1972b. *A Quiet Revolution: Probation Subsidy.* Prepared by R. L. Smith. Ibid., DHEW Publication No. (SRS) 72-26011.

———. November 1973 and January 1974. *Youth Reporter* (monthly newsletter). Washington, D.C.: Office of Public Information, OYD.

———. 1974. *Juvenile Court Statistics, 1972.* Washington, D.C.: U.S. Government Printing Office.

Warren, M. Q. 1969. The Case for Differential Treatment of Delinquents. *Annals of the American Academy of Political and Social Science* 38:47-59.

Warren, M. Q., and staff. 1966. *See* State of California Youth Authority, 1966b.

Weeks, H. A. 1958. *Youthful Offenders at Highfields: An Evaluation of the Effects of the Short-Term Treatment of Delinquent Boys.* Ann Arbor: University of Michigan Press.

Wheeler, S., ed. 1968. *Controlling Delinquents.* New York: John Wiley and Sons.

Wheeler, S.; Cottrell, L. S.; and Romasco, A. 1966. *Juvenile Delinquency: Its Prevention and Control.* New York: Russell Sage Foundation.

Whitlatch, W. C. 1973. Practical Aspects of Reducing Detention Home Population. *Juvenile Justice* 24:17-30.

Wilson, J. Q. 1968. *Varieties of Police Behavior.* Cambridge: Harvard University Press.

Zimring, F. E. 1971. *See* National Institute of Mental Health, 1971c.

Zimring, F. E., and Hawkins, G. J. 1973. *Deterrence: The Legal Threat in Crime Control.* Chicago: University of Chicago Press.

Index

Adams, S. A., 20–22, 50
Age: CYA wards, 131; parole risks
by, 133–34, 184–85; probation
risk by, 112
Assumptions of probation subsidy
program, 112–19, 124; rationale
behind, 110, 111, 126, 129. *See
also* Goals
Attitudinal change, 56–58

Bailey, J. S., 12
Bailey, W., 96
Barnard, J., 96, 215, 216
Becker, H., 218
Bed space: net gain of (1966–72),
14, 178–82; relationship of
detention to, 47, 74, 189–90. *See
also* Institutions (state level)
Beker, J., 5, 71–72
Beverly, R. F., 94, 129
Black, D. J., 64
Board of CYA: detention proce-
dures of, 48–49, 75–77; revoca-
tion decision by, 60–61, 65–66,
91; screening by, of CTP youth,

21–22; supervision of parole
agents by, 86–87. *See also* De-
tention by CYA parole
Borgatta, E. F., 96
Bremner, R. H., 96, 215, 216
Briar, S., 64
Bureau of Criminal Statistics, 136,
140, 142, 145, 147

California Psychological Inventory
(CPI), 56–58
California Youth Authority. *See*
Board of CYA; Career costs;
Institutional costs; Institutions
(state); Parole; Population
characteristics; Staff of CYA;
Standards
Career costs: assumptions underlying, 172–74; computing, while
controlling for inflation, 177–
78; CTP vs. regular, 67–69; historical data on, 174–76; post-
subsidy rise in, 163–65, 169. *See
also* Fiscal costs; Institutional
costs

249

Community adjustment, 55–56
Community Delinquency Control Project (CYA—Los Angeles), 69
Community treatment policy, deficiencies and alternative strategies of, 220–27; criteria for assessing, 204–5; definition of, 2–3; historical development of, 215–17
Community Treatment Project (CTP): actual program design, 30–35, 50–54; administration of, 23–24; assessment of, by federal commissions, 4; assessment of, by nonfederal sources, 4–5, 69–72; assessment of program of control and treatment in, 35–41; costs of research program of, 24; description of, 3–4; goals and assumptions, 20–23; ideal program design, 21–22; impact of, 55–77, 129 (see also Detention by CYA parole; Fiscal savings; Youth behavior); measuring effectiveness of, 22–23, 55–57, 65–67; research program of, 21–22, 31–32, 229–37; use of agent time in, 33–34. See also Career costs, CTP vs. regular; Social costs/impact; Goals
CTP Research Reports: No. 1, 23, 36, 50; No. 2, 45; No. 3, 31, 35, 37, 51; No. 5, 31, 32, 67–68; No. 6, 31, 32, 55–56, 60, 229; No. 7, 32, 37–40, 53, 56–57, 60, 65, 229–30, 233, 235; No. 8, 32, 33, 39; No. 9, 36, 60, 61, 230–33; No. 10, 56, 58
Correctional history, 215–17
Correctional research utilization, 196–97, 224
Cottrell, L., 219
Counties: patterns of decision making in, 142–45; problems for, in subsidy program, 115–19, 123–24; subsidy caseload

proportions in, 136. See also Detention by California counties; Institutions (county level)

Davis, E. F., 150
Davis, G. F., 112, 133
Davis, K. C., 6, 59, 78–79
Decision making: altering, 113–14, 125; detention and county patterns of, 142–45; influences on correctional, 186, 191, 216–20; omission of critical, 125, 154; problems of, posed for counties, 115; program, in CTP, 6–8. See also Discretion in CTP; Discretion in probation subsidy; Parole violations
Delinquency, 92–95, 224; definition of, 79–83; expansion of meaning of, 217–19; measurement of, 58–63, 90–92. See also Youth behavior
Department of Corrections, 129; expected and actual commitments to, 159–61; expected and actual costs to, 163–65; reduced use of facilities of, by CYA, 131; rise in career costs of, 169, 172–74
Detention by California counties: description of, 15; discretion and, 197–99; fiscal consequences of increases in, 182–83; legal reasons for, 145; length of stay in, 152–53; reasons for increased use of, 150–51; types of offenses and reasons for, 145–48, 198; variable county cooperation with CTP via, 48; 1960, 1965, and 1970 patterns of, 142–45. See also Counties; Institutions (county level)
Detention by CTP: assessment by CYA Task Force of, 42–45; description of, 6–7; measurement of use of, 35–41; operational problems in, 47–50; rationale for use of, 41–47

Detention by CYA parole: description of, 14, 72–73; policy manual authorization of, 75–76, 189–90; relation of, to special projects, 73–75; statistics of, 73, 190; temporary, and probation subsidy, 189–92. *See also* Board of CYA

Detention outside California: in Chicago, 215–16; in Cuyahoga County, 213–14; national statistics for, 211–13

Deviance theory, 217–20. *See also* Delinquency; Youth behavior

Discretion in CTP: advantages of, 78–79; consequences of, 6–7, 79–90, 208; definition of, 59; detention decisions and, 5–6, 42–50, 76–77; honorable discharge from parole and, 66, 235; influence of, on recidivism rates, 58–67; intensive treatment strategy and, 30–33; organization of, 6, 14; policy issues of, 79–95. *See also* Decision-making

Discretion in probation subsidy: administrative, 116–17, 209–10; county corrections and, 197–99; state corrections and, 192–96; use of, in setting program standards, 121–23. *See also* Decision-making

Due process in corrections: basic elements of, 84–86, 88–90, 202–3. *See also* Social costs/impact

Earnings formula for probation subsidy, 108–10, 115–19, 123–24

Effectiveness: assumptions of, 5, 112–13, 125, 208; CTP, 58–67; of probation subsidy, 156, 203. *See also* Ineffectiveness

Empey, L. T., 11, 97, 211

Evaluation of probation subsidy, 12–13, 107–8; research reports of, 109, 122, 136–37, 156–57,

171. *See also Progress Report to the Legislature, 1966-1973; Report to the Legislature, 1966-68*

Fairness, 84–86, 88–90, 202–3

Federal commissions: assessment of CTP by, 2–4, 20; assessment of probation subsidy by, 12–13; and policy evaluation, 204

Fiscal costs: computing anticipated, 165–69; increased detention and, 182–83; overall rise in, 183–87; probation subsidy rise in, 162–65; regulation of, 98–101; remedies for reducing, 193–95; run-ups in, 68–69, 100–101, 169–76. *See also* Career costs; Institutional costs; Policy

Fiscal savings, 157–69; hypothetical, for new construction, 182

Fixsen, D. L., 12

Gemigani, R. J., 108

Goals: of CTP, 20–23, 188; of probation subsidy, 201–3. *See also* Assumptions of probation subsidy program; Community Treatment Project, goals and assumptions

Hareven, T. K., 96, 215, 216

Heyman, D. S., 5, 71–72

Highfields Project, 11, 130, 204

Hood, R. H., 96

Ineffectiveness in policy formation, 95–98, 125, 195, 203. *See also* Effectiveness

Inflation: controlling for, 177–78; impact of, 172–76, 186–87

Institutional costs: actual, 128, 130; projected, and potential savings, 114; rise in, 162–65. *See also* Career costs; Fiscal costs

Institutions (county level): probation subsidy and, 138–45, 191; type of offense and, 145–49. *See*

also Detention by California counties; Social costs/impact
Institutions (state level): closing and opening of, 178-82; commitments to, 152-53, 159-61; length of stay in, 128, 131; master plan for building, 127-28; population characteristics of, 132-33; population pressure in, 129; ratio of wards to staff, 131, 135. *See also* Bed space in institutions; Length of stay; Social costs/impact
Intensification of institutional treatment, 131-38, 155, 184-87; consequence of, 193, 203
Interpersonal Maturity Level Classification: Juvenile [I-Level], 24-29, 36, 70-72, 231-34

Jesness Inventory, 56
Joint Study by CYA and Department of Finance, 157, 162-63, 165, 168, 172, 186
Jones, W. C., 96
Justice. *See* Due process in corrections; Social costs/impact
Juvenile court, 143-44, 215-16
Juvenile status offenses, 224. *See also* Delinquency; Deviance theory; Youth behavior

Labeling theory, 218-19
Legal reform, 222-24
Legislation for probation subsidy: amendments to, 138, 151, 172; initial, 109-12, 116-17, 119-24
Legislative analyst, 180
Lemert, E. M., 8, 218, 221
Length of stay, 128, 131, 135, 172-74, 190. *See also* Institutions (county level); Institutions (state level)
Lerman, P. S., 4, 61, 95, 213, 224
Lohman et al. *See* Robison, J.
Los Angeles County Probation Department, 70-71, 117
Lubeck, S. G., 11

McGee, T. A., 74
Marris, P., 222
Mennel, R. M., 96, 215-17
Methodology, and CTP, 229-37
Meyer, H. J., 96
Molof, M. J., 94

National Commission on the Causes and Prevention of Violence, 2-4
National Council on Crime and Delinquency, 183, 211
National Institute of Mental Health (NIMH), Center for the Study of Crime and Delinquency, 4, 5, 19-20, 98, 236
Newland, G. C., 11

Oakland Community Delinquency Control Project (CYA), 49-50
Organizational survival, 135, 137, 185-86

Palmer, T. B., 51, 52, 61, 66, 67, 96, 229-37
Parole: cost of, 68, 173; discharge from, 5, 61, 66-67; early release to, 129; impact of CTP on work of, 72, 77, 85, 103-4; length of supervision on, 14, 33, 190; revocation of, 60-61, 65, 67, 81, 86, 91-93; suspension of, 37, 60-61, 81, 82, 91-92, 229-30. *See also* Detention by CYA parole
Parole violations: changes in ratio of, 191; release cohort studies of, 133-34, 238; violence risk and, 239. *See also* Detention by CYA parole; Parole
Payments to counties for probation subsidy: actual amounts of, 109, 118, 160; basis for obtaining, 108-9, 120, 124, 159-61. See also *Joint Study by CYA and Department of Finance*
Phillips, E. L., 12
Pilliavin, I., 64

Platt, A., 217
Police: arrest rates by, 142–43,
    145–47, 217–18; probation
    referrals by, 143; and subsidy,
    150–51
Policy: ideal vs. operational, 30;
    issues for correctional, 78–104,
    188–203, 205–25; framework
    for, analysis, 5–15, 104, 204–5.
    See also Fiscal costs; Social
    costs/impact
Political reform, 221–23
Pond, E., 69
Population characteristics, 129,
    132–33, 136–37, 139
Powers, E., 96, 204
President's Commission on Law
    Enforcement and the Adminis-
    tration of Justice, 2–4, 20, 204
Probation subsidy program: adop-
    tion by other states of, 107–8;
    CYA administration of, 119–20,
    122; comparison of, and CTP,
    123, 125, 188; description of, 13,
    108–9; candidates for, 120; or-
    ganizational criteria in, 124;
    traditional standards in, 121–
    23. See also Assumptions of pro-
    bation subsidy program; Earn-
    ings formula for probation sub-
    sidy; Evaluation of probation
    subsidy; Legislation for proba-
    tion subsidy; Payments to coun-
    ties for probation subsidy
Professionalization: impact of, on
    social control systems, 199–
    201, 216–19. See also Social
    control
Progress Report to the Legislature,
    1966–1973, 156, 201–3

Reckless, W., 57
Reduction of county commitments
    to CYA: actual, 152–53; poten-
    tial, 113–15; certification of,
    115; in computing state savings,
    158–62, 165–69; in statutory
    formula, 108–9

Rein, M., 222
Reiss, A. J., 64
Report to the Legislature, 1966–
    68, 165, 170
Robison, J., 5, 9, 95, 151
Romasco, A., 219
Rothman, D. J., 215

Saleeby, G., 107, 110–11, 114, 139,
    141
Sanders, W. B., 216
Sanctions. See Social control
Sarri, R., 213
Scarpitti, F. R., 57
Schur, E. M., 5, 218
Schwitzgebel, R., 10
Seckel, J. P., 130
Sellin, T., 95
Smith, G., 5, 9, 95, 151
Smith, R., 13, 108, 111, 112, 114,
    116–18, 127, 135, 137, 141, 157,
    170, 178–82
Social control: assessment of CTP
    use of, 101–4; assessment of
    statewide impact of, 152–56;
    definition of, 8–10; dominance
    of, in CTP, 35–41, 50–54; ideal
    CTP strategy of, 25–29; national
    trends of, 211–12; participation
    of corrections in, 8–12, 15;
    strategies of reduction, 220–25;
    systems of, 212–20
Social costs/impact: CTP, 90, 97–
    98, 101, 206–8; probation sub-
    sidy, 152–56, 193, 197–98, 201–
    3, 208–10. See also Detention by
    CYA parole; Due process in cor-
    rections; Institutions (county
    level); Institutions (state level);
    Policy; Social control
Sparks, R., 96
Staff of CYA: administrative dis-
    cretion by, 116; framing of leg-
    islation by, 110, 116; onsite in-
    spections by, 122; recommenda-
    tion for parole by, 114; and sub-
    sidy, 124, 195–96
Standards, 128–30; proposed, for

freezing detention rates, 198–
99; use of, in approving pro-
grams, 109, 119–22, 124
Stapleton, W. V., 223
State Aid for Probation Service.
See Probation subsidy program
Statewide correctional system,
152–56, 210–13

Teitelbaum, L. E., 223
*Temporary Detention Task Force
Report* (CYA), 38, 39, 42–50,
53–54. *See also* Detention by
CTP
Treatment: intensification of institutional, 131–38; decisions,
checking of, 87–90; operational
meaning of, 33–35; vs. social
control, 10–12

Warren, M. Q., 20–22, 25, 28, 50
Weeks, H. A., 11, 130, 204
Welfare and Institutions Code
(California), 81, 116, 117, 119,
122, 138, 145, 151, 192
Wheeler, S., 200, 219
Whitlatch, W. C., 213–14
Wilson, J. Q., 67, 217, 219
Witmer, H., 96, 204
Wolf, M. M., 12
Wolfgang, M. E., 95

Youth behavior: vs. adult behavior, 64–67; parole violation rates
and, 191–92; problems in measuring, 58–64, 90–95; trends in,
142–49, 202. *See also* Delinquency; Deviance theory

Zimring, F. E., 10